Restructuring The Schools

THE NATIONAL SOCIETY
FOR THE STUDY OF EDUCATION

The Series on Contemporary Educational Issues
Kenneth J. Rehage, Series Editor

The 1992 Titles

  School Boards: Changing Local Control, Patricia F. First and
    Herbert J. Walberg, editors
  Restructuring the Schools: Problems and Prospects, John J. Lane and
    Edgar G. Epps, editors

The Ninety-first Yearbook of the National Society for the Study of
Education, published in 1992, contains two volumes:

  The Changing Contexts of Teaching, edited by Ann Lieberman
  The Arts, Education, and Aesthetic Knowing, edited by Bennett Reimer
    and Ralph A. Smith

All members of the Society receive its two-volume Yearbook. Members who take the Comprehensive Membership also receive the two current volumes in the Series on Contemporary Educational Issues.

Membership in the Society is open to any who desire to receive its publications. Inquiries regarding membership, including current dues, may be addressed to the Secretary-Treasurer, NSSE, 5835 Kimbark Ave., Chicago, IL 60637.

Restructuring
The Schools:
Problems and Prospects

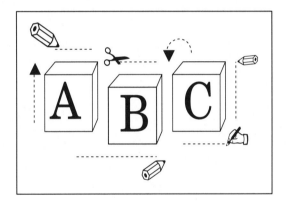

Edited by
John J. Lane
DePaul University
and
Edgar G. Epps
University of Chicago

McCutchan Publishing Corporation
P.O. Box 774, 2940 San Pablo Ave., Berkeley, CA 94702

ISBN 0–8211–1116–7

Library of Congress Catalog Card Number 91-66584

Copyright © 1992 by McCutchan Publishing Corporation

Printed in the United States of America

Contents

Contributors

Evans Clinchy, Institute for Responsive Education, Boston, Massachusetts

Bruce S. Cooper, Fordham University

John C. Daresh, University of Northern Colorado

John Egermeier, U.S. Department of Education

Edgar G. Epps, The University of Chicago

Eugene E. Eubanks, University of Missouri at Kansas City

John J. Lane, DePaul University

Daniel U. Levine, University of Missouri at Kansas City

Betty Malen, The University of Washington

Hunter Moorman, U.S. Department of Education

Leonard O. Pellicer, University of South Carolina at Columbia

Rodney T. Ogawa, The University of Utah

Albert Shanker, American Federation of Teachers

Kenneth R. Stevenson, University of South Carolina at Columbia

Introduction and Overview

John J. Lane and Edgar G. Epps

After a decade of efforts to reform the American schools, the major educational problems remain. By most standard measures, children do not seem to be learning more or better now than they were ten years ago. Parents and community members continue to feel disenfranchised from the schools they are expected to support. While salaries have improved and student-teacher ratios have been reduced, other working conditions of teachers have not substantially improved. Dropout rates remain unchanged, hovering around 50 percent in our large urban areas. Minority and other at-risk children are still in jeopardy. Job prospects—even for those who remain in high school— are bleak. In big cities, employers cannot find qualified applicants even for entry-level jobs.

WAVES OF REFORM

Clearly, reform efforts to date have not gone far enough to alleviate the major problems plaguing American schools. Since the early 1980s, reforms have come in three waves. The first wave is appropriately characterized as "top down." Governors, state legislatures, and influential members of the business community, with little or no advice from the professional education community, initiated omnibus education bills that contained numerous regulations designed to improve education. Notable among the attempted reforms of the first wave were improvement in teacher preparation, merit pay, differentiated staffing, and demand for more accountability from educators. By 1986, a survey sponsored by the Education Commission of the States reported that forty-five states had increased high school graduation requirements. Six states had increased the length of the school year. Also, a number of states increased their requirements for mathematics, science, and social studies (Pipho, 1986).

By the mid 1980s, a "bottom-up" approach to reform, the second wave, was beginning to emerge. A new spate of reports like *Tomorrow's Teachers: A Report of the Holmes Group* and the Carnegie Forum's *A Nation Prepared: Teachers for the 21st Century* argued that teachers must have the professional preparation consistent with their awesome societal responsibility. About the same time, efforts were underway in a number of urban areas to end the stifling effects of bureaucratic control of the local schools by excessively centralized district offices.

Teacher empowerment initiatives and school-based management as well as a favorable political and social climate have helped to usher in a new, third, wave of reform that requires a radical examination of the very design of the schools—restructuring.

Definitions of restructuring vary depending on which reform group does the defining. But Hanson (1991, p. 370) observes that restructuring suggests a nationwide movement to reform the organization, management, processes, and instructional content of the schools. Restructuring also suggests a holistic concern for the reformation of the local community school as well as the statewide professional education system.

Elmore (1990, p. 5) notes the emergence of a general agreement that restructuring is "about" at least three types of changes: (1) teaching and learning in schools; (2) the conditions of teachers' work in schools; and (3) the governance and incentive structures in schools. Accordingly, he has developed three models with alternative forms of what restructured schools look like if restructuring were guided by one or another of these types of change. His first model focuses on reforming the core technology of the school. He speculates about what configuration schools would take if they were designed around the best available knowledge about teaching and learning.

The second model is teacher-oriented and suggests that schools could be organized to approximate the conditions of professional workplaces. He calls the third model the "client model," where restructuring is guided not by the principles of school-based management but by principles derived from proposals for parental choice. In Elmore's view, restructuring is a highly complex process subject to the influence of various political interests. Contributors to this volume demonstrate the validity of his perspective.

Schlechty (1990, p. 63) suggests that anyone who would restructure the schools must first answer the question: "What are the present rules, roles, and relationships that impede the capacity of schools and teachers to respond to the needs of students and invent schoolwork products that satisfy those needs." Schools and school districts and statewide systems of education need to find answers to these questions and to create schools that help children to learn.

In nineteenth-century American society, plans to develop a system of education had one characteristic in common—centralization. Rules, roles, and relationships were quite clear. In addition, for the last several decades, federal and state support of schools allowed the traditional bureaucratic school structures to prosper. As we move toward the twenty-first century, our problem is quite different. Holding the belief that local schools are the authentic unit of improvement, educators, lawmakers, and an increasing number of the general public are convinced that schools will improve only when we decentralize them.

NO COMMON VISION

Devolving power to the local schools or any concerted effort to transform the schools in the United States is made all the more complex because there is no common vision of the common schools. To be sure, alternative strategies to improve the schools abound. But lacking a coherent sense of what schools are to accomplish, the American public, or at least that portion of the public that is aware of the crisis in the schools, remains unwilling to support partial remedies for the ills of the schools. As at least one of the authors in this volume suggests, it may well be that efforts to restructure the schools—to fashion each school to meet the needs of students from a particular locale—may eventually lead to the development of a shared vision of what public schools should accomplish.

Schools are not alike nor should they be. But differences can be accommodated within a set of commonly held principles about the purpose of schooling. Sizer (1989, p. 1) observed:

> Good schools sensitively reflect their communities—both the students and teachers within the school building and the wider neighborhood it serves. A good school respectfully accommodates the best of its neighborhood, not abjectly—playing whatever tune any particular interest group might demand—but sensibly, balancing the claims of national values with those of the immediate community. . . . A good school is the special creation of its own faculty—its teachers, counselors, and administrators.

OVERVIEW

This book, then, is about what it will take to create good schools. As many have observed, including contributors to this volume, incremental, no-risk innovations that merely tinker with the systems will not improve our schools. Our desire for better schools must be grounded in more radical stuff. The authors raise no false hopes. Neither do they provide definitive answers to the vexing questions they raise. But their reflections on current educational problems and the nature of restructuring and their reports on the progress of schools and school districts, taken together with their concern for the effect of current restructuring efforts on minorities and disadvantaged children, form a useful guide through the complex maze of issues relating to restructuring and school-based management. The book is organized into three sections. The first deals with the concepts and theories that relate to school restructuring in general and to school-based management in particular. The second provides examples of school restructuring. The final section, though including additional examples of restructuring, explores several policy implications of restructuring.

In "The Crisis in Education and the Limits of the Traditional Model of Schooling," Albert Shanker expresses doubt that the American public has accepted the seriousness of the situation in the schools. Worse, he suspects that even those who see the problems have such faith in the traditional bureaucratic structure of the schools that they believe only minor repairs will have the system up and running the way it seemed to work for them a generation or so ago. He cites the need for schools to be competitive and to be capable of self-renewal.

The evidence, he suggests, points in just the opposite direction. Rather than being self-directing and self-renewing, schools are on the verge of being run by state departments of education. Increasingly, businesses are deciding what the agenda of the public schools will be. Like it or not, ready or not, the general public must acknowledge that the schools must change radically.

In "Educational Restructuring: Generative Metaphor and New Vision," Hunter Moorman and John Egermeier explore the range of meanings and implications of restructuring. In the process, they provide a framework for productive public dialogue about the major challenges facing schools today. In particular, they show how restructuring serves as a conceptual tool for sorting and matching educational problems, solutions, and opportunities for choice. Their investigations of current problems also provide readers with a current review of the reform literature. The authors indicate that a new consensus is forming around a set of educational values and beliefs occasioned by efforts to restructure. Restructuring, they believe, is essentially a process for establishing community of purpose. While most reforms of the past fifty years have been largely technical, restructuring offers the hope of developing a guiding ethos for American education.

In "Site-Based Management: Engine for Reform or Pipedream? Problems, Prospects, Pitfalls, and Prerequisites for Success," Daniel Levine and Eugene Eubanks review and assess selected research and practice relating to school-based management. They examine also the problems and obstacles that attend implementation of school-based management. Among these obstacles are inadequate time, training, technical assistance, resistance to change, leadership, school board policies, and state and federal regulations. Overcoming these obstacles will itself take time. Yet they provide encouraging examples of multischool improvement projects and the strategies used to create them. Throughout the chapter, the authors examine school improvement and school-based management in light of what seems possible based on research findings.

Today, more than at any time in recent history, international data are available to make possible comparison of the relative educational progress of one nation to another. Nonetheless, the general public knows little about the structures that support various national educational systems. In "Local School Reform in Great Britain and the United States: Points of Comparison—Points of Departure," Bruce Cooper compares and contrasts school reform in Great Britain and the United States, nations with very different kinds of ideologies, governments, and school systems. His analysis is illuminating in a number of ways. First, it sharpens one's understanding of the nature of reform by forcing the reader to reassess the rhetoric and definitions of reform. Second, his analysis provides a comprehensive review and critique of the many recent restructuring initiatives. He examines the results to date of efforts in both cultures to transform the schools. One of the interesting comparisons and analyses he makes concerns the effects of authority on reform. England's prime minister has power over the local schools; presidents of the United States do not.

It is one thing to propose reform and to criticize those who resist change. It is quite another to step out of the professorial role and get involved at the grassroots level and at the implementation stage of school-based management. In "Impressions of School-Based Management: The Cincinnati Story," John Daresh provides an insider's view of Cincinnati's early experiences with a local school advisory committee. He provides realistic examples to show that the road to community empowerment is rocky. He argues that school-based management will fail unless considerable resources are allocated to the formal preparation and in-service education of every participant in the school management team, including the principal.

Nowhere is the need to restructure the schools more evident than in our large urban school systems, where often most of the students are minority. How has reform benefited these students? To what extent have the schools accepted parents as full-fledged partners in the education of their children? In "School-Based Management in South Carolina: Balancing State-Directed Reform with Local Decision Making," Kenneth Stevenson and Leonard Pellicer describe that state's effort to be responsive to the needs of local school districts. Half the school districts in South Carolina have undergone some form of restructuring in order to empower teachers, parents, principals, and superintendents with considerably more authority over school matters than they enjoyed in the past. The authors' recent statewide survey of principals and superintendents leads them to believe that principals and other local authorities have not been given sufficient control over resources to ensure successful implementation of South Carolina's ambitious plans for school improvement. In addition, the authors show what happens when educational priorities among state authorities, superintendents, and principals are not congruent.

Beginning with a brief history of the community control movement, Edgar Epps discusses the role of parental involvement in the education of minority students. To illustrate his points, he draws on current research and examines several models and experimental programs, including restructuring efforts in Chicago. The themes he develops in "School-Based Management: Implications for Minority Parents" are both realistic and optimistic. Epps argues convincingly that with proper encouragement and care, every child can become an effective learner.

Of all the forms restructuring might take, choice offers the greatest opportunity for empowerment for parents and students. In "Public Schools of Choice: School Reform in the Desegregating Urban Districts of Massachusetts," Evans Clinchy describes and evaluates experiences with "controlled choice" within magnet schools in three Massachusetts school systems. Based in part on the alternative school models of the 1960s, magnet schools were created to give minority and nonminority parents a major voice in choosing the kind of education they want for their children. The three experiments described in this chapter support the view that it is possible to empower each school community to determine its own educational philosophy and to develop a curriculum and school structure to match that philosophy. Clinchy notes that this new effort to restructure the schools is evident in nearly every sector of the country and may quite possibly replace the school systems we now have.

In "Site-Based Management: Disconcerting Policy Issues, Critical Policy Choices," Betty Malen and Rodney Ogawa raise three questions critical to successful implementation of site-based management. Do site-based management plans really change the formal decision-making arrangements in schools? Do they change traditional influence arrangements as well? And, do schools become more bureaucratic or less bureaucratic when they attempt to move from traditional school governance structures to site-based management? Their answers to these questions are instructive for anyone interested in restructuring and school-based management. The authors are very aware that the research findings on school-based management and restructuring are preliminary and tentative. They note that much of what has been written about school-based management is only impressionistic. Nonetheless, what does exist can provide guidelines for future innovators. The chapter concludes with an examination of several critical policy choices for educational decision makers.

REFERENCES

Elmore, Richard F., and associates. *Restructuring Schools: The Next Generation of Educational Reform*. San Francisco: Jossey-Bass, 1990.

Hanson, E. Mark. *Educational Administration and Organization Behavior*. Boston: Allyn and Bacon, 1991.

Pipho, Chris. "Kappan Special Report: States Move Reform Closer to Reality," *Phi Delta Kappan* 68 (December 1986): K5.

Schlechty, Phillip C. *Schools for the 21st Century: Leadership Imperatives for Educational Reform*. San Francisco: Jossey-Bass, 1990.

Sizer, Theodore R. "Diverse Practice, Shared Ideas: The Essential Schools." In *Organizing for Learning: Toward the Twenty-first Century*, edited by Herbert J. Walberg and John J. Lane. Reston, Va.: National Association of Secondary School Principals, 1989.

Part One

The Concepts: Restructuring and School-Based Management

CHAPTER 1

The Crisis in Education and the Limits of the Traditional Model of Schooling

Albert Shanker

Our public schools are in deep trouble, but that's hardly news. Commission reports, analyses by public policy experts, and op ed articles in daily newspapers all agree that unless something is done, the American system of public education will collapse. And because the people within public education seem unwilling or unable to handle the crisis, others have stepped in with remedies that once would have been considered desperate or foolish. Radical measures like the state takeover of the Jersey City schools, the surrender of a public school system to a private university in Chelsea, Massachusetts, and the state-mandated creation of parent-majority school councils for each school in Chicago are becoming routine. Efforts to initiate tuition tax credits and vouchers continue, now at state and even local levels. How can it be that nearly a decade after *A Nation at Risk*, as others take the initiative, the public education enterprise is still searching for a way to reform our schools? Why have there been so few efforts at change and so few signs of improvement?

One explanation is that many people simply have not accepted the seriousness of the situation. Of course, they know about failing schools and poorly prepared students, but these problems belong to the school district across town or across the state. And even people who see that our whole education system is in trouble often define its problems too narrowly because they fundamentally believe in the traditional model of schooling. As a result, they suggest minor adjustments like adding another year of English to the graduation requirements or preventing students who do not keep a C average from playing sports or toughening up the teacher evaluation system. This approach will not work. The problems in our schools are structural ones that cannot be fixed by merely tinkering with the system. We have reached the limits of our traditional model of education, and the whole system requires rethinking and reworking.

What do students know? What skills have they learned? These are the test of any education system. And anyone who needs convincing about the magnitude of the problems in our system should look at the results of standardized tests measuring what our students know about geography, American history and literature, mathematics, and so forth and some of the other tests comparing our students with students in other industrialized countries. The results of the National Assessment of Educational Progress (NAEP) are a reasonably good measure of student achievement in certain skills, and the results for seventeen-year-olds are particularly sobering. But since most youngsters who are going to drop out are gone by then, the 25 percent of students who are likely to be the lowest achievers are gone; thus the sample is skewed positively. However, only 20 percent of the remaining students can write an adequate persuasive letter to a principal or to the manager of a supermarket in applying for a job. And when NAEP says "adequate," it does not mean anything very complex.

For instance, a letter of application to the supermarket manager needs to include at least one reason why the writer should get the job. It might say, "I used to work in a candy store, and I know how difficult it is to get help at the last minute, so you can count on me to be there every day." Or "I used to be the treasurer of my Boy Scout troop, and I know how easy it is to lose money when you don't count change accurately. I've had that experience and I'll be a good employee." The letter can even have some spelling or grammatical errors and still be considered adequate, but only 20 percent of those seventeen-year-olds were able to write such a letter. Only 12 percent could take six common fractions and arrange them in order by size. And only 6 percent could solve this problem: "Christine borrowed $850 for one year from the Friendly Finance Company. If she paid 12 percent simple interest on the loan, what was the total amount she repaid?"

None of these questions has much intellectual content. Students do not have to display a knowledge of Shakespeare or Dickens or solve calculus problems, and there are no difficult concepts in the history or science assessments. They call only for the kind of knowledge a person who has completed high school should have in order to find his or her way around in the world.

This is not, as some would like to think, a problem of minorities only. NAEP results show that minorities are rapidly catching up. They need and deserve special help, but when they reach the same levels of achievement as the majority population in this country, we will still have an educational disaster on our hands. NAEP figures show that depending on how high the standards are set, we are doing a good job at educating about 10 percent, 15 percent, or 20 percent of the students—the higher the figure, the looser the standards. But no rational person could examine the results of these NAEP tests and maintain that we are educating 40 percent of the youngsters in this country.

How do our results compare with results of student assessments in other countries? We will forget about Japan because their society is so different from ours and look instead at other democratic, industrial countries like Great Britain, France, West Germany, Holland, and Belgium. These countries do not have a national assessment like ours, but they all have either national or provincial examinations for students graduating from secondary school, and these exams are much harder than the NAEP tests. Some of them take days, and they involve essays and problems in mathematics and science; in West Germany, there are still oral examinations.

Every student in these countries who does well enough on these exams to get into college would be in NAEP's top category. In Great Britain, where the percentage is smallest, 15 to 17 percent of students pass examinations more difficult than NAEP, as compared with our 4 to 6 percent who attain the highest level in NAEP. Approximately 22 percent do so in France and 27 percent in West Germany. In other words, in these other countries, the percentage of students tested who attain the highest achievement levels is four or five times greater than the percentage of students tested in the United States who achieve comparable levels.

But many Americans are very satisfied with their schools because they see that the majority of our high school graduates go on to college: 55 percent according to recent U.S. Department of Education statistics. If our students were judged by European standards, only about 4 to 6 percent would go, but of course parents do not apply these standards. They compare their children with those next door, and if they feel their children are doing a little better than the neighbors', they are pleased. They fail to realize that their sons and daughters are going to college only because most colleges have very low standards; and they do not see that the majority of our students who do go to college are getting their junior high school and high school education there.

However, few businesses are satisfied with the education our students are getting. They complain bitterly about high school graduates' inadequate skills, and they will soon have even more reason to complain. When European countries unite in 1992 and form a single economic bloc, we will face competition from a united Europe in addition to what we now have from Japan, Korea, and Singapore. Our free trade agreement with Canada will probably also intensify Canadian competition. And we cannot look forward to a very prosperous future if education systems in other countries produce as many as 30 percent of students who can function at a level where perhaps 5 percent of our students can function.

How can we explain these differences between the achievement of our children and that of students from other countries? Our students are not less intelligent, but certainly our system of public education is different. A look at some of the reasons for the differences will bring our problems into focus and might suggest some routes to change.

Local school governance. The lay community school board is a unique American institution. In many countries, the national government runs the schools; in others, the states or provinces control them. Nowhere else is there anything like our sixteen thousand elected school governments, each with substantial powers to hire staff; make textbook, curriculum, and testing choices; and determine salaries and conditions of employment.

The rationale for this arrangement is that the people who pay school taxes and send their children to the schools are best suited to decide what the schools should be. The result is that professional staff here has less to say about how schools are run than in other countries, and our schools are more subject to local politics. For example, the school system head, the superintendent, must face the school board in a public meeting at least once a month and answer for any mishap that has occurred in the schools. He must manage a system at the same time as he tries to protect his job by maintaining majority support on the school board. Perhaps schools are "too important to be left to educators," as supporters of local lay school boards often say, but we do seem to be the only country where the people, whose principal qualification may be that they went to public schools, get to run them.

National goals and standards. Most industrialized nations have national or provincial curriculums. They have agreed on what their students should know and be able to do, and these things are taught in their schools. This idea has always made Americans nervous. It sounds like regimentation, like the federal government meddling in what should be a state and local matter. As a result, we have a fragmented curriculum in which fifty states and sixteen thousand separate school boards decide for themselves how much and what kind of mathematics, science, history, and so forth students get and what the curriculum and textbooks will be.

To the extent that we have a national curriculum and national standards, they are what the private textbook and testing companies set; and because these companies are in the business of pleasing their customers and their customers have a hodge-podge of interests and demands, our standards are very low indeed.

The problem is compounded at the school level. In most school districts, teachers are given huge course syllabuses, which contain much more than a class can possibly cover. Teachers who try to follow a syllabus faithfully find they are simply stuffing facts into students' heads, and they realize they must select. But select what? What must students know and be able to do? Since we have no national goals or standards, teachers have no basis for selecting which topics they must cover and which are optional. Teachers should be free to exercise judgment about methods, but we need to agree about a common core of knowledge.

Standardized, multiple-choice tests. No other country shares our infatuation with standardized, multiple-choice tests. In fact, some do not use them at all, preferring essay questions and in a couple of cases, oral exams. We, on the other hand, start administering these idiotic exams to children in kindergarten and continue on through college and beyond. Things have gotten worse since the first wave of school reform, too, because standardized multiple-choice tests are now driving the curriculum and are seen as a technique for finding out which schools are improving and which are not.

The results of these tests are often worthless. The low-level skills they test do not have much to do with real learning. And Dr. John Jacob Cannell's discovery of the "Lake Wobegon Effect" in testing—that is, the majority of children taking the most commonly used achievement tests got above-average scores—suggests that the scores are not reliable anyway. The problem goes beyond the inefficiencies of wasting time in preparing for and giving the tests and wasting money in purchasing and scoring them; these tests now have an important and undesirable effect on what teachers teach and children learn.

Comparing the way a teacher would prepare students for a test consisting of essay questions with how he would get them ready for a multiple-choice exam makes the effect clear. In taking an essay exam, children must know how to write sentences and paragraphs. They need to be able to select details that will make their points and to put the points together convincingly. In contrast, in taking a multiple-choice test, children need only the ability to recognize the right answer. They do not even have to go into their memories to pull up the correct word or phrase. They just have to recognize it on the page and make their mark beside it.

In other words, students need only passive knowledge to do well on multiple-choice tests, but students need active knowledge to do well on essay tests. It is like two different ways of knowing a language. The visitor to a foreign country who has a passive knowledge of its language will be able to read road signs, a restaurant menu, and the hotel bill. He will be able to respond to written cues and probably recognize enough words to stay out of trouble, but that is it. The person with an active knowledge of the language will be able to communicate with the natives, do business, go to the theater, and so forth.

A curriculum driven by tests like the ones we commonly use in the United States is painfully limited. It might be acceptable if we were trying to turn out workers who were each assigned one simple, repetitive task on a production line. But work is no longer organized in that way, and the tests that drive our curricula need to reflect that new reality.

The quality of our teachers. What can we say about the quality of our teachers in comparison with those in Europe? The test results I have already cited tell part of the story. In Europe, the only students who go on to college are the 20 percent or so who score at the highest level in their school-leaving exams. We send nearly 60 percent of our graduates to college, though only 5 percent, more or less, score at the highest level in the NAEP. So every teacher in Germany or Great

Britain or France comes from a group of students that performs at a level comparable to the top 5 percent of *all* American students. In other words, we do not have as large a pool of talent from which to draw our teachers as they do in European countries.

Moreover, the rewards of public school teaching are much greater in Europe than they are here. Teachers there are considered to be professionals, so they enjoy the independence and the respect that we save for physicians and lawyers, and also they receive some of the top salaries among public employees. It is no surprise, then, that top students in Europe are more likely to become and remain teachers than are top students here.

Incentives. Another difference between our system and the European system is in the area of student incentives. As John Bishop, a professor of labor and industrial relations at Cornell University, points out, American teenagers who go directly from high school into the workforce have no incentive to work hard in high school. They know that a potential employer will ask only one question: "Do you have your high school diploma?" The employer is not going to ask about the courses students took or the grades they got or their attendance records. It would be no surprise for someone who barely passed and cut school one day in every four to be hired alongside another new graduate who took tough courses and did well in them. The two new graduates would probably both start with the same salary, too. School does not count when you are looking for a job, and our students know it.

It is different in other industrialized countries. There, the subjects students study and the marks they get make a difference as to who gets a job first and what the starting salary is. It is therefore not surprising that students in these countries work harder and take school more seriously than ours do. Our kids are not unintelligent or lazy; they are accurately interpreting the cues we give them about the importance of school in getting a job.

The situation is similar for students going on to college. It is true that students who want to get into selective colleges work hard, but they are only a very small percentage of students. The ones who want to go to less selective schools can work or not, as they choose, because as long as they have a diploma, they will be able to find a college— and probably two or three—that will admit them. Money, not achievement, is the main entrance requirement. Like employers, colleges are sending students the message that what they do in high school does not count; and there is no doubt that students are getting the message.

Tracking. The education systems in most other industrialized countries handle the differences among youngsters differently from the way we do. In West Germany, for example, they give all the students an examination in the fourth grade and send them off to three different kinds of schools. Those who are most academically inclined go to a school where the standards are very rigorous. The second group, students who seem less promising academically, go to a less demanding school. And the students who are really not good at academic work go to a third school where they follow a vocationally based curriculum. No one comes out of any of these schools without mathematics, science, languages, and so forth. But each school handles the curriculum in a different way, one that is presumed to fit the abilities and needs of the students.

In this country, we have the same individual differences, but we are politically, socially, and philosophically opposed to separating students formally in the way I have just described. Of course, residential patterns, informal sorting, specialty schools, and the choice of courses in school do separate students, but we still have less tracking than any of the other countries I have been talking about. In the absence of tracking, it seems obvious that an education system needs to take the differences among students into account in planning the way instruction is delivered in the school and classroom.

But obvious or not, we do not do this. We use the same basic instructional delivery system you would use with a rather narrow tracking system in schools and classrooms where we have a broad range of abilities. A teacher in a one-room schoolhouse who had three first graders, two second graders, and so forth all the way up to eighth grade would be very unlikely to stand up in front of the class and give the same lecture to all the children. But it is possible to find a group of students in the same class who have almost as great a range in where they are in mathematics or in English as the children in the one-room school. And we expect a teacher to use the same methods and give the same lesson to this extremely heterogeneous class.

Educational bureaucracy. When the subject of reform comes up, people often remark on how much money we already spend on education—more than many of the countries discussed here—and how little we get for it. The point is well taken, but so is the teachers' point that their schools, especially those in cities, are starved for resources. So where does the money go?

When Martin Mayer wrote *The Schools* in the early 1960s, he found that there were more supervisors, administrators, inspectors—more central office administration—in New York City than in all of France and more in New York State than in all of Europe. This should have been no surprise: European schools do not have the elaborate bureaucratic structure at the local level that New York City and, indeed, most of our school systems have. Many of our large school districts have one administrator per 560 students, which probably translates into one administrator for every sixteen to twenty teachers. Compare this with the Holweide Comprehensive School in Cologne, West Germany, where a principal and two deputies take care of the administrative duties in a school of 2,200 students and teach, too.

But however we saddled ourselves with a system that requires an army of administrators, who need middle managers to support them, who need support staff to support them, and so on, it is clear that there are more effective and efficient ways of spending scarce education dollars.

Am I suggesting we should alter our education system along the lines of the European system I have sketched here? Not really. European educational practices can help put our problems into perspective. They raise questions that we need to answer, but they do not provide the answers. And the questions are pressing:

- Can we reconcile our tradition of local control with the need for more sophisticated standards of what students should know and be able to do, standards that reflect the new demands of a global economy and a changed society? The Education Summit in 1989 correctly perceived the need for national agreement about our goals for schools and students. But will we be able to come up with standards that will be acceptable to the various governing bodies and diverse populations in our sixteen thousand school districts and yet rigorous enough to be worth something?
- How can we meet the challenge of finding enough qualified teachers, particularly in a time of labor shortage? Will we need to think more about restructuring the teaching profession, as the medical profession and, to a lesser extent, the legal profession have restructured themselves? Can technology help provide an answer?
- How will we solve the problem of variations in student ability that European education systems have typically dealt with by explicit, formal tracking and that we have generally tried to avoid? Is some form of cooperative learning, a system in which small, mixed-ability learning groups work together and compete

with other groups, a useful answer? Is technology a possible answer here, too? What about a version of Australia's Victorian Curriculum, where coursework is organized like a Boy or Girl Scout Merit badge and students get course credit by performing specified tasks?

- Can we transform our system of standardized testing so that it assesses worthwhile skills and achievements instead of the low-level skills, which are tested in most multiple-choice exams?

We are unlikely to find solutions to these problems unless we call on the creativity of the people in our schools and encourage them to experiment, learn from their mistakes, and experiment some more. Bureaucratic institutions—and most schools are bureaucracies—do not foster this kind of daring in their people. The bureaucratic approach is to try to solve a problem by adding some new programs with some new staff to administer them, while leaving the basic structure unchanged. So we will need to be creative in figuring out how to encourage school systems and schools to be flexible and creative and productive. The most useful guidance comes from our market economy, the private sector. This is not to suggest that schools be privatized—far from it, for that would only compound our problems. Rather, it is to suggest that many of the fundamental principles of our market economy may be as applicable to the public sector as they are to the private.

A company manufacturing a product serves the market better than its competitors do or it goes out of business. And it must be ready to change when other companies improve their products and when the market and the economy change. For example, during the oil crisis of the mid 1970s, companies that depended on a plentiful supply of cheap energy had to rethink the way they did business or go under. And again, ten years later, when the dollar became strong in world financial markets, companies for whom foreign markets were important had to figure out how to cut their costs drastically or risk not being able to sell their products abroad.

This system of self-examination and self-renewal does not wait for times of crisis to go into operation. Successful businesses are constantly on the lookout for new ways of doing things. Their survival depends on their ability to see what changes need to be made and to make them, even if they hurt.

How might we set up mechanisms that will make schools responsive to change and able to renew themselves? Competition is the spur in business and success the reward. So, with schools, we must find mechanisms to ensure that improving student achievement brings great rewards and continuing failure to do so brings punishment or other negative consequences. Creating such mechanisms for our schools will require giving them flexibility and time for experimentation. We do not yet know what will move people over periods of time and encourage them to make tough decisions. We do know from bitter and repeated experience that we do not need some one-size-fits-all education policy that might work today but will close out possibilities for change tomorrow.

A similar point about the sources of self-renewal was made by Wei Jingsheng, a Chinese dissident, a little over a decade ago, when Chairman Mao had just left office and the current Chinese government had taken over. The new government decided to solve the problems of China by modernizing manufacturing and agriculture—in fact, they planned "four modernizations" of various sectors of the society. Wei Jingsheng countered by proposing a "fifth modernization," democracy. He saw democracy as a system of self-criticism, adjustment, and renewal, and without it, he believed, the other four would never succeed.

Wherever we find this principle of self-renewal for public education and whatever we call it, we have to realize that we do not have the option of remaining with our present system of public education. It will be abandoned because it does not work. And we do not have much time.

The signs are clear. The Illinois legislature has already taken the responsibility for running Chicago's schools away from Chicago's school board, administrators, and professionals and given it to parent-majority councils in individual schools. Similar proposals are being considered for other big cities like Detroit and New York City. New Jersey has used its educational bankruptcy law to take over the Jersey City school system and remove its superintendent and elected school board. Kentucky has also taken over "educationally bankrupt" school districts. More takeovers are likely to follow. In Chelsea, Massachusetts, the school board has admitted defeat and handed over the power to run its schools to Boston University. The university hopes this will be the first of many such takeovers.

The movement for tuition tax credits is also gaining popularity at the state level. Wisconsin plans a major move for vouchers, which will include vouchers for nonpublic schools. And in Kansas City, a court case is seeking vouchers for black students to attend private schools.

I wish I could say that I feel optimistic about the prospects of our finding a fifth modernization for American public education. Doing it will take nerve and boldness and a willingness to take risks, and these qualities are rare in any group of people. In the meantime, the news could not be worse. We are getting closer and closer to vouchers, closer to schools being run from state departments of education, closer to businesses coming up with our answers for us. Some of us still act as though the public education system, run the way we run it now, will go on forever. We had better wise up because it will not.

CHAPTER 2

Educational Restructuring: Generative Metaphor and New Vision

Hunter Moorman and John Egermeier

INTRODUCTION

What is educational restructuring? How can we better understand it, constructively criticize it, and help promote it? Is there a chance that American education can be improved by it? Our aim in this chapter is to provide a context and conceptual framework that can help in formulating answers to these questions.

The concept of restructuring has come to encompass a myriad of educational problems, programs, and philosophies. While no consensus definition exists, there is some emerging agreement around what "it" is or should be and what its guiding principles and key elements are in practice.

Restructuring is

- *A metaphor* for educational change that conveys the image of starting anew, of changing not only content but also form, of shifting from tinkering with the old order to inventing a new order founded on new assumptions, values, and vision.
- *A national public policy debate,* made possible by the metaphor, in

search of new grounds for public agreement over enduring issues of national purpose and identity as well as over the ends and means of education.

- *A loose collection of prescriptions* for school reform that in sum call for change in four domains of schooling: programs and services for students, roles and relationships, rules and regularities, and accountability (National LEADership Network, 1991).

- *A codification of maturing beliefs* about the ideal performance of the educational system, organizational and pedagogical processes suited to it, and ways of making changes that will result in desired processes and performance, comprising an inchoate but promising new vision for American education.

We seek here not to *define* restructuring but to *appreciate* it—not to reduce it to some smaller-than-life formula but to develop a context and framework for understanding its richness and power.

Restructuring, we believe, is first and foremost a potent "generative metaphor" (Schön, 1979), a powerful trope stimulating interesting, inventive new thought in the problematic areas of educational policy and practice. We describe the metaphor at work using three different perspectives on education: as a proxy area for the broader debate over national purpose and direction, as an organizational "garbage can," and as a "wicked" public policy problem. The oft-decried messy, imprecise, and unmanageable character of restructuring is the consequence of the conflicting, ambiguous public policy arena it is a part of.

Restructuring is also an operational undertaking to define and implement an emerging consensus in answer to the two guiding questions of educational reform: In what ways do we want to improve *performance* in education? and, How can we best bring about the *changes* needed to meet the performance objectives we set for education? Restructuring is thus an effort to crystallize from disparate parts of knowledge and belief an alternative conceptualization of what education can and should be and of how we can achieve this new vision. We believe it constitutes an important culminating or consolidating stage in which several theories of educational improvement and change gel to form an important new understanding of education and related public policy.

From its unshapely mass in the context of public dialogue and problem finding, we see coalescing a vision of potentially striking coherence and power that seems to hold forth significant prospects for reform. We describe this inchoate picture first in a sketch of field initiatives and a simple conceptual framework for organizing such efforts and then in terms of the reform thought it generates. We then assess how prospects for reform can be enhanced or diminished by actions the public and the education profession choose to take with respect to certain internal contradictions and constraints of restructuring, to the processes of change that might guide it, and to the combination of "tight integration" and "loose coupling" that can cause change in education either to blossom or to wither. After examining these factors, we conclude with an optimistic observation about the future of restructuring in American education.

RESTRUCTURING AS GENERATIVE METAPHOR: THREE PUBLIC POLICY CONTEXTS

Generative Metaphor

A "generative metaphor" is an image that encompasses divergent values or perspectives on a problematic situation in a way that permits fruitful thought and action (Schön, 1979). The Cold War was such a metaphor. It encompassed the dual notions of ongoing, hostile competition and peaceful coexistence in a way that enlisted public support and guided the formulation of a coherent, persuasive foreign policy.

We see restructuring as such a metaphor. This image, borrowed from the business world (see, for example, Business International S.A., 1987), embraces a host of divergent ideas and appeals— problems with education (human capital and international competitiveness, human dignity and character and intellect); rejection of discredited approaches to improving education (new wines souring in old skins); invocation of an enduring American value (business enterprise); and a quest for new ways to "solve the problem" through optimistic, inventive, and collaborative social action.

Conceiving of the issue as one of restructuring creates new conceptual ground to stand on and makes possible ideas and alliances precluded by prior analyses and positions. The metaphor helps us to escape the bounds of ordinary experience and to reach new insights and more powerful perceptions. In shifting to new ground, it sets aside stalemated values and ideas and opens the way for discovery or crafting of new common interests and goals. Agreement among people and across positions that could not be reconciled under prior conceptual terms has become possible under the metaphoric stimulus of restructuring.

Restructuring suggests the need to rethink the mission of education in light of changing conditions and imperatives of the coming century, to exchange traditional forms of schooling for pedagogical and organizational processes that fit new missions, to shift from one set of guiding values and assumptions to another, and, perhaps, to embark on an ongoing process of transformation instead of seeking static solutions to fixed problems.

Metaphors are powerful, but they are not especially precise. The tropic responses the metaphoric vehicle evokes are as varied as there are contexts and imaginations. The gain in insight and understanding a good metaphor sparks is possible in fact only by virtue of the freedom from definitional constraint it enjoys. The cost of metaphoric gain here is acceptance of the diversity, contradiction, and tentativeness metaphors entail. We come in a later section to a meatier formulation of restructuring for those who hunger for definitional repasts. In this section, we look to three public policy contexts—national dialogue, "wicked" problems, and the organizational "garbage can"—for an appreciation of the messy side of restructuring.

Educational Reform as Proxy Debate

It is a common lament that American schools reform "again, again, and again" (Cuban, 1990). To some, America's pursuit of educational innovation and reform seems both endless and feckless. We suggest, though, that it is a healthy if imperfect quest.

In times of national crisis, the country turns toward education and the schools. The nation wants a better, certainly a more stable, future in one or more important dimensions where personal and national values are at stake: national security, social order, economic well-being, social justice, and realization of human potential. These themes, arranged here roughly to correspond to Maslow's hierarchical formulation of human needs, are recurrent in the national debate and dialogue regarding education. They are continually debated in many forums but they rise to public consciousness chiefly during periods when perception of national crisis or threat is widely shared.

There are three possible explanations for this focus on education in times of crisis. First, Americans believe education is the social tool for constructing a better future, either because governing elites choose schools as the indirect but safer avenue to change in such volatile areas as poverty and racism, or because society trusts in the meliorative powers of knowledge and socialization that schools are thought to provide (Cuban, 1990). Second, education entrepreneurs use periods of uncertainty, unrest, or distress as occasions to advance ideas or to seek opportunity that more settled times foreclose. This possibility is discussed under the "garbage can" thesis in a following section. And third, education is a national stage where citizens block out fundamental values and directions of society (Tyack and Hansot, 1982). What the polity is unable or unwilling to do in other institutional venues, it struggles to work through in the crucible of education.

National debate over education may constitute the most vital examination of fundamental questions of national problems, purpose, and policies the American public engages in. Directions set for education may well signal the resolution (for the time being) of conflicts over urgent public values expressed in new coalitions, consensus, and meaning that transfer to other social sectors and problems. Educational debate plays this role because it incorporates the major issues and conflicting values of the larger society and because it provides a more vigorous intellectual and institutional forum than does the rest of the public sphere.

America was born amidst a swirl of disparate political and social ideologies. Its political and governmental processes have institutionalized diverse commitments and values, suspended uneasily between an embrace of national power and rejection of central authority. This legacy has been reflected through the years in ongoing struggles between cherished but clashing values: equality and quality, equity and efficiency, liberty and equality, among others. The full realization of any one element in a pair is hampered by the contrary pull of the other. Much of the contest of national policymaking is the weighing, negotiating, and working out of a balance among the competing values that will hold at any given period of time—a balance that enables productive, cooperative action greater than would otherwise be possible under some other balance.

The United States, like the industrialized West and most other advanced countries, has a small public sphere. Society is highly organized (Scott and Hart, 1979) and is shaped chiefly by private corporate and professional values and influences. The scope for public consideration of the ends of society has shrunk to meager proportions (Arendt, 1958). It was not always so. The pre-Enlightenment world, for example, was largely a public world, where basic values and societal directions were worked out within the Church, community, and workplace.

It is not only that the overall *institutional* scope of public as opposed to private life has declined over the generations. Cultural bases of public life have lost force as well. Conventions about the relationship of the individual to the community have changed, such that the scope of individual interests has increased relative to the scope of commitments and obligations to the group (Bellah et al., 1985; Horkheimer, 1974; Lasch, 1979). The geographical borders of local communities and the common values they contain, along with the interpersonal bonds they provide, have deteriorated (Coleman, 1985), and the shared values that give society symbolic grounds for cooperative action have eroded (Vickers, 1983).

Moreover, the governmental institutions through which public values are expressed and realized are themselves at a low state of efficacy. Congress has long been criticized for its "impediments to democracy" (Dahl, 1977). Recent reforms intended to overcome those impediments have themselves become a part of the problem, leading to near legislative paralysis through a balkan array of subcommittees, lack of leadership continuity, and party disarray. At the same time, voters express irreconcilable preferences. They demand both fiscal and foreign policy conservancy and expansion of domestic assistance and opportunity, putting executive and legislative branches at loggerheads. Lacking satisfaction through formal democratic procedures, the American public has organized an army of interest groups that besieges the executive branch (Lowi, 1979). As presidents have seen their office grow correspondingly visible and potent, they have been impelled to govern more firmly and to be more responsive to partisan interests, with the result that the executive branch has grown increasingly centralized and politicized (Moe, 1982) and government efficiency and overall citizen participation have been reduced. The terms of political debate are locked now in doctrinaire and sterile antagonism (Dionne, 1991). Productive discussion of major issues and solutions to critical social problems are obstructed by partisan dogma serving primarily to perpetuate the power of parties and politicians.

Education is the most pervasive public service and generally the smallest local unit of government in America today. It serves as an arena for public debate about key societal values, dilemmas, and directions that extend far beyond the schoolhouse. In this context, it is possible to see restructuring as the forum for the development of the "universe of discourse" necessary for the evolution of public values and determination of effective social action. To the degree that a robust debate over restructuring persists, it may well help formulate the new terms and coalitions for effective action along similar lines in other sectors.

How should our society be organized, and what kinds of opportunities should we make available to whom? Where does responsibility rest for individual and community advancement, and what kinds of public policies best promote expression of that responsibility? What do we mean as a society by community and by individualism? What is the proper balance between them, and how should we try to achieve that balance? What kinds of human relations are desirable and just? What is the extent of both public and private good in this society, and how are decisions about the distribution of those goods best reached? Is human nature such that it responds best to competition and incentives, or to cooperation and enablements—and if there are circumstances in which one is more fitting than the other, what are they and how can they be incorporated in sound public policy?

Restructuring couches the debate over such essential questions in terms that transcend the limitations of contemporary political discourse. It provides the metaphoric ground for examining these questions in fresh terms and for negotiating new meaning to the age-old conflicts they represent. It provides the basis for reframing problematic situations so that effective social action can be taken. It is helping the nation engage in a productive but safe airing out and catharsis of deeply troubling and often intractable problems. And it gives symbolic expression to society's concern for certain values, even if they are more largely honored in theory than realized in policy and action (Cohen and Rosenberg, 1977).

Education as a "Wicked" Problem

In addition to serving as a conversation over national values, restructuring is also the public and professional process of conducting a renewed, reinvigorated debate over the two problematic issues in education: What constitutes satisfactory system performance? and, What is the best way to manage the change needed to achieve that performance?

Restructuring, again, serves as a generative metaphor that stimulates and channels the working through of specific problems in education. The concept of restructuring as a generative metaphor is particularly powerful in this context because of the peculiar nature of education as a "wicked" problem and the resulting need to seek solutions through negotiation of meaning and "reframing" rather than through rational decision making and technically oriented "solutions."

In what sense is education a "wicked" problem? Scholars have coined the terms "tame" and "wicked" to draw the distinction in public policy between sets of problems that yield to technical solutions and those that defy such solution (Rittel and Webber, 1973). "Tame" problems may be formidable but they can be usefully defined and solved in technical terms. "Wicked" problems are of a different order.

Rittel and Webber note the following characteristics (among others) of wicked problems: there is no "definitive formulation" of these problems; there is no way of telling when the problems have been fully understood or "solved"; prospective solutions cannot be objectively determined but only assessed as a matter of judgment; the consequences of any operation on the problems elude precise measurement, even over long periods of time; every such problem is essentially unique, conforming to no meaningfully established pattern; causation is interdependent and indeterminate; problems are overdetermined—they are the products of several factors, any one of which alone would be a sufficient cause; and the consequences of faulty action may be severe—planners and policymakers have no room for error.

Crime, poverty, and race relations fit this definition. So does education, where the "problem" is one of resources, technology, children or parents, environment, structure, goals, values, professionalism, too little discretion or too little initiative, overcontrol or lack of accountability, poorly integrated services, racism, poverty, mediocrity or competence short of excellence. When and by what criteria the problem is "solved," what standards to set, what time horizon to scan, whom to involve, how to summon the will, and where to focus the corrective technology—all these are characteristic dilemmas of wicked problems. The definition of the problem is ipso facto the statement of the solution; but both are inextricably bound up in the tangle of interdependent, problematic social conditions.

It can be useful to think of wicked problems less as "problems" than as "problematic situations" (Schön, 1979) or as "systems of problems"—"messes"—in Ackoff's (1974) pithy terms. They are best approached not in hopes of finding a ready technical solution but as situations to be appreciated and managed (Ackoff, 1974).

Given its wicked nature, education needs to be placed in a "problem setting"; that is, a context of relevant factors and interactions in which an extended process of "reframing" can unfold (Rein and Schön, 1977). The analyst frames the problem, formulates an initial solution, judges the outcome, and lets that result lead to a richer, more interesting reformulation of the problem, progressing thus in an iterative "conversation with the situation" (Schön, 1983; 1984).

Americans tend to believe that new knowledge, or more facts, will provide needed answers to social dilemmas of policy. But social sciences research and professional social inquiry are limited tools. Wicked problems are by nature beyond the reach of rational methods, and policy is by nature concerned with competing interests and values that are not directly resolvable by knowledge. Analytic problem solving methods are usually inadequate in the face of interdependent problem situations. Indeed they may cause damage where they are intended to help (Dunn, 1981). Where individuals and social units are engaged in interlocked behaviors too complex to chart fully, analysis and instrumental action are as likely as not to make matters worse (Weick, 1979; March and Olsen, 1976).

What analytic inquiry *can* do is to inform the debate in a variety of ways. It can help set the problem, clarify policy choices, weigh the costs and benefits of trade-offs between competing values and policies (Rein and White, 1977). Research knowledge gives power to those who have it, can help arrange coalitions around developing ideologies, and can satisfy public demand for accountability. It can help complicate matters productively by pointing out new issues, dimensions, and complexities; and it can confirm or cast doubt on unscientific but strongly held perceptions, opinion, and convictions (Cohen and Lindblom, 1979).

But it is the guiding metaphor that inspires new interest among the public, stimulates imaginative reconceptualizations of problematic situations that are amenable to more effective social action, and consolidates public commitment and political will. Restructuring has begun to reframe the problematic situation of education. How this is so, and the extent to which it is occurring, are issues explored in later sections of this chapter.

The Educational "Garbage Can"

There is one sense in which it does not do to look for too much logic or coherence in the restructuring movement. It may instead be useful to view restructuring as part of an organizational phenomenon that Cohen, March, and Olsen (1972) have dubbed the "garbage can." This evocative term reflects the anarchic, ambiguity-laden, and irrational dimension of organizational life. It may aptly characterize education and the early stages of restructuring.

Ambiguity and dissension prevail at both the unit and overall system level in education. The scope of authoritative views is large and uncertain. The "industry" is fragmented across fifty states and nearly sixteen thousand local education agencies. In addition to several groups generally acknowledged as having a legitimate share of power in educational matters—parents, teachers, administrators, state and local boards, and state legislators, among others—it encompasses many noneducational members such as test publishers, accrediting agencies, and textbook publishers that exercise a considerable influence over educational decision making. Agreement on the purposes of education and on the means for achieving them is uncommon. The core technology is itself still poorly understood.

Any such extensive, complex, amorphous and ambiguity-prone organization as our national "system" of education invariably plays host to an anarchic gathering of problems and solutions seeking a match, and of prospective decision makers shopping for choices to make. The mix lacks the order and logic of a recipe; instead, it resembles a "garbage can" where problems, solutions, and choice situations mix indiscriminately and at random in the flow of organizational events (Cohen, March, and Olsen, 1976).

To liken education at the overall system level to an organizational "garbage can" is to be neither cynical nor derogatory but to acknowledge the range of interests and potential represented in industry-level reform movements. The image helps portray how so much activity and so many ideas—some of them new, some familiar—can gather under the rubric of restructuring.

The processes that match problems, solutions, and choice situations are usually poorly structured themselves. Solutions casting about for problems to solve and problems searching for solutions to justify may form mismatched attachments.

When faced with opportunities for choice, decision makers may embrace problems or solutions prematurely or too late. Various rules and devices of an organization structure the "garbage can" and determine what kinds of connections are created, for better or worse, between the bits and pieces. Under ideal conditions, organizational filters reduce the flow of problems and advance the flow of solutions, creating the most favorable ratio for good matches and sound decisions.

The restructuring metaphor has stirred up the "garbage can," bringing to light problems and solutions that have been buried or strewn about the edges. The dawn of the current interest in reform, let us say for the sake of convenience with publication of *A Nation at Risk* (National Commission on Excellence in Education, 1983), and the more recent adoption of the term "restructuring" in an educational context, have provided a convenient forum for the convergence of problems, solutions, and opportunities for making decisions. Advocates advance their particular interests, hoping to find under the "restructuring" rubric the occasion to put to use their particular problem, solution, or choice point.

Restructuring has been a movement in flux (Lewis, 1989). It has served well by providing a forum where the lessons about processes of innovation and institutional change and their implications for the roles and practices of state and local educational agencies could be paraded, where the concerns of industry and communities and the professions could be sounded, where publicity and interest could be stimulated for otherwise obscure or uninteresting reform practices, and where experimentation could be undertaken on a larger-than-usual scale without undue fear of failure.

It has also begun to serve as the organizational structuring device, a conceptual tool for sorting and matching problems, solutions, and choice opportunities. It has effectively begun to shift the discourse about reform from specific programs to general principles. Content is being complemented with process, and goals with transformation. Restructuring is leading to a codification of emerging principles— some rediscovered from times past, some minted from newly mined research—that may be advancing toward a new guiding ethos for education.

RESTRUCTURING INITIATIVES AND CONCEPTUAL FRAMEWORK

A handful of influential reports appear to have provided the early inspiration for restructuring. Works such as *Horace's Compromise: The*

Dilemma of the American High School (Sizer, 1985), *A Place Called School: Prospects for the Future* (Goodlad, 1984), *A Nation Prepared: Teachers for the 21st Century* (Carnegie Forum on Education and the Economy, Task Force on Teaching as a Profession, 1986), and *Restructuring the Education System: Agenda for the '90s* (Cohen, M., 1987) painted a dismal picture of American education. They found teachers and students to have colluded in a pact of mediocrity, teachers to lack the discretion and accountability of other professionals, curriculum and instruction to discourage independent, critical thinking, and schools to be rigid, numbing environments.

Their prescriptions for change drew from unlike philosophical bases and led in many directions, but they converged along a common theme of restructuring. Sizer (1985) proposed an "experiment" where schools would concentrate on development of mind and character; teacher and student would commit to roles as coach and worker; attitudes of unanxious expectation, decency, and trust would prevail; staff, budget, and decision making would be tailored to the school goals under the discretion of principal and teachers; and students would strive to master work and to demonstrate mastery as the sign of completing school. Goodlad (1984) pinpointed pedagogy and the quality of the teacher workforce as the key ingredient in school effectiveness and in preparing young citizens for participating in a democracy. Improvements in teacher competence would have to occur in tandem with changes in the school environment. School change would have to proceed principally at the individual building level, but school change and restructuring of teacher education could best be accomplished through school-university partnerships. Carnegie's Task Force on Teaching as a Profession (Carnegie Forum on Education and the Economy, 1986) called for a "transformation of the environment for teaching" (p. 55) that would confer professional autonomy on teachers; engage them in a collegium with lead teachers; provide adequate staff support and maintain stable student-teacher ratios; substitute alternative leadership models for the bureaucratically managed hierarchy; encourage building autonomy through school-site budgeting and state deregulation; and balance autonomy with greater teacher accountability. Michael Cohen (1987) emphasized the need for significant change in "the nature, level, and distribution of student outcomes" (p. 5) and for overall restructuring capable of realizing the productivity gains achieving such outcomes would require. So that *all* children could master higher-order cognitive skills, the entire system of education—not just the schools—

would have to be restructured. States would have to set goals, assess performance, provide rewards for good performance or disincentives for poor performance, and promote diversity and experimentation. Districts would have to shift discretion for decision making and allocation of resources to the schools. At the school building level, academic goals, time, space, curriculum, instruction, and teacher roles would have to change in ways determined by local conditions and the overall commitment to students' higher cognitive performance.

Early Field Initiatives

Much else has been written about restructuring since those early reports, but those studies' influence in the field still predominates. Overall, while restructuring appears still to be far better developed in theory than in practice, there also does seem to be steady growth in policy and practice aimed at radical school change.

Not even the most informed observers can say how widespread the restructuring movement in the field is. We estimate that perhaps 3 to 5 percent of the schools in the country are involved in some kind of restructuring. As of mid 1991, at least five major national restructuring programs were underway, several lighthouse districts were moving from infancy into "school-age," and numerous state programs had been initiated by governors or legislatures.

The *Coalition of Essential Schools* engages 170 schools in restructuring according to the nine principles of "essential schools" developed in *Horace's Compromise* (Sizer, 1985). Schools work out the implementation of the principles in their own ways. The coalition offers the support of shared commitment to common ideas and of access to others engaged in the enterprise.

Re: Learning is a partnership among the Coalition of Essential Schools, the Education Commission of the States, and seven participating states, begun in 1988 to provide essential state and district support for schools engaged in restructuring. State governors have made commitments to support ten to fifteen schools in their development as "essential schools." Several other states with schools active in the coalition are working toward making the commitments needed to join Re: Learning.

The National Center for Innovation at the National Education Association has recently consolidated, refocused, and expanded the association's program on restructuring. The center has five program thrusts that together constitute an overall system for innovation:

- *Excellence in Action.*   An effort to identify exemplary programs in schools (e.g., teaching of English, dropout prevention). The center identifies approximately eight sites per year, aiming for a total of about twenty exemplars.
- *Mastery In Learning Consortium.*   Thirty-two school-level sites at the forefront of change host research and demonstration to learn in depth what is necessary for restructuring.
- *Learning Laboratories Initiatives.*   Twenty district-level sites, with five or six added each year until there will be one such site in each state, serve as laboratories for investigating how all schools in a district can successfully restructure.
- *Teachers' Education Initiative.*   Collaborations in several states among school sites, colleges and universities, and state teachers associations are working to develop new ways of preparing teachers to take new roles in restructuring schools.
- *School Renewal Network.*   Teachers at restructuring sites, along with prominent researchers, network through electronic conferences on ten pertinent topics.

The *Center for Restructuring*, of the American Federation of Teachers, supports a range of program development and technical assistance to advance restructuring. Several projects are developing ways to train teachers in forms of alternative assessment in different subject areas and to help teachers and administrators implement alternative assessment programs in their schools. The center has pilot-tested a prototype CD-ROM on school restructuring in fifty schools. "Professional practice schools" have been started in three different states. The Urban District Leadership Consortium links and supports superintendents, board members, and teachers' union presidents in urban districts undertaking restructuring.

John Goodlad's *Center* and *National Network for Educational Renewal* are committed to the concurrent reform of teacher education and the restructuring of schools. Participating members pursue school change at the building level in partnership with universities responsible for teacher preparation. Their overarching aim is to prepare citizens to take responsible roles in a humane society. The network links the efforts of fourteen school-university partnerships with 115 school districts and sixteen participating universities (Education Commission of the States, 1991).

The *National Alliance for Restructuring Education*, sponsored by the National Center on Education and the Economy, supports twelve schools and districts in restructuring. Sites exemplify the kinds of broad, systemic change restructuring demands. Participants in the alliance concentrate on developing alternative student assessment, boosting performance through innovative incentive and accountability mechanisms, and introducing processes for managing change at school and district levels. Member sites also work on such problems as creating new roles at state and district levels, designing effective communication and decision-making processes, and building community support for achieving better student performance (Regional Laboratory for Educational Improvement of the Northeast and Islands Newsletter, 1991).

State restructuring initiatives, some of them overlapping with the Coalition of Essential Schools and Re:Learning, are numerous. Some, like Governor Romer's Creativity Schools project in Colorado, have been initiated by state executives. Others are the result of legislative mandate—in Texas and New York, for example, school-based management is now required by law. Washington State legislation permits some schools to restructure under its "Schools for the 21st Century" program. Maine has encouraged district restructuring following individual plans approved by the state department of education and has provided grant funds for some.

Pioneering restructuring initiatives in several communities are persisting, though not without trouble. Programs in Dade County (Miami) and Broward County (Ft. Lauderdale) in Florida; Hammond, Indiana; San Diego, California; Greece and Rochester in New York; and Bellevue, Washington, among several other notable examples, are entering the stage where early plans and commitment will be tested. Prickly issues—of follow through, expansion and consolidation, outcomes and their comportment with expectations, and the limits of program, technique, and will—have already arisen or can be expected to arise in these sites, as they must elsewhere. (See Chira, 1991; Timar, 1989.)

Starting Points and Organizing Dimensions

The restructuring metaphor and these various restructuring initiatives clearly encompass a very broad range of ideas and approaches to restructuring. We think a simple conceptual framework of three dimensions can help in sorting out and thinking through the various approaches to or rationales for restructuring. Impetus for restructuring tends to start within one or another of these dimensions: *mission*, *organizational systems*, and *environmental imperatives*. The more robust rationales or initiatives extend along the remaining dimensions, following the logic established by their initial starting point. The particular value or problem statement of the starting point usually drives the choice of elements in the other dimensions.

Mission.   Restructuring efforts are driven by varying assumptions about school *mission*. Missions commonly advanced for restructuring schools emphasize development of intellect and character, preparation of a competitive workforce, and provision of education programs that meet, in both structure and content, the diverse needs of a heterogeneous student population. Each rests on different assumptions about the nature of society and schooling, and each suggests a somewhat different approach to school restructuring.

The argument on behalf of education for intellect and character is that American schools have labored under an impossibly broad and incoherent mission, with the result that school programs lack substance and focus and that school organization and processes impede learning and development of maturity. Schools should pare down and revamp the curriculum, it is argued, recast the roles of teacher as "coach" and student and as "worker," and employ Socratic or other instructional methods geared to the development of critical thinking skills and independent habits of mind. Missions reconceived along these lines lead of necessity to changes in the form and content of schooling, including fewer subjects, longer or varied class periods, interdisciplinary instruction, and authentic relationships between teachers and students. This approach is exemplified in The Study of High Schools, chaired by Theodore Sizer, and the ensuing work of the Coalition of Essential Schools, in earlier work of the Paedeia Group, in much of what is coming to be called "schools of thought" (Brown, 1991; Chion-Kenney, 1991), and in some of the projects of the National Governors' Association.

Preparation of a competitive workforce is a mission evolving out of twin concerns for America's declining economic competitiveness in a changing world economy and its poor performance on standardized measures of international academic achievement. The world economy has changed, it is said, and so have America's students. The international marketplace has shifted from low technology basic manufacturing, from heavy industry, and from personal services to high-tech communications and electronics and to sophisticated, abstract services, requiring relatively more complex reading, writing, and computational skills as well as the capacity to "learn to learn." While the educational systems in many other Western and Pacific Rim countries are producing workers skilled in higher-order thinking and problem solving, American youth, it is argued, lack the intellectual skills and productive workplace attitudes industry needs. While American students' scores on standardized tests have improved relative to those of their predecessors, the rate of improvement of American students still lags behind the improvement rate of their overseas contemporaries. For America to remain competitive, or to regain its competitive position, its schools must develop an improved, competitive product.

American industry asserts that the quality of high school and college graduates is sufficient to meet the workforce needs of the largest and foremost firms. But they contend that the bulk of these graduates do not have adequate skills to meet the needs of the rest of the industrial sector. Schools, then, have a dual challenge. They must shift from programs emphasizing basic skills and test mastery to programs that will develop higher-order thinking skills and intellectual independence. And they must serve not only the top and bottom layers, the most traditionally promising and the needy students, but also the large and typically neglected group in the middle. More rigorous academic programs, new forms of testing, new curricula and materials, and different ways of organizing instruction to reach all students effectively are required.

The *equality of access* mission is based on the belief that schools as presently designed are incompatible with the needs of large numbers of students at risk in American society today (Kershner and Connolly, 1991; Shedlin, 1990). It is the, or one, mission of schools to ensure that minority, urban, and low-income children at risk of failing to advance in school and in society are given the means for sharing equitably in both. Schools designed to develop intellect and character, or to provide a competitive workforce, it is held, may ignore or further damage these children by adopting narrow conceptions of intelligence, failing to recognize and reward effort, and neglecting students' cognitive and affective needs for stable, cooperative, and individually tailored programs. Where social disintegration is well advanced, it is argued that schools are the *only* social institution capable of serving this population (Howard, 1991), and they must do so with programs that emphasize cooperative learning strategies, diverse teaching styles, perhaps multicultural curriculum, and coordination of several community and social services through the school.

Organizational Systems. Organizations can be thought of as operating along a variety of dimensions. Bolman and Deal (1984) have described organizations in terms of four "frames" corresponding to the major lines of organizational theory: structure, human relations, power, and culture. Another common analytic distinction is made between organizational "authority" and "task" structures. Restructuring at present concerns two major dimensions of organizational systems drawn from a combination of these perspectives: authority/structure and task (sometimes called "core technology").

Authority/structure concerns the organizational forms for getting work done through specialization and integration. It includes the organization's roles, relationships, goals, communication, and allocation of authority. In traditional schools, principals and teachers, with some special support personnel, occupy well-defined roles, and two or three levels of organization fulfill given functions in working toward school goals, according to clear lines of communication and authority.

Task, or "core technology," concerns the conduct (as opposed to the organization) of the basic work of the organization. Learning and instruction and such related technologies as testing, classroom management, and curriculum development constitute the task substance of the school organization.

Proponents of restructuring, then, tend to argue from the logic of either *micropolitics* or *pedagogy*. Those who are primarily concerned about the uses and distribution of power advocate changes in the discretion school members have to act and in the way decisions are made. More managerial discretion closer to the action, or less hierarchical domination, or more participation in decisions are held to lead to better management and decision making, to instructional choices in line with the school's intended mission, and to more wholehearted implementation of the decisions. School-based management and shared decision making are examples of shifting discretion (and accountability) and reorienting the relationships according to which power is shared and used in a school. Corbett (1989a) is careful to note that these and other forms of expanded decision making—or "empowerment"—will be hollow or even counterproductive absent fundamental alterations in the patterns of rules, roles, relationships, and results embodied in the organization.

Others whose primary concerns start with the purposes and nature of sound school technology—teaching and learning, curriculum and instruction—advocate increased emphasis on higher-order thinking skills, alternative conceptions of cognition, revised forms of curriculum and testing, or improved teacher competence and professionalism. Michael Cohen (1987), the Carnegie Task Force on Teaching as a Profession (Carnegie Forum on Education and the Economy, 1986), and Goodlad (1984) exemplify this approach. The choice of micropolitical or pedagogical starting points might well lead to very similar or very different forms of restructuring. Both, for example, could lead to more flexible scheduling or allocation of time (class periods), or to a conception of teachers as coaches or leaders instead of as inculcators of knowledge. But in theory, it could just as readily happen that shared decision making leads a school team to select a more traditional program of instruction, and an alternative pedagogical approach could rest on traditional lines of organizational authority and decision making. In practice, the perspectives tend to converge—redistribution of power leads to autonomy and increased professionalism, and increased professional competence is said to require nonhierarchical, collegial work settings.

Environmental Imperatives. These are the complex of factors within the broader school environment that influence school goals, programs, and processes. In an earlier paper (Moorman and Egermeier, 1990), we used the term "institutional orientation," coined by scholars at the Center for Policy Research in Education (Center for Policy Research in Education, 1988), to suggest that technical, professional, and client orientations characterized approaches to restructuring. It seems to us now on further reflection that the technical perspective is captured under the notion of organizational processes described above, and that "professional" and "client" belong to a larger nest of environmental imperatives acting on the schools. We identify these imperatives as the values and incentives inherent in *professional, political*, and *market* forces at play in the environment. Each force embodies an implicit theory about the purposes of education, human nature, and accountability in education.

According to the *professional* orientation, changes in the working conditions and professional norms of the education workforce will produce improvements in the classroom and in the overall operation of the school. (See Carnegie Forum on Education and the Economy, Task Force on Teaching as a Profession, 1986; Goodlad, 1984; Little, 1982; and Wise, 1990.) The professionalization of teaching will, for example, attract keener aspirants, introduce internal control over members' quality and competence, and substitute desirable norms of professional commitment and collegiality for those of bureaucratic loyalty and autonomy. These changes will lead in turn to better teaching and more authentic human relationships that will result in greater student learning and intellectual development.

The *political* model emphasizes change and control exercised through negotiation of competing interests. Here individual preferences are sorted through political processes, responsibility for their expression is delegated to state government and school boards, and negotiation and compromise result in a formulation of public will that guides the conduct of education.

In the ideal, the public debates preferences and elects state officials and school boards (or the officials who appoint the boards), the boards negotiate policy, and the superintendent and school staff carry out the policy in an untroubled, coherent sequence of policy implementation. Things are different in reality. Three levels of government, and separate bodies within each one, have generated uncoordinated streams of policy. Mandates, regulations, and programs treating isolated groups or problem areas have created a balkanized administrative and program structure. Based on inadequate understanding of local conditions and of processes of change, policies have had limited or unintended effects.

In acknowledgment of these conditions, analysts of restructuring have increasingly begun to think of it in terms of *systemic reform* in which state and local governments have a significant, if modified, role (see Cohen, M., 1987; Harvey and Crandall, 1988; Timar, 1989; Smith and O'Day, 1990). Though the school building may be the basic unit of restructuring, individual schools cannot make and sustain needed change on their own. A strategy of systemic change has to combine "bottom-up" change with new forms of support from the central office and the state (Cohen, M., 1987; Smith and O'Day, 1990). Common purpose must guide a coherent system of educational governance replacing today's hodge-podge policy process (Timar, 1989; Smith and O'Day, 1990). States must shift from use of mandates to facilitating and enabling activity (McLaughlin, 1989; Timar,

1989), and they must set goals and assess performance, providing appropriate rewards and disincentives (Cohen, M., 1987; Smith and O'Day, 1990). Both state and district offices must decentralize decision making and control of resources and ensure that a supportive climate nourishes local initiative and experimentation (Cohen, M., 1987).

The *market* approach assumes that a match can be achieved between consumer preferences and educational programs through the market forces of supply and demand. Advocates of "educational choice" argue that the market model achieves the most efficient client service and the most accountable operation of schools. Attendance at school would be determined on the basis not of geographical zones but of participation entitlements valid at the school of choice.

Overall, consumer preferences are identified, sorted, summed, and ordered, and alternative programs are stimulated or discouraged according to their success in responding to consumer preference. Consumers would be motivated to seek out the best available information concerning market offerings and their match with preferences, and to use this information in choosing a school. Suppliers would be motivated to survive and to achieve success (or make a profit) by appealing to an increasing market share, perhaps even finding creative ways to affect consumer preferences and enlarge demand for the product.

These starting points, and the connections across dimensions they lead advocates of restructuring to choose, reflect their answers, if only implicitly, to such questions as these: What characterizes a just, stable, and productive society? How should the goods and responsibilities of this society be allocated between public and private sectors, and across different societal institutions? What kinds of decisions are crucial in education? What are the incentives and values that should guide educational decision making? Who should make these decisions? How can decision makers be held accountable for their decisions? Predictably, answers are as varied as are public and private values. Where one starts along these dimensions is less important than the journey that follows. Reformers who limit their interests to one of these elements or dimensions may be working to improve schools, but they are not restructuring. For that, a comprehensive vision, broad consensus, systemwide coordination, and time are needed. We turn now to this vision of restructuring.

NEW VISION OF REFORM

In what may be a powerful synthesis across these perspectives, a new vision of reform through restructuring is taking shape. Supporting the vision is a foundation of new assumptions about *education outcomes, human and organizational behavior,* and *institutional performance and change.*

Outcomes

Restructuring has introduced, or reinforced, a new level and quality of emphasis on outcomes. It comes in part from concern with organizational performance. Comparative state and international assessments show that some systems perform less well than other systems, and our nation not so well as other nations. Analysis of workforce needs and international economic competitiveness bares the need for better preparation of school graduates. This perspective is enhanced by the emphasis organization theory and total quality work currently give to organizational results in diagnosing and improving performance.

What outcomes are of particular interest? Two appear to rise above all others: the acquisition of higher-order thinking skills, and academic success for *all* children. New knowledge about learning and instruction and new social and economic conditions have come together as the basis for a new understanding of how best to balance equity, equality, excellence, and efficiency.

The focus on higher levels of cognition stems from developments in "the new learning theory" (see Bransford and Vye, 1989; Resnick, 1987) indicating that learners actively construct the knowledge they acquire and that higher-order skills are used even in the initial development of subject-area knowledge. Passive learning, particularly for those judged incapable of more sophisticated processes, and using basic skills acquisition as a floor standard, can no longer be defended (Cohen, M., 1987; Smith and O'Day, 1990).

Similarly, once the artificial distinction between "basic" and "higher-order" thinking skills is removed, there can be no justification for choosing to educate different children to different levels. Moreover, the demands of the workplace and international competition require that we make the most of our human resources; a wasting or side-tracking of human development that might once have been excused under some other rationale can no longer be tolerated under current economic imperatives. All students must be helped to achieve at a high level.

What may be even more significant than this concentration on particular outcomes, however, is the more general attention paid to the importance of vision, goals, and coherent sense of direction in the education enterprise. The importance of these elements in education is not a new idea. They are widely cited as characteristics of effective organizations and essential tools of sound leadership. Yet at the aggregate system level of organization in education, at state and national levels where the organizational verges onto the political, Americans have been loath to talk of goals and coherence. There lurks the specter of centralization, fear of suffocating diversity and experimentation and of suppressing minority or nonconformist points of view.

At the simplest, operational level, the message of restructuring is that organizations must have some fairly explicit and meaningful sense of mission or goals in order to perform well. At the school level, precisely what mission is selected is less important than that there be one that guides what the school does in a way its participants believe is special (Hill, Foster, and Gendler, 1990).

But the literature of restructuring extends this emphasis on mission and goals beyond the school. Duttweiler and Hord (1987) maintain that "policymakers must visualize and articulate the outcomes their system should strive to achieve" (p. 11). Michael Cohen's (1987) education agenda for the 1990s on restructuring, prepared for the National Governors' Association (NGA), called for states to set goals that they could assess and hold others accountable to, an appeal that later NGA reports have reiterated (National Governors' Association, 1989). In its "call to restructure schools," the National Association of State Boards of Education (undated) argued that states should set "goals and expectations for schools and students" (p. 16). The National Education Goals formulated by the governors and president in 1989 at the Charlottesville, Virginia, "education summit" have been made the centerpiece of the Bush administration's education strategy in *America 2000* (U.S. Department of Education, 1991). The strategy calls for development of standards and voluntary commitment to national testing in pursuit of the goals, and the National Education Goals Panel worked through the summer of 1991 to develop such standards.

Goals and missions connote agreement. And indeed a growing chorus of voices is calling not for goals alone, but for some more fundamental kind of consensus, coherence, and unity to American education. Multiplying state mandates, and regulations and programs intended to satisfy diverse interest groups, fragment the education system and threaten to stymie educational reform (Timar, 1989). A "fragmented, complex, multi-layered educational policy system" significantly impedes education change (Smith and O'Day, 1990, p. 6). In addition to their intended effects, some legislative and legal remedies to inequities in education have intensified political dissension and social conflict (Cohen, D., 1982). The steadying center of gravity in education has come apart under the centripetal assaults of "baroque bureaucracy," conflict within both community and school systems, patchwork federal programs, union activism, and such nonsystem forces as textbook publishers and test developers (Tyack and Hansot, 1982; Smith and O'Day, 1990). If American schools are to change for the better, if meaningful reform is to work, and indeed if public education is to fulfill its commitment to the American dream, then we must establish "a broad consensus about the purpose of schooling" (Timar, 1989, p. 275) served by a "unifying vision and goals" (Smith and O'Day, 1990, p. 18). Restructuring is more than a search for improved organizational performance in education; it is a quest for common purpose, a crusade to unify the American public around a common vision for the future of its children.

Human and Organizational Behavior

Fresh assumptions about the nature of reality, knowledge, and human behavior also contribute to the emerging synthesis. Whether or not they are sufficient to constitute a *new paradigm* for education, we cannot say at this point. But it does seem at least that this is an effort to bring together two existing social science paradigms, to leaven the traditional positivism of education with the yeast of interpretive or constructivist assumptions. The picture of education that emerges is more robust, complex, and promising, and more challenging, uncertain, and precarious as well. It has profound implications for educational policy and practice.

In brief, the resulting synthesis establishes a new set of guiding tenets for education:

- Schools and the education system can best be understood as a *combination of rationality and indeterminacy*, such that organizational processes are governed to some degree by linear cause-and-effect relationships amenable to prediction and control and to some degree by ambiguous, mutually causative, interdependent relationships best engaged in through creative problem finding and acts of sense making.

- Schools as organizations exist in some part as pregiven, *external entities* independent of the individuals within them, and in some part as *organized streams of experience*, which participants shape through implicit agreements negotiated and confirmed among themselves over time.

- Students, teachers, administrators, and other participants in education are most productive and fulfilled when they act within *organizational frameworks that are both deterministic and voluntaristic*, with some processes that rationally constrain and induce behavior toward organizational goals, and others that engage and enable participants to express, create, and give meaning to significant individual and group values.

- The means participants use to regulate their interactions with one another and their functions in the school environment are ideally a combination of *bureaucratic and participatory democratic processes*: one for achieving control through division of labor, specialization, and hierarchical allocation of information and "decision premises" and the other for achieving community of purpose through mutual enablement and collaborative inquiry.

The implications of these tenets for education are profound. The tenets require fundamental revision of the basic assumptions, values, and beliefs about education in America. Restructuring reaches to the deepest level of culture in society.

American education is structured in accordance with a set of deeply ingrained beliefs about the proper form of schooling. We are struck at the prominence of this theme in the literature across the generations. Scholars and analysts speak of "the real school" (Metz, 1988) and the "deep structure of schooling" (Tye, 1987). The processes of schooling are guided by a set of "unalterable truths" (Eurich, 1969). Schools teach the "hidden curriculum," based on "occult foundations" (Illich, 1972).

These beliefs reflect the "techno-rational ethic" (Denhardt, 1984) of American culture. A pervasive epistemological paradigm, this ethic contains a set of implicit rules for what we know and how we know it, and establishes a set of implicit assumptions and beliefs about the nature of education (Bernstein, 1976; Fay, 1975). Schools institutionalize the "rational myths" society holds and expects to see in its institutions (Scott and Meyer, 1983; Meyer and Rowan, 1978). They mirror the "theories-in-use" shared across the population in the purposes and expectations society has for them, in the uniform structure of their physical arrangements, in the sameness of their curriculum and materials, and in the homogeneity of student behavior.

The form of school organization incorporating the rational-technical ethic is commonly referred to as the "factory model" (Schlechty, 1990). In imitation of the successful model for industrial production, the school is organized as a manufacturing bureaucracy, with division of labor, specialized tasks, routinized processes, and hierarchical communication and control. The model prizes and maximizes predictability and control. These are gained at a cost. Just as the worker with only a hammer sees all problems as nails to be struck, schools in the business of predictability and control turn human interaction and educational content into linear, means-ends relationships. Reductive, numbing curriculum and instruction, impersonal and nonprofessional contact among teachers and between teachers and administrators, and organizational rules that both legitimate the school and isolate it from its environment are the (predictable) results.

Instrumentalism infects the larger educational system as well. Much state and national policy is developed in response to discrete problems and group interests, and in consequence, many educational services are fragmented and uncoordinated (Smith and O'Day, 1990; Timar, 1989; Tyack and Hansot, 1982). Because they tend to expand and partition along lines dictated by policies and resources at higher levels, state and local administrative offices operate without central purpose or coordination. Legislative, administrative, and judicial efforts to distribute access and power more equitably have instead increased conflict and magnified the powerlessness of the empowered (Cohen, D., 1982).

Fundamental change in American education has to confront these underlying conditions. A new set of assumptions and the vision of education they support must be substituted. Societies will always seek to provide order, stability, and predictability through given categories of institutions and behavioral conventions. Restructuring will not be an attempt to banish order and institutional legitimacy. But what constitutes order and what satisfies the public's need for understanding and confidence in its institutions will change. The restructuring movement is an effort to accomplish this paradigmatic shift.

The content of the movement is not a model or program, or a prescribed goal for education, but a set of beliefs about educational purpose, organizational performance, and institutional change that challenge established thought in each of these areas. These beliefs constitute an overall vision, or perhaps ethos, of education that gives meaning and guidance to specific efforts to improve schools, whatever their particular content.

The logic of restructuring is systemic, interactive, cultural. In lieu of the traditional emphasis given to linear processes and adaptation to external interventions, restructuring engages participants in self-determined processes of discovery and invention. No single element of the system can alone produce change on the order called for. All interdependent elements and levels of the system must be involved in common effort.

Restructuring gives priority to qualitative over quantitative improvements. Programs are chosen because of their fit with mission; teaching quality is enhanced through norms of collegiality and professionalism; teacher and student roles and relationships define the environment for learning. Judgment assumes greater importance in assessing where participants are with respect to where they want to be, and in charting the course to bridge any gap; appeals to outside expertise and authority are diminished.

A holistic concern for the interrelationship among inputs, outputs, and the school structure overrides single-factor and linear prescriptions. Educational reform has traditionally emphasized inputs (e.g., teachers, curriculum, and funding). Restructuring also underscores outputs, and it is argued that there has been a paradigm shift toward output-oriented reform (Finn, 1990). Notions of how to define outputs and where to attribute them have also changed (Schlechty, 1990). We differentiate between district, building, and student outputs; we use a variety of output measures to determine effectiveness; and we hold persons accountable for outputs they can control from their location in the system.

Institutional Performance and Change

Concerning the performance of educational organizations, then, restructuring is based on these beliefs:

- Higher-order thinking skills, critical thinking and problem solving skills, and independent habits of mind are essential to even basic mastery and application of knowledge, and these can be mastered by all learners, not only by an intellectual elite.
- The academic content of schooling must support the missions schools define for themselves. Conversely, no matter what missions they espouse, incompatible content will drive schools away from the missions.
- The so-called "factory model" of schooling is obsolete. It must be replaced by organizations and processes designed to balance competition with cooperation, incentives with enablement, bureaucracy with professionalism, and dependency with self-directed behavior.
- A school's task and authority structure must reinforce the school's purpose and function. It must also permit each member of the organization to fulfill a responsible role consistent with the school's overall focus. It is especially important to acknowledge and provide for the human and professional needs of *workers* as well as of *products* and *outcomes*.
- Teachers do not educate students. Students educate themselves with the abilities developed through instruction. Schools must provide instruction and nourish education.
- Schools are social systems in which "social capital" (Coleman, 1985) is as important as physical capital and labor. Attitudes, relationships, and expectations that exist among the school community must be consistent with the school mission and engage its members in ongoing development of increasingly worthy values.
- Communities formed in order to work with common purpose to alter their shared physical and social reality must have some effective means of assessing their progress and of holding themselves accountable for their contributions. Communities should be held accountable for their own commitment to work, rather than for work imposed by others, and should be measured in terms of things truly within their purview.
- Education is at all levels equifinal. There is no one formula for

achieving desired results. What is key is that schools be able to adopt clear and persuasive missions sufficient to distinguish them in meaningful ways from other alternatives, that they implement programs that concentrate resources and effort toward achievement of their missions, and that they be able to learn systematically from their own experience and continually make corrections for shortcomings in their performance.

Concerning the processes of change to achieve the performance ideal, restructuring is based on these beliefs:

- We must set aside limiting assumptions and challenge constraining, dominant societal myths with new versions of meaning and order in education.
- Change must be systemic. Systemic forces as well as the unique qualities of individual sites determine performance and outcome. They must be integrated into and perform as a coherent, mutually reinforcing system.
- There is, again, no one model for the goal or process of school change. Like community development, restructuring must be a self-determined process of local innovation facilitated and supported by the larger environment.
- The major problems with change are not technical but political and conceptual. The sine qua non of change is public commitment and political will. Where they exist, technical requirements can be readily met; where they are lacking, no amount of technical capacity will suffice.
- Coercion has only a small role to play in change. It is usually ineffective or counterproductive. Vision and enablement—in the form of purpose, knowledge, funds, faith, tolerance for risk, guidance, and peer contact—are the more effective determinants of change.
- Finally, restructuring is a process, not a goal. The ideal of education is the creation of learning communities in which all participants are continually engaged in the development of increasingly sophisticated and worthy values. We seek through change not substitution of one static condition for another, but the inherent logic of ongoing system transformation.

Thus, we can say that restructuring is a complex, purposeful process of social evolution that transforms the educational system and

institutions by reordering the organizational rules, roles, and relationships and engaging participants in work that develops and expresses increasingly interesting, worthwhile academic and social
values so that desired changes result in what schools do and in the
kinds of outcomes they produce.

CONDITIONS NEEDED TO SUSTAIN RESTRUCTURING

If the movement for restructuring is to sustain its momentum and
advance productively in coming months and years, at least three
conditions will have to be met. First, certain constraints or contradictions internal to restructuring will have to be resolved. Second,
appropriate large-scale change strategies will have to be employed.
And third, the right combination of key symbolic and structural
characteristics of the education system will have to be found.

Internal Constraints and Contradictions

Some pitfalls common to all reform movements and some particular to restructuring await in the path of this reform movement. Rist
(1972) identified the phenomenon of internal constraints and contradictions impeding reforms of the 1960s. For example, reforms that
gave community schools local control also bred new forms of institutional intolerance as the new boards cut other groups out of the
governance process. There are similar constraints and contradictions
at work in restructuring.

There is a tension in educational institutions between legitimacy
and innovation. Legitimacy is often the product of conformance with
deep social myths. Innovation of lasting value requires that long-held
assumptions be shed. Both legitimacy and innovation are key ingredients of restructuring; neither can be traded against the other.
Successful restructuring will require the development of a new sense
of common purpose and shared commitment to education to serve as
a guiding framework for pursuit of legitimacy and innovation.

Reform in American education is too often ensnared in the "programmatic trap" (Timar, 1989). Limits of time, resources, breadth of
commitment, and sometimes imagination induce reformers to adopt

new programs and practices rather than to revise underlying assumptions and restructure the system. Newer generations of restructurers could easily be lured by the initial successes or appeal of restructuring into adopting easy programmatic trappings of restructuring, as could bruised veterans be tempted to retreat to the apparent comfort of similar programs.

Accountability and local discretion, both watchwords of restructuring, may also run counter to each other (McDonnell, 1990). The shift in emphasis from inputs to outputs, and the corresponding emphasis on teacher, school, district, and state accountability, could threaten to usurp the discretion and professional judgment of each of these groups. To the degree that accountability is simply a maintenance of the social control value, the initiative and professionalism critical to restructuring will be crippled. Accountability programs will enhance reform only if they include such elements as "authentic testing" and measures of performance actually under the domain of the subject. By the same token, professionals will have to be willing to surrender some of their autonomy and to commit more fully to the communities both of their craft and of their clients.

"Choice" and unity of purpose could also come into conflict. Choice presumes the availability of a variety of options to meet different interests. Unity of purpose presumes the existence of a sufficiently shared vision of education that services and policies can be well coordinated. If decision making is turned over to the market to the extent that central office or other higher-level agents cannot coordinate systemwide change, or if no common purpose exists to organize the efforts of community and schools, then the fragmentation and programmatic orientation that have bedeviled education and reform endeavors to this point will continue to plague them. We might expect to see a large number of perhaps interesting and successful school improvement sites, but not restructuring.

"Professionalization" can appear in benign or less congenial guises. Where it enlarges teachers' discretion to make pedagogical decisions and enable student learning, and also holds teachers appropriately accountable to client, customer, and colleague, professionalization can improve schooling. There is, though, the danger that the more highly structured or specialized profession merely substitutes one set of rigid, expert-oriented values for another. To found the professionalization of American teachers on the growing body of impressive research on effective teaching, including the "new learning theory" and apposite instructional strategies, and on increased autonomy in professional decision making alone, without adequate emphasis on teachers' responsibilities to practice reflectively; to treat students with decency and trust; to model adult virtues to encourage the young to develop increasingly interesting values; and to meet their pledge of public trust, is to build a castle on the sand.

A lesser order of practical problems or issues also vies for attention.

- *Mapping the scope of the activity*—identifying the important undertakings and developing empirical descriptions of what is underway.
- *Guidance on implementation.* Associations and officials note the absence of guidance in strategic planning, of staff development for jobs that do not yet exist, and of tested procedures for creating tomorrow's new structure while continuing to meet today's ongoing commitments.
- *Doing the work involved in restructuring.* The intellectual, emotional, and physical resources called for in total system change are immense, risk and uncertainty drain energy, and clear indicators of progress are elusive.
- *Support for local endeavors.* Technologies, money, and system support are in short supply. Much can be done without any of these, but teachers and building administrators report that at some point, there is an absolute limit to what they can do without such support.
- *Coordination at many levels.* Expansion of local and state initiatives creates the need for coordination to help diverse sponsor groups work together, clarify implications of local experience for state policy, multiply the effects of limited resources, and promote exchange of information and technical assistance. Although restructuring must be conducted as a building initiative, central office support and overall district commitment is necessary for comprehensive change over the long term.
- *Follow through.* Reports from some major urban districts indicate problems with follow through, both in expanding early innovations to larger parts of the district and in sustaining initial commitments to innovations after the excitement of the early stages begins to wane.
- *Backlash.* Restructurers see a backlash over the horizon if the emotional, political, and financial investments in restructuring, and the hopes they raise, seem to go unrewarded.

Change Strategies and Restructuring

Restructuring as a reform movement differs from broad-based "effective schools" or "school improvement" movements and from other reform efforts in significant ways.

Restructuring is not school improvement. Although Corbett (1989b) and others have categorized restructuring as a subelement of school improvement overall, we believe it is important to view it as something qualitatively different.

School improvement can refer to any systematic effort to improve the conditions or effects of schooling. In the current context of educational reform, we define it as the systematic application of a research-based process or model in a significant, multi-stage effort to strengthen selected determinants of performance or outcomes in one or more participating schools (Moorman and Egermeier, 1990).

Intended changes may be large or small, comprehensive or limited. They may address the core technology or the authority structure, and they may emphasize curriculum, instruction, training, leadership, physical arrangements, or all of these. But they do not challenge the basic assumptions that underlie the system as it stands. The values and beliefs that dictate the establishment of a *certain kind* of order, control, accountability, legitimacy, and pattern of relationships persist. Thus it is possible to pursue a school improvement strategy on a building-by-building basis (although here too, as in restructuring, it may be more effective to work at the district level). It is possible to ensconce the reformed practice within a system that continues to operate as before. Although concrete changes in the school program and in student effects may occur, the bedrock assumptions about what to do in schools and how to do it survive.

By contrast, it is precisely these assumptions restructuring seeks to overturn. Because such great change is in order, some practitioners of change argue the case for a *synoptic* approach—that is, for specifying in advance and in complete form an ideal end state to substitute for the present state. In our view, a better case can be made for a modified *incremental* approach that allows participants to shape both the vision of the ideal and the way it is actually put to work.

A thoughtful example of synoptic change is the "redesign" proposal offered by Basom and Crandall (1989) and to some extent by Banathy and Jenks (1990). Redesign is an approach to educational change in which social systems inquiry is applied to the complete reconfiguration of the system under a new paradigm (Basom and Crandall, 1989). The approach assumes the present system is near the maximum of its current capacity with little room for improvement. The system is a problem tangle that cannot be unraveled by picking at only one side. Thus, incremental improvement is rejected in favor of redesign. Redesign may proceed in stages, under the assumptions that the logistics of change take time and that the program to be replaced must continue to function while the new program is being constructed. But there is nevertheless an "ideal solution" (design) that precedes and motivates the change, and a "planned change" process is followed to implement the ideal.

As alternatives to synoptic change, incremental processes are criticized for their lack of vision, acceptance of "things as they are," and partial efforts. Yet Quinn's (1989) "logical incrementalism" offers an imaginative synthesis of the best of the redesign and incremental tacks. "Logical incrementalism" views change as an unfolding and unpredictable process impelled by a guiding but tentative, flexible vision. Realities of power and behavior and the limits to rationality call for an incremental approach that maximizes opportunities for learning, testing of assumptions and alternatives without deep commitment, development of commitment and incorporation of new ideas, and natural coordination of otherwise uncontrollable systems. Because the precise nature of the problems or decisions cannot be known in advance, and the complexities of the system and environment prevent prediction and control of relevant responses, the guiding vision may itself change during the evolutionary change process or may become clear only after the change is well underway.

Quinn's strategy for change nicely captures the best of both traditions of planned change and natural systems change. "Logical incrementalism" seems to build on a more realistic view of organizing. It acknowledges the limits of rationality in human systems, of control over power, behavior, and events, and of capacity to imagine and invent desired future states in advance of action. It treats the unexpected not as unwanted but as possibly interesting new information and an opportunity for innovation. Moreover, the strategy fits neatly with the kind of syntheses across other restructuring strategies we would like to see between educational procedure and principle (Lieberman and Miller, 1990), policy mandates and enablements, and charismatic and democratic leadership. (See Reich, 1987; Heifetz and Sinder, 1987.)

Symbolic and Structural Characteristics: Loose Coupling, Tight Integration

In our view, the greatest challenge to restructuring arises from the cultural contradictions inherent in American education. It will be essential to find some way to resolve or transcend these contradictions if restructuring is to avoid the fate of other reform movements. Two characteristics of organizations—"tight integration" and "loose coupling"—are particularly significant in education and will influence the course of restructuring.

The education system and the processes in individual schools are loosely coupled (Weick, 1976; Rosenblum and Louis, 1981; Firestone and Wilson, 1985). Loose coupling in a system means that only a very strong or sustained stimulus in one element of the system is felt in another part of the system. In effect, stable subassemblies in the overall system operate relatively autonomously, independent of larger system or environmental forces. On the other hand, the system is remarkably uniform (Goodlad, 1984; Sizer, 1985). Despite its being a highly decentralized system and comprising thousands of elements, the education system in the United States is remarkably homogeneous. Wayland (1964) noted long ago that while the system is not tightly coupled, it is highly integrated. In the analogy of a railroad system, tracks and cars are built to uniform specifications. Tracks may be laid hither and yon, and cars may roll from location to location at the whim of their owners. But the system is so highly integrated that any car may go virtually anywhere.

It is the combination of loose coupling and tight integration that so strongly influences education and that could profoundly affect the course of restructuring. Loose coupling can affect change in several ways. It can facilitate change and development of diversity. It can blunt the stimulus of change and stifle movement from the status quo. Or it can produce too little of some desired response or too much of an unwanted reaction. Deal, Meyer, and Scott (1975) indicate that the loosely coupled, or "doubly segmented," nature of schools can result in a relatively high level of local change (though they doubt that the changes would be sustained without formal linkages with the system hierarchy). Weick (1979) seems to suggest that the loose coupling can promote variety and experimentation. Weick (1976), Meyer and Rowan (1978), and others have also noted that loose coupling can serve as a barrier to policies or outside influences that would be either unworkable, inappropriate, or embarrassing. It protects systems from the encroachments of the environment, and it preserves a degree of flexibility and variety, valuable either for the sake of pluralism per se or for ready responsiveness to new circumstances. It may also guarantee a needed degree of stability and predictability in the system.

Tight integration, too, may either stifle or promote change. "Tight integration" refers to a particular aspect of uniformity characteristic of organizations in a common environment. It is especially well described by the theories of "institutional" sociology (see Scott, 1987). Scholars in this area have found, among other things, that institutions of society purchase legitimacy and the confidence of their supporters through the incorporation of dominant myths of society. American schools have incorporated the "rational myths" that characterize this nation's psyche. That is, to be a school in America means to include certain pervasive "categories" by which society defines schooling—classroom structure, accreditation, grade structure and grading, established texts, testing and accountability functions, and so on (Meyer, Scott, and Deal, 1981). If schools ignore these categories, they sacrifice the legitimacy and claim to resources on which schools depend. The categories are so fundamentally held that to question them can be literally unthinkable. They stand not as the exemplar but as the implicit idea of schooling.

Meyer, Scott, and Deal (1981) characterize the institutionalization of societal myth as an organizational act that insulates the organization's technical core from the influence of the environment even as it purchases legitimacy by corresponding to societal expectations for form and structure. Institutionalization of societal myth and loose coupling are in effect reciprocals. We suggest, then, that loose coupling and tight integration are conditions that reflect opposing cultural orientations embedded within a common cultural field. Loose coupling is an organizational expression of inherent American values of opposition to centralized authority, individuality and autonomy, diversity, and local innovation. Tight integration is the expression of cultural myths concerning technical rationality and control, the "melting pot" that creates one out of many, and the power of institutions to subdue nature and engineer a desired future. American social institutions, schools foremost among them, operate from the hidden dimension of these deeply held cultural assumptions and reflect their opposed drives and constraints.

Firestone and Wilson (1985) have suggested that loosely coupled organizations can be integrated through "cultural linkages," symbolic influences that align the various parts of an organization in the direction of some common belief, value, or vision. Their recognition of the integrating function of cultural forms is significant. We add to their formulation the notion that loose coupling is itself a cultural phenomenon, that the interaction between what we describe as tight integration and loose coupling is therefore a phenomenon that is at bottom cultural, and that the nature of that interaction can be influenced by the quality of the cultural forces that are brought together.

The "wrong" combination of tight integration and loose coupling in education may bring too much of an undesirable response in a process called *schismogenesis*. Schismogenesis is the anthropological term (Bateson, 1972) that describes cultural interactions resulting in vicious circles. The *asymmetrical* form of this phenomenon entails interlocked behavior in which group A's response to group B prompts a more extreme form of B's initial act, which in turn stimulates a more extreme response on A's part. This process is elsewhere known as "degenerative" and as "deviation-reinforcing" (Weick, 1979).

Policy mandates and loose coupling in education provide us with a model of schismogenesis. Wise (1979) has documented the hyperrationalization of American education, in which increasing efforts to control and mandate are applied by policymakers and decision makers in the field. He notes that there is a theoretical limit to the schools' capacity to absorb these procedures without fundamental redesign. Other scholars have noted a variety of limitations to the use of rational mandates to effectuate policy goals (Elmore, 1980; Marshall, C., 1988; McDonnell and Elmore, 1987; McLaughlin, 1987). The most telling argument against the "hyperrational" approach seems to us to lie in its interactive effects with loose coupling.

We suggest that the greater the efforts of the environment to *control* the technical functions of schooling, the greater are the preservative reactions of loose coupling. When, as a result of the loose coupling, the efforts to achieve control are frustrated, the typical response of those in control will be to try to exert even greater control (Elmore, 1980). Control is typically the logic of the policy system, and a system will tend to interpret events in the terms of its primary logic. A vicious circle of extreme control and extreme loose coupling is underway.

At the level of intersocietal dynamics, schismogenesis of this sort stops only because the parties grow exhausted or are diverted (Bateson, 1972). However, at a smaller organizational level than society, it should be possible to halt degenerative cycles in other ways. Individual behavior can be changed or substituted, so that a different response is evoked by a preexisting stimulus. The number of interacting variables can be changed, or an intervening variable can be introduced to correct deviations and achieve a homeostatic balance. For example, a state department of education oriented toward enabling and facilitative technical assistance could be inserted between the legislature and the school district; and the same could be said analogously for the district's central office staff. Or the development of new myths, metaphors, and values could replace the prevailing set of variables with another, establishing an entirely new and possibly more productive interaction.

In lieu of control, and even stronger assertion of the prevailing myths of society, what is needed for successful educational reform is the extensive, sustained assertion of some equally powerful integrative myth that emphasizes coordination and enablement and that stimulates behavior more in line with the loosely coupled nature of the education system.

A NEW COMMUNITY OF PURPOSE

Two important characteristics of the restructuring movement lead us to be optimistic about the prospects for success with the problems of internal constraints, change strategies, and cultural dynamics noted above. These are the intellectual content of restructuring and the evolving, guiding myth of American education that restructuring is helping to nurture.

Historian Lawrence Cremin (1964) wrote some time ago that reformist energy absent intellectual direction leads to decadence. Successful reform movements must be made of sound intellectual material. Restructuring is richly endowed with intellectual content. In what has been compared to a paradigm shift (Finn, 1990), the logic of inputs has been replaced by the logic of outcomes. Far more sophisticated appreciations of human and organizational behavior enlighten the process. Compelling syntheses of new research in such areas as learning and cognition, school performance, and "cultural" leadership open new vistas of possibilities in student achievement. This framework of guiding content grows more robust with each day.

A new, persuasive "myth" of American education is also emerging. From the midpoint of this century up to the present time, there has been no overall integrating myth about American education other than that provided by the deep, structural forms of the rational-technical ethic. The protestant-republican common school philosophy and the ideology of centralization, scientific management, and expertise, which for decades provided a common ideology and community of purpose in education, disintegrated under an onslaught of mid-century pressures, and no new organizing myth has evolved (Tyack and Hansot, 1982).

Near the end of their rich analysis of public school leadership in America, Tyack and Hansot (1982) ask whether a "new coherence and community of commitment" in public education are possible. They answer this question with guarded hope. In the roughly ten years since they wrote, reason for hope seems to have grown greater. The importance of vision or guiding ethos in education is now widely acknowledged. It is abundantly clear just how fragmented the structure and community of education are. National association officials and scholars call for a renaissance of shared commitment and common purpose. The felt need is there, but is there more than that? We believe there is, and that it is to be found in the context of restructuring.

Restructuring is at bottom a process for establishing community of purpose. The first achievement of the restructuring movement has been to quicken the realization that shared vision and commitment are essential to effective societies, whether nations or schools. This basic truth that defines how "human systems are different," to use Geoffrey Vickers's phrase (1983), has been rediscovered.

Moreover, consensus is forming around a set of specific beliefs and values. We have already outlined restructuring's new beliefs about school performance and change. It is not necessary that all of these enter the nation's consciousness. Some are pertinent chiefly to those closest to the schools—those who work in them and guide them through the process of change. But many citizens, educators, scholars, and policymakers of all stripes seem to agree on a set of notions abstracted from that larger list:

- There is a direct relationship between goals, effort, and outcome in both student achievement and educational policy.
- Society can no longer afford to educate only selected portions of its children; whether for reasons of equity or national economic development, it is impossible to reach societal goals and continue our waste of human resources. All children and all parts of

society must be schooled in ways that ensure their own good and that of the larger community. School curriculum and instruction should be designed to encourage and reward both student effort and the many forms of intellectual ability students have.

- A community should base its faith in a school not on the school's conformance with a structure thought to provide predictability and control but on the strength of the school's mission and plans for achieving it.

One does not have to search far in the literature on education to find such sentiments as these expressed: "The secret to good education is to find good people and let them do good work." Or: "We can have the education system we want. We must decide what it is we want and then go after it." It was the central message of *A Nation at Risk* (National Commission on Excellence in Education, 1983), in fact, that we were getting just the educational performance we demanded, and deserved—mediocrity.

Yet reforms over the past half century have been overwhelmingly technical in nature, and none has effectively altered the fundamental structure or academic outcomes of schooling. They have, by intention or by implication, demeaned both the teacher workforce and student population, denying each a responsible role in school, as though education were too important a task to be entrusted to either. Expanding resources have permitted the nation to serve an expanding population and school mission without having to face one incontrovertible fact: that teachers and children, by and large, do well when they work hard, and schools (and homes) are effective when they are places in which teachers and students want to, and can, work hard (Marshall, 1988; Tomlinson and Cross, in press; Office of Educational Research and Improvement, forthcoming).

Talk of values, community of purpose, and ethos is not so easy to ground on empirical confirmation as are findings of learning theory and policy implementation. Yet, to paraphrase William James, it is often only our faith in an uncertified outcome that guarantees the result we seek. With continued commitment to the emerging principles of restructuring, a guiding ethos for American education may yet be found.

REFERENCES

Ackoff, Russell. *Redesigning the Future: A Systems Approach to Societal Problems.* New York: John Wiley and Sons, 1974.

Arendt, Hannah. *The Human Condition.* Chicago: University of Chicago Press, 1958.

Banathy, Bela H., and Jenks, C. Lynn. *The Transformation of Education by Design.* San Francisco: Far West Laboratory for Educational Research and Development, 1990.

Basom, Richard E., Jr., and Crandall, David P. "Implementing a Redesign Strategy: Lessons from Educational Change." Paper presented at a conference of the International Society for General Systems Research, Edinburgh, Scotland, July, 1989. Andover, Mass.: Regional Laboratory for Educational Improvement of the Northeast and Islands, 1989.

Bateson, Gregory. *Steps to an Ecology of Mind.* New York: Ballantine Books, 1972.

Bellah, Robert N.; Madsen, Richard; Sullivan, William M.; Swidler, Ann; and Tipton, Steven M. *Habits of the Heart: Individualism and Commitment in American Life.* New York: Harper & Row, 1985.

Bernstein, Richard J. *The Restructuring of Social and Political Theory.* New York: Harcourt Brace Jovanovich, 1976.

Bolman, Lee G., and Deal, Terrence E. *Modern Approaches to Understanding and Managing Organizations.* San Francisco: Jossey-Bass, 1984.

Bransford, John D., and Vye, Nancy J. "A Perspective on Cognitive Research and Its Implications for Instruction." In *Toward the Thinking Curriculum: Current Cognitive Research,* edited by Lauren B. Resnick and Leopold E. Klopfer. 1989 Yearbook of the Association for Supervision and Curriculum Development. Alexandria, Va.: Association for Supervision and Curriculum Development, 1989. Pp. 173–205.

Brown, Rexford G. *Schools of Thought.* San Francisco: Jossey-Bass, 1991.

Business International S.A. *Restructuring and Turnaround Experience.* Geneva, Switzerland: Business International S.A., 1987.

Carnegie Forum on Education and the Economy, Task Force on Teaching as a Profession. *A Nation Prepared: Teachers for the 21st Century.* New York: Carnegie Forum on Education and the Economy, 1986.

Center for Policy Research in Education. *Continuation Application for Years 4–5, Vol. I: Technical Document.* Submitted to the Office of Educational Research and Improvement, U. S. Department of Education, Washington, D.C., 1988.

Chion-Kenney, Linda. "Schools of Thought," *Washington Post,* 15 April 1991.

Chira, Susan. "Rochester: Uneasy Symbol of School Reform," *New York Times,* 10 April 1991.

Cohen, David K. "Policy and Education: The Impact of State and Federal Education Policy in School Governance," *Harvard Educational Review* 52 (1982): 474–499.

Cohen, David K., and Lindblom, Charles E. *Usable Knowledge.* New Haven, Conn.: Yale University Press, 1979.

Cohen, David K., and Rosenberg, B. H. "Function and Fantasies: Understanding Schools in Capitalistic America," *History of Education Quarterly* 17 (1977): 113–137.

Cohen, Michael. *Restructuring the Education System: Agenda for the '90s.* Washington, D.C.: National Governors' Association, 1987.

Cohen, Michael D.; March, James G.; and Olsen, Johan P. "A Garbage Can Model of Organizational Choice," *Administrative Science Quarterly* 17 (1972): 1–25.

Cohen, Michael D.; March, James G.; and Olsen, Johan P. "People, Problems, Solutions, and the Ambiguity of Relevance." In James G. March and Johan P. Olsen, *Ambiguity and Choice in Organizations.* Bergen-Oslo-Tromso: Universitetsforlaget, 1976. Pp. 24–37.

Coleman, James S. "Schools and the Communities They Serve," *Phi Delta Kappan* 66 (1985): 527–537.

Corbett, H. Dickson. "Empowerment and Restructuring." Unpublished paper based on work performed by Research for Better Schools, Philadelphia, Penn., under contract from the Office of Educational Research and Improvement, U.S. Department of Education. Washington, D.C., 1989a.

Corbett, H. Dickson. "On the Meaning of Restructuring." Paper based on work performed by Research for Better Schools, Philadelphia, Penn., under contract from the Office of Educational Research and Improvement, U. S. Department of Education. Washington, D.C., 1989b.

Cremin, Lawrence A. *The Transformation of the School: Progressivism in American Education 1867–1957.* New York: Vintage Books, 1964.

Cuban, Larry. "Reforming Again, Again, and Again," *Educational Researcher* 19, no. 1 (January–February, 1990): 3–13.

Dahl, Robert A. "On Removing Certain Impediments to Democracy in the United States," *Political Science Quarterly* 92 (1977): 1–20.

Deal, Terrence E.; Meyer, John W.; and Scott, Richard W. "Organizational Influences on Educational Innovation." In *Managing Change in Educational Organizations,* edited by J. Victor Baldridge and Terrence E. Deal. Berkeley, Calif.: McCutchan Publishing Corp., 1975. Pp. 109–132.

Denhardt, Robert B. *Theories of Public Organization.* Monterey, Calif.: Brooks/Cole Publishing Co., 1984.

Dionne, E. J. *Why Americans Hate Politics.* New York: Simon & Schuster, 1991.

Dunn, William N. *Public Policy Analysis: An Introduction.* Englewood Cliffs, N.J.: Prentice-Hall, 1981.

Duttweiler, Patricia C., and Hord, Shirley M. *Dimensions of Effective Leadership.* Austin, Texas: Southwest Educational Development Laboratory, 1987.

Education Commission of the States. *Exploring Policy Options to Restructure Education.* Denver, Colo.: Education Commission of the States, 1991.

Elmore, Richard F. *Complexity and Control: What Legislators and Administrators Can Do about Implementing Public Policy.* Washington, D.C.: National Institute of Education, 1980.

Eurich, Alvin C. *Reforming American Education.* New York: Harper & Row, 1969.

Fay, Brian. *Social Theory and Political Practice.* London: George Allen & Unwin, 1975.

Firestone, William A., and Wilson, Bruce L. "Using Bureaucratic and Cultural Linkages to Improve Instruction: The Principal's Contribution," *Educational Administration Quarterly* 21 (1985): 7–30.

Goodlad, John I. *A Place Called School: Prospects for the Future.* New York: McGraw-Hill, 1984.

Harvey, Glen, and Crandall, David P. "A Beginning Look at the What and How of Restructuring." Andover, Mass.: Regional Laboratory for Educational Improvement of the Northeast and Islands, 1988.

Heifetz, Ronald A., and Sinder, Riley M. "Political Leadership: Managing the Public's Problem Solving." In *The Power of Public Ideas*, edited by Robert B. Reich. Cambridge, Mass.: Ballinger Books, 1987. Pp. 179–203.

Hill, Paul T.; Foster, Gail E.; and Gendler, Tamar. *High Schools with Character*. Santa Monica, Calif.: Rand Corporation, 1990.

Horkheimer, Max. *Eclipse of Reason*, rev. ed. New York: Seabury Press, 1974.

Howard, Jeffrey. Keynote presentation at the National Network of Principals' Centers Eighth Annual Conversation, St. Louis, Missouri, April 26, 1991.

Illich, Ivan. "The Alternative to Schooling." In *Restructuring American Education: Innovations and Alternatives*, edited by Ray C. Rist. New Brunswick, N.J.: Transaction Books, 1972. Pp. 257–274.

Kershner, Keith M., and Connolly, John A. *At Risk Students and School Restructuring*. Philadelphia, Penn.: Research for Better Schools, 1991.

Lasch, Christopher. *The Culture of Narcissism*. New York: Warner Books, 1979.

Lewis, Anne. *Restructuring America's Schools*. Arlington, Va.: American Association of School Administrators, 1989.

Lieberman, Ann, and Miller, Lynne. "Restructuring Schools: What Matters and What Works," *Phi Delta Kappan* 71 (1990): 759–764.

Little, Judith Warren. "Norms of Collegiality and Experimentation: Workplace Conditions of School Success," *American Educational Research Journal* 19 (1982): 325–340.

Lowi, Theodore J. *The End of Liberalism: The Second Republic of the United States*, 2d ed. New York: Norton Books, 1979.

March, James G., and Olsen, Johan P. *Ambiguity and Choice in Organizations*. Bergen-Oslo-Tromso: Universitetsforlaget, 1976.

Marshall, Catherine. "Bridging the Chasm between Policymakers and Educators," *Theory into Practice* 27 (1988): 98–105.

Marshall, Hermine H. "Work or Learning: Implications of Classroom Metaphors," *Educational Researcher* 17, no. 9 (December 1988): 9–16.

McDonnell, Lorraine M. "Accountability and School Restructuring: Resolving the Dilemma." Paper prepared at the Rand Corporation for the Office of Educational Research and Improvement, U. S. Department of Education, Washington, D.C., 1990.

McDonnell, Lorraine M., and Elmore, Richard F. "Getting the Job Done: Alternative Policy Instruments," *Educational Evaluation and Policy Analysis* 9 (1987): 133–152.

McLaughlin, Milbrey W. "Learning from Experience: Lessons from Past Implementation Research," *Educational Evaluation and Policy Analysis* 9 (1987): 171–178.

McLaughlin, Milbrey W. *The RAND Study Ten Years Later: Macro Realities*. Palo Alto, Calif.: Center for Research on the Context of Secondary School Teaching, Stanford University, 1989.

Metz, Mary H. "Some Missing Elements in the School Reform Movement," *Educational Administration Quarterly* 24 (1988): 446–460.

Meyer, John W., and Rowan, Brian. "The Structure of Educational Organizations." In Marshall W. Meyer and Associates, *Environments and Organizations*. San Francisco: Jossey-Bass, 1978. Pp. 78–109.

Meyer, John W.; Scott, W. Richard; and Deal, Terrence E. "Institutional and Technical Sources of Organizational Structure: Explaining the Structure of

Educational Organizations." In *Organization and the Human Services: Cross-Disciplinary Reflections*, edited by Herman D. Stein. Philadelphia: Temple University Press, 1981. Pp. 151–179.

Moe, Terry M. "Regulatory Performance and Presidential Administration," *American Journal of Political Science* 26 (1982): 197–224.

Moorman, Hunter, and Egermeier, John. "Educational Restructuring and School Improvement." In North Central Regional Educational Laboratory, *Restructuring to Promote Learning in America's Schools: Selected Readings*. Vol. 1 for Video Conferences 1–4. Columbus, Ohio: Zaner Blosser, Inc., 1990. Pp. 5–11.

National Association of State Boards of Education. *Today's Children, Tomorrow's Schools: A Call to Restructure Schools*. Alexandria, Va.: National Association of State Boards of Education, n.d.

National Commission on Excellence in Education. *A Nation at Risk*. Washington, D.C.: U. S. Department of Education, 1983.

National Governors' Association. *Results in Education: 1989*. Washington, D.C.: National Governors' Association, 1989.

National Leadership Network. *Developing Leaders for Restructuring Schools: New Habits of Mind and Heart*. Washington, D.C.: U. S. Department of Education, 1991.

Office of Educational Research and Improvement. *Hard Work and Higher Expectations: Motivating Students to Learn*. Summary report of a conference held November 8–9, 1990. Washington, D.C.: U. S. Department of Education, forthcoming.

Quinn, James Brian. "Strategic Change: 'Logical Incrementalism'." SMR Classic Reprint. *Sloan Management Review* 30 (Summer 1989): 45–60.

Regional Laboratory for Educational Improvement of the Northeast and Islands Newsletter. *Regional Lab Reports: On Restructuring*. Andover, Mass.: Regional Laboratory for Educational Improvement of the Northeast and Islands, March, 1991.

Reich, Robert B. "Introduction." In *The Power of Public Ideas*, edited by Robert B. Reich. Cambridge, Mass.: Ballinger Books, 1987. Pp. 1–11.

Rein, Martin, and Schön, Donald A. "Problem Setting in Policy Research." In *Using Social Research in Public Policy Making*, edited by Carol H. Weiss, Lexington Mass.: D. C. Heath, 1977. Pp. 235–251.

Rein, Martin, and White, Sheldon H. "Can Policy Research Help Policy?" *Public Interest* 49 (1977): 119–136.

Resnick, Lauren B. *Education and Learning to Think*. Washington D.C.: National Academy Press, 1987.

Rist, Ray C. "Introduction." In *Restructuring American Education: Innovations and Alternatives*, edited by Ray C. Rist. New Brunswick, N.J.: Transaction Books, 1972.

Rittel, Horst W. J., and Webber, Melvin M. "Dilemmas in a General Theory of Planning," *Policy Sciences* 4 (1973): 155–169.

Rosenblum, Sheila, and Louis, Karen Seashore. *Stability and Change: Innovation in an Educational Context*. New York: Plenum Press, 1981.

Schlechty, Phillip C. *Schools for the 21st Century: Leadership Imperatives for Educational Reform*. San Francisco: Jossey-Bass, 1990.

Schön, Donald A. "Generative Metaphor: A Perspective on Problem Setting in Social Policy." In *Metaphor and Thought*, edited by Andrew Ortony. Cambridge and New York: Cambridge University Press, 1979. Pp. 254–283.

Schön, Donald A. "Leadership as Reflection-in-Action." In *Leadership and Organiza-*

tional Culture, edited by Thomas J. Sergiovanni and John E. Corbally. Urbana: University of Illinois Press, 1984.

Schön, Donald A. *The Reflective Practitioner*. New York: Basic Books, 1983.

Scott, W. Richard. "The Adolescence of Institutional Theory," *Administrative Science Quarterly* 32 (1987): 493–511.

Scott, W. Richard, and Meyer, John W. "The Organization of Societal Sectors." In John W. Meyer, W. Richard Scott, et al., *Organizational Environments: Ritual and Rationality*. Beverly Hills, Calif.: Sage, 1983. Pp. 129–153.

Scott, William A., and Hart, David K. *Organizational America*. Boston: Houghton Mifflin, 1979.

Shedlin, Allan, Jr. "Shelter from the Storm," *American School Board Journal* 177 (1990): 12–16.

Sizer, Theodore R. *Horace's Compromise: The Dilemma of the American High School*. Boston: Houghton Mifflin, 1985.

Smith, Marshall S., and O'Day, Jennifer. "Systemic School Reform." In *The Politics of Curriculum and Testing*, edited by Susan Fuhrman and Betty Malen. Bristol, Penn.: Falmer Press, 1990. Summarized as "Putting the Pieces Together: Systemic School Reform," in *Center for Policy Research in Education (CPRE) Policy Briefs*, RB-06-4/91.

Timar, Thomas. "The Politics of School Restructuring," *Phi Delta Kappan* 70 (1989): 265–275.

Tomlinson, Tommy M., and Cross, Christopher T. "Academic Effort: What's in It for Students?" *Educational Leadership*, in press.

Tyack, David, and Hansot, Elizabeth. *Managers of Virtue*. New York: Basic Books, 1982.

Tye, Barbara Benham. "The Deep Structure of Schooling," *Phi Delta Kappan* 69 (1987): 281–284.

U. S. Department of Education. *America 2000: An Education Strategy*. Washington, D.C.: U.S. Department of Education, 1991.

Vickers, Sir Geoffrey. *Human Systems Are Different*. London: Harper & Row, 1983.

Wayland, Sloan R. "Structural Features of American Education as Basic Factors in Innovation." In *Innovation in Education*, edited by Matthew Miles. New York: Teachers College, Columbia University, 1964.

Weick, Karl E. "Educational Organizations as Loosely Coupled Systems," *Administrative Science Quarterly* 21 (1976): 1–19.

Weick, Karl E. *The Social Psychology of Organizing*, 2d ed. Reading, Mass.: Addison-Wesley, 1979.

Wise, Arthur E. *Legislated Learning: The Bureaucratization of the American Classroom*. Berkeley: University of California Press, 1979.

Wise, Arthur E. "Six Steps to Teacher Professionalism," *Educational Leadership* 47 (1990): 57–60.

CHAPTER 3

Site-Based Management: Engine for Reform or Pipedream? Problems, Prospects, Pitfalls, and Prerequisites for Success

Daniel U. Levine and
Eugene E. Eubanks

During the past three decades, many approaches to local school reform have come and gone, then come again in altered guise. In the 1960s and 1970s, one of the most popular approaches was *decentralization*, which largely involved the establishment of regional or sub-regional offices and, sometimes, governing or advisory boards of education encompassing groups of schools within large big-city districts. Reflecting a growing recognition in the 1970s and 1980s that regulations and policies require intelligent adaptation and flexible implementation at the building level if they are to be implemented successfully, *site councils* were created to work on planning and carrying out building-level improvements in many school districts. Establishment of site councils constituted a major step toward *site-based management*.

Responding to a variety of national and local concerns as well as ideologies stressing possibilities for improving productivity in schools and other organizations through enhanced employee participation, many school districts in the 1980s initiated *empowerment* approaches to expand and formalize participation in decision making by teachers and other parties as part of the operation of decentralized site councils.

This chapter briefly reviews and assesses selected research and practice dealing with possibilities for attaining local school reform through site-based management. We define site-based management as the establishment and functioning of site councils and the companion efforts to empower teachers and other parties at the school building level.

PLUSES OF THE SITE-BASED MANAGEMENT MOVEMENT

Recent emphasis on site-based management as a tool for reform is positive in that such management recognizes and incorporates some of the major conclusions and generalizations derived from two decades of research on efforts to change and improve public schools. In addition, the recent emphasis on empowerment theoretically may help in addressing severe obstacles and pitfalls that have hampered earlier reform efforts. We limit our discussion here to a brief citation of practices that have received substantial support in research on change in education.

1. *School-based management.* In emphasizing the importance of reform at the building level, site-based management recognizes that positive change cannot be simply mandated from the outside but is a school-by-school phenomenon (Fullan, 1991; Marburger, 1985).

2. *Long-range and multiyear efforts.* Many if not most attempts to empower teachers, administrators, and other participants in local school reform explicitly recognize that fundamental and lasting improvement requires at least two or three years to initiate, and vigorous continuing action thereafter (Louis and Miles, 1990).

3. *Faculty input in decision making.* Research on schools that are unusually effective in producing achievement (taking into account their students' socioeconomic background) indicates that their faculties are active participants in making decisions about instruction and other matters (Purkey and Smith, 1983). In addition, unusually effective schools tend to exemplify high levels of coordination of

curriculum and instruction across classrooms; alignment of curriculum, instruction, and testing; and adaptation of methods and materials for classroom use (Levine and Lezotte, 1990). Attainment of these characteristics requires active participation and initiative on the part of teachers. Thus effective schools research indicates that faculty should be active and vigorous in determining how to shape and implement instruction in their schools—a major goal of site-based management. Indeed, successful "effective schools" projects designed to enhance frequently cited "effectiveness correlates" such as outstanding leadership, orderly environment, high expectations for students, and focus on key learning skills usually have placed considerable emphasis on increasing teacher participation in decision making through site-plan councils and similar mechanisms (Levine, 1991; Levine and Lezotte, 1990; Taylor and Lezotte, 1990).

Problems and Obstacles in Local School Reform Through Site Councils and Empowerment

Although efforts to improve public schools fundamentally through site councils and empowerment of participants at the building level are theoretically attractive and eventually may help in bringing about positive reform, they also are inherently problematic in several important respects, and severe obstacles usually are present to hinder their development. Among the problems and obstacles that researchers and analysts have identified are the following:

1. *Inadequate time, training, and technical assistance.* Numerous observers have remarked on the extent to which participation in decision making dealing with fundamental school improvement and reorganization requires very large expenditures of time and energy from teachers, administrators, and other participants (e.g., Brown, 1990; Clune and White, 1988; Duttweiler, 1988; Kelly and Willner, 1988; Mauriel and Lindquist, 1989; Sagor, 1991; Short and Greer, 1989). As pointed out by Clune and White (1988), planning at the site level can be a "very time-consuming process" for principals and teachers who are "already overburdened with time-consuming activities" (p. 28). Furthermore, lack of adequate time can lead to what Firestone and Corbett (1988) have called "mock participation."

Similarly, many observers have concluded that training and technical assistance requirements in working to improve instruction through site-based decision making also are very great (e.g. Collins, 1988;

Duttweiler, 1988; Harrison, Killion, and Mitchell, 1989; Kelly and Willner, 1988; Strusinksi, 1989). The importance of training was emphasized as follows (Clune and White, 1988) in a study of thirty-one school districts attempting to initiate one or another approach to school-based management (SBM): "Increased training is an obvious response to the difficulty of roles involved in SBM. . . . [When] very little training was provided, participants complained that they had been given inadequate orientation" (pp. 28–29). The situation in education seems to resemble that in business and industry, regarding which management consultant W. Patrick Dolan (quoted in Hoerr, 1988) stated, "Very few companies" endeavoring to install self-management teams "understand how deep the change must be. . . . Training is always a peripheral, secondary consideration, and when push comes to shove, it keeps sliding" (p. 58).

2. *Difficulties in stimulating consideration and acceptance of inconvenient changes*. Some of the actions required to make schools more effective may run counter to teachers' desires or perceived self-interests. For example, substantial improvement of achievement is likely to require more time and effort outside the usual working day at many schools, and both acquisition and utilization of new instructional approaches is a painful task for many teachers (Kirby, 1991). This argument can and perhaps should be turned around in pointing out that it is precisely the "hardships" of change that may make participation a prerequisite for gaining teachers' commitment to it, but the potentially counterproductive effects of teachers' perceived self-interest also suggest caution in moving toward radical increases in participation and empowerment (Hart and Murphy, 1989; Levine, 1991; Levine and Taylor, 1991; Levine and Lezotte, 1990).

An indication that inconvenient reforms have not received serious consideration is when decision makers at schools engaged in site-level budgeting distribute the same amount of resources to most or all teachers (Levine and Lezotte, 1990). For example, if every teacher receives the same assistance from paraprofessionals, or a discretionary fund is divided equally among all classrooms, or funds are allocated or reallocated to reduce class size everywhere by one or two students, faculty probably have taken "the easy way out" rather than identifying and addressing central but difficult problems in their schools.

3. *Unresolved issues involving administrative leadership and enhanced power among other participants*. One of the best-established findings in research on unusually effective schools is that the principals and other school leaders in these schools display vigorous leadership and initiative

(Stringfield and Teddlie, 1987, 1988; Levine and Lezotte, 1990). By way of contrast, many site-level empowerment approaches provide for and indeed are based on expanding opportunities for teachers, and sometimes for parents and students, to participate formally in a wider range of decisions, frequently with an influence sufficient to override administrators. While participation in decision making is not necessarily a zero-sum game that universally reduces the power of administrators (Goldman, Dunlap, and Conley, 1991; Shoemaker, 1984; Tannenbaum, 1968) and while major actors in a participative approach need not be in fundamental disagreement, neither is it clear at this time how or how well tensions between administrative leadership and enhancements in the power of teachers, parents, and other participants can be harmonized in the service of school improvement (Brown, 1990; Conley, Schmidle, and Shedd, 1988; Ford, 1991). This dilemma cannot be resolved successfully on the basis of flip ideological claims that empowering teachers will somehow automatically transform them into members of a cohesive faculty committed in practice to the difficult work involved in reforming schools.

4. *Constraints on teacher participation in decision making.* In addition to issues involving time, energy, and technical assistance referred to above, frequently mentioned constraints include (a) lack of interest of some or many teachers in participating in some types of decisions; (b) absence of a schoolwide perspective on many problems and possibilities for change; (c) lack of consensus among faculty but, conversely, stifling of initiative when consensus does emerge; (d) reluctance to take responsibility for decisions; and (e) lack of an adequate knowledge base and relevant research to inform decision making (Brown, 1990; Carrano, 1990; Duke, Showers, and Imber, 1980; Mann, 1990; Clune and White, 1988; Fleming, 1988; Hansen, 1988; Kirby, 1991; Malen, Ogawa, and Kranz, 1990; Short and Greer, 1989). Another frequent constraint that can quickly dissipate teachers' motivation to participate involves lack of significant discretionary funds that would facilitate implementation of action plans to promote instructional reform (Goldman, Dunlap, and Conley, 1991; Kelly and Willner, 1988; Levine and Lezotte, 1990; Short and Greer, 1989).

5. *Reluctance of administrators at all levels to give up traditional prerogatives.* Some analysts believe that significant attempts to empower faculties at the building level are certain to encounter substantial resistance from administrators who perceive or fear that empowerment will reduce their power and prerogatives. Apart from the difficulties (discussed above) inherently involved in trying to harmonize

the decision-making roles of various parties, administrative resistance can create crippling obstacles because success in improving schools through empowerment still depends—as does any other reform effort—on outstanding leadership and supportive management. Viewed charitably, administrators are likely to be concerned that empowerment will reduce school and teacher accountability for carrying out a unified improvement plan if it places decision-making authority in the hands of untrained and unprepared persons (Conley, 1989a, 1989b; Ford, 1991; Kirby, 1991). Viewed suspiciously or cynically, they are concerned mostly with maintaining their power and privileges. Whichever view predominates, administrators are likely to raise serious questions about large-scale movement toward comprehensive teacher participation in decision making.

6. *Restrictions imposed by school board, state, and federal regulations and by contracts with teacher organizations.* Even if faculties want to introduce substantial instructional changes that might produce higher student achievement, implementation frequently is blocked by governmental regulations or negotiated agreements with teachers' bargaining units (Hansen, 1988; Malen, Ogawa, and Kranz, 1990; Mann, 1990; Mauriel and Lindquist, 1989; Short and Greer, 1989). Of course, the existence of such impediments to improved effectiveness is one of the major reasons for moving toward empowerment arrangements through which faculties may be able to reduce or circumvent unproductive external constraints. (Possibilities for doing so are discussed in a later section of this chapter.) Nevertheless, until such regulation actually is reduced through empowerment or some other means, external restrictions constitute a massive obstacle to the success of school-based management activities.

RECENT RESEARCH ON THE IMPLEMENTATION AND SUCCESS OF SITE-BASED MANAGEMENT

As the empowerment movement has coalesced and spread rapidly during the past few years, researchers have begun to assess outcomes in districts that have been early adopters of one or another approach to site-based management or enhanced faculty collaboration in decision making. Given the many difficult problems and obstacles such as those enumerated above, perhaps it is no surprise that research to date generally has reported conclusions that appear more neutral and disappointing than positive and encouraging. (As Wagner and Gooding [1987] and Beer, Eisenstat, and Spector [1990] have pointed out, research on participative decision making in business also clearly indicates that such participation frequently fails to produce major benefits.) We present here some examples of recent findings in education.

1. Mauriel and Lindquist (1989) carried out an intensive study of two school-based management (SBM) projects, and reported the following conclusions:

> The conflicts over delegation and advocacy, the need for training, the requirements for time and resources, and the fact that many site councils begin to falter after early bursts of enthusiasm, point up the size and scope of the problems involved. . . . For many school systems the adoption of SBM means a major change in organizational structure, management style, allocation of power and resources, a need for new accountability systems, and a serious renegotiation of the respective governance roles and authority of the school board, the teacher union, the central office, and the community stakeholders. Otherwise, SBM will be just another moderately helpful public relations/ communications vehicle tinkering with the peripheral issues of school governance and management. [P. 22]

2. Brown (1990) studied school-based management in a group of Canadian schools and concluded:

> How schools produce learning remains an intriguing black box. . . . Do principals supervise their teachers differently? . . . Is it possible that equality of educational opportunity . . . is attained in some way? How? . . . Does school-based management actually "make a difference" on these dimensions? Clearly, many more research resources are needed to investigate these topics. [Pp. 265–266]

3. Based on an examination carried out for the National Governors' Association of efforts to introduce various approaches to decentralized decision making, David (1989a, 1989b) summarized the available research on school-based management as follows:

> In districts that practice school-based management essentials, research studies find a range of positive effects, from increased teacher satisfaction and professionalism to new arrangements and practices within schools. . . . There are [only] a few examples of second-order change, schools that have altered the daily schedule to allow more time for teachers to work together or to increase time devoted to reading. . . . This is not surprising, since studies of school

improvement find that school councils rarely tackle even instructional issues, let alone second-order change; dealing with such issues is much more difficult than creating a new discipline policy or decorating the entranceway. [1989b, pp. 50–51]

4. A recent study (Buttram and Kruse, 1988) of a school improvement project in Maryland found no relationship between extent of teacher participation in program planning and movement toward greater effectiveness on "challenge" dimensions selected by participants at each school.

5. Clune and White's (1988) examination of school-based management in thirty-one districts concluded:

> Criteria of success for SBM programs . . . [generally have pertained] to process rather than outcomes (increased autonomy, flexibility, communication). Systematic monitoring is rare, whether of student achievement or other outcomes. Implementation problems revolve around the difficulty of new roles. . . . Principals may lack the disposition and training. . . . Teachers may lack time and resources; . . . participation of parents and students . . . is often difficult to maintain. . . . The most conspicuous outstanding research issue flows out of the findings of program diversity and the typical lack of systematic evaluation. . . . Given a very large range of decentralization, and practically uniform expressions of satisfaction, the obvious question is whether type and degree of decentralization make any difference. [Pp. 23–31]

6. Wohlsetter and Buffet (1991) studied developments with respect to school-based budgeting in five big-city districts in four states and found that "state and local initiatives to encourage school-based management (and budgeting) were developed independently and remain uncoordinated" (p. 12). They further concluded that school-based management has limited potential for encouraging "systemic reform" if it is not part of a "coordinated effort to improve school productivity" (p. 13).

7. After examining the operation of site councils at eight schools in Salt Lake City, Ogawa and Malen (1989) reported that "shared governance had done more than simply fail to alter traditional decision-making relationships; it had actually worked to reaffirm them" by (1) diffusing potentially contentious issues from the district office to school councils; (2) sustaining "zone of indifference" agendas on the councils; (3) defusing potentially explosive issues on school councils; (4) evoking empathy from council members for administrators and teachers; and (5) developing loyalty toward schools and their councils (pp. 2–3). In "light of the history of previous attempts to decentralize

and democratize schools," they further concluded that it "seems appropriate to examine site-based management as a political response to conflict and a strategy to stabilize school systems," rather than primarily as an attempt to improve education through local school reform (p. 10).

8. As part of a relatively intensive examination of conditions and problems in five big-city school districts, Corcoran, Walker, and White (1988) found that two of the five had established site councils in every school, and that

> the actual influence of the councils and the scope of their decision making varies enormously . . . "One problem was that authority was not well defined . . ." In addition, district officials did not appear to be holding the principals accountable for making the school councils work. There were policies specifying the composition of the councils and the frequency with which they should meet, but there was no monitoring of their implementation. Sometimes district policies seemed to be in conflict. "The district is going through an identity crisis, trying to raise standards and decentralize decisions at the same time," said one respondent. [P. 68]

The preceding citations and quotations make it clear that empowerment and other site-based management approaches are relatively new in many school districts and will take years to develop. They may or may not eventually prove successful in bringing about substantial educational improvements on a widespread basis. Recognizing the complexity and promise of the burgeoning school-based management movement, some analysts are trying to identify the most important theoretical and practical issues and considerations that should receive attention in implementing this approach to local school reform.

For example, Conley (1989a, 1989b) has described much of the confusion that currently exists with respect to site-based management. She has pointed out that progress probably will be haphazard unless appropriate distinctions are made between "technical," "managerial," and "strategic" decisions, and also between decisions respectively involving organizational resource allocation, work allocation, professional/client-organization interface, and teaching process (1989a, pp. 11, 13). Alternately, Richardson (1986) examined school-based management projects in twelve districts and concluded that analysis and implementation might be enhanced by classifying budget, personnel, and instructional issues into three, eight, and six subcategories, respectively, with attention in implementing each aspect given to staffing, staff development, participant training, data accessibility, veto powers, and local accountability (p. 3).

In a somewhat similar analysis, study of developments in nine school districts participating in the "Empowered School District Project" led Short and Greer (1989) to identify ten kinds of district policies (e.g., composition of school faculty, student promotion and retention) and ten types of site-level "areas" (e.g., organization of the school day, use of space) that seem likely to receive considerable attention in working to implement participative decision making and shared governance. Regarding organizational analysis in general (as distinguished from analyses focusing primarily on elementary and secondary education), Hackman and Walton (1986) have identified five general types of "conditions" that promote the effectiveness of self-managed units: (1) clear, engaging direction; (2) enabling of performance (includes "well-structured" group tasks and "well-composed" groups); (3) positive norms that regulate behavior and foster active scanning and planning; (4) available expert coaching; and (5) adequate material resources (pp. 90–92). Each of these conditions depends on "critical leadership functions" involving both diagnostic and predictive monitoring as well as "taking action" that has external as well as internal effects. Case studies presented by these authors not only indicate that the effectiveness of self-managed units sometimes depends on availability of "unlimited resources on call," but also suggest that the process of creating and operating such units is a complicated and difficult matter that probably has not been thought through very well by most proponents in education and other fields.

PROMISING APPROACHES AND COMPONENTS

Although school-based management is still for the most part a relatively new innovation for bringing about local school reform, and although knowledge and understanding concerning prerequisites for its successful implementation are still rudimentary, several components of approaches being developed in the field are particularly promising from both an analytical and a practical point of view. Several such components are described briefly here.

1. *Waiver strategies.* As we noted above, external regulations constitute some of the most important obstacles to successful school-based management, not to mention to school effectiveness in general. In-

deed, school-based management frequently is viewed primarily as a way to reduce or overcome external constraints. As numerous analysts have emphasized and advocated, combining school-based management with opportunities to waive unproductive local, state, and federal regulations and dysfunctional provisions of bargaining unit contracts may represent a feasible approach for substantially improving the performance of elementary and secondary schools (Elmore, 1988; Hansen, 1988; Hill, Wise, and Shapiro, 1989; Mann, 1990).

For example, the New York State Board of Regents Committee on the New York City Schools (1988) recently concluded that a "mammoth system, plus tenure, plus union protection, and an uncertain technology, currently combine to make the school building impregnable" against demands for accountability and reform. The committee recommended that schools failing to meet specific improvement goals should participate in a process of "conditional deregulation," which would provide them with *flexible compliance* with state "regulations, mandates, and reporting/auditing requirements"; *lump sum budgets* that "repackaged" existing state aid programs into block grants; *contract waivers* with the United Federation of Teachers (UFT) to extend existing "school-based option" opportunities; and *additional personnel* provided in part through reassignment of central office and state personnel to the school level. Developments at conditionally deregulated schools would be closely monitored to determine whether they are meeting "negotiated performance targets," and failure to meet targets would result in district consideration of possible additional remedies including appointment of new leadership and/or thorough reorganization and reconstitution of a school and its faculty.

Several big-city districts that are moving to enhance school empowerment are placing considerable emphasis on developing policies and practices involving waivers of existing regulations and controls. For example, a 1987 contractual agreement between the New York City Board of Education and the UFT provided teachers with greater opportunity to challenge supervisors' decisions regarding grading of students, curriculum, and other matters, and also enhanced possibilities for waiver of some contractual provisions that restrict flexibility in redesigning instruction. As of March 1989, forty to fifty waivers had been approved by district and union representatives, though information on their nature and content has not been compiled.

In Dade County, Florida, which is the big-city district that has moved furthest and most comprehensively toward instituting various aspects of empowerment, waiver strategies seem to be playing an increasingly important and central part in the reform effort. Probably more than in any other big-city district, Dade's approach encourages faculties to view their budget allocation as constituting a "lump sum," which they can reallocate based on analysis of particular school needs. To a greater or lesser degree, such reallocations frequently involve either waiving of districtwide policies or, at the least, official clarification concerning the permissibility of departures from standard or previous practices. As of the spring of 1989, fourteen of the thirty-three schools participating in Dade's School-Based Management/ Shared Decision-making Project had received permission to waive one or more existing regulations or policies (Collins, 1988, 1991).

2. *Selection of teachers.* Research on unusually effective schools indicates that one of their distinguishing characteristics frequently involves the vigor with which their principals and other school leaders have acted to select and recruit capable faculty and to replace those who are not making a significant contribution in carrying out the school's mission (Levine and Eubanks, 1989; Levine and Lezotte, 1990; Stringfield and Teddlie, 1987, 1988). It is not surprising that unusually effective schools exemplify this characteristic inasmuch as existence of a positive organizational culture and shared sense of mission among faculty is an important element in determining school effectiveness (Purkey and Smith, 1983; Taylor and Lezotte, 1990). Vigor in selecting and replacing faculty in turn can make a decisive difference in building a cohesive and effective faculty. When teacher empowerment and other school-based management activities include meaningful faculty participation in selecting new teachers, substantial improvement in school effectiveness may not be so dependent on the availability of an unusually outstanding principal as has been true in the past.

3. *District or project-level support and interventions.* As we pointed out above, success in school-based management requires provision of considerable training, technical assistance, and other forms of support for participating schools. Faculties must receive help, direction, and encouragement in dealing with difficult instructional issues and in overcoming a multitude of obstacles that hamper the development and implementation of site-level action plans for improvement (Louis and Miles, 1990). When combined with systematic and comprehensive efforts to improve instructional programming and delivery, site-based planning and faculty empowerment can make an important and perhaps in some cases indispensable contribution to local school reform (Harrison, Killion, and Mitchell, 1989; Levine and Lezotte,

1990). Examples of practices that appear to have produced encouraging results as part of multischool improvement projects and should be considered for inclusion in implementing site-based management include the following:

1. Provision of parallel and coordinated training for administrators and teachers at participating schools (Everson, Scollay, Fabert, and Garcia, 1986; Heim, Flowers, and Anderson, 1989).
2. Assignment of new or weak principals for several weeks of observation and shadowing of more effective principals (O'Neill and Shoemaker, 1989).
3. Assignment of part-time evaluators to assist faculties in collecting and analyzing data (Strusinski, 1989).
4. Use of a "central office intervention team, consisting of representatives from the basic skills, bilingual, staff development, and records and evaluation division," to confer with school improvement teams at ten of the lower-achieving schools in a districtwide effective-schools project involving elementary schools in Newark, New Jersey (Azumi, 1987, p. 6).
5. Designation of and reimbursement for teacher leaders who function as a link between their school faculty, the central office, external resources, and project personnel.
6. Assignment of former (i.e., retired) principals to serve as mentors for principals of schools engaged in site-based planning as part of an effective schools project (Johnson-Lewis, 1988).
7. Monthly meetings of clusters of participating principals who "share successes, failures, strategies, and frustrations and . . . work collaboratively to solve common problems" (Harrison, Killion, and Mitchell, 1989, p. 57).

MAJOR CONCERNS

The preceding analysis indicates that site-based management represents a theoretically promising and attractive approach to local school reform, particularly when it aims to release or relieve schools from unproductive or debilitating external constraints, emphasizes reconstitution of the staff so as to develop and enhance a common faculty mission, and involves substantial district or project-level interventions designed to support systematic and comprehensive efforts to improve instruction. However, as we also pointed out, there are many serious obstacles to successful site-based management, and numerous pitfalls and dangers to be overcome. Among the trends and dangers that have been most worrisome in the recent past and are likely to be most damaging in the near future are those enumerated next.

1. *Confusion between satisfaction and performance.* One of the key arguments frequently offered in favor of site-based management is that it may help increase teachers' satisfaction and commitment, and thereby reduce attrition from the profession. Indeed, Clune and White's (1988) study of site-based management in thirty-one locations indicated that it has almost "uniformly" been perceived as initially improving the satisfaction of participants.

However, research on organizational behavior has shown that employee satisfaction by no means automatically translates into improvements in productivity or other performance outputs. As long ago as 1970, Schwab and Cummings (1970) reviewed decades of research bearing on relationships between satisfaction and productivity, and concluded that because these variables interact in a complex way with many others, satisfaction generally has little influence on performance in the absence of numerous (poorly understood) moderating variables involving employee traits, abilities, and commitment of effort; perceived equity and value of rewards; role definitions and perceptions; and other considerations. We know of nothing in organizational analysis since 1970 that suggests a simple or straight-line relationship between satisfaction and performance.

Given the predictable temptations and tendencies for faculties in site-based management projects to emphasize possibilities for change that are least difficult and inconvenient (see above), the fact that participants frequently express satisfaction may warrant more skepticism than optimism, particularly since there are few if any indications that early movement toward site-based management has been associated with substantial change in instructional delivery or student performance. To a significant degree, satisfaction may have been attained precisely through neglecting requirements for inconvenient institutional reform; from this point of view, one might prefer to find an increase in certain kinds of dissatisfaction that reflected unhappiness with the extent and effectiveness of instructional change. Unless site-based management is clearly part of a much more comprehensive and serious reform effort in the future, indications of increase in faculty satisfaction should not necessarily be interpreted as a positive development.

2. *Substitution of site-based management approaches for central responsibilities involving initiation and support of comprehensive school reform efforts.* Just as satisfaction may in effect substitute for and sometimes even undercut difficult instructional reform possibilities at the school level, district thrusts toward site-based management may divert attention from central decision makers' responsibility for initiating and supporting comprehensive and fundamental reforms in the design and delivery of educational services. If power and resources can be shifted to the school level, central authorities also may be able to shift most or all of the responsibility for failure to improve student performance to teachers and administrators in the schools. As noted above, researchers examining "shared governance" in Salt Lake City concluded that site-based management in practice can be viewed more accurately as a "political response to conflict and a strategy to stabilize school systems" than as an effort to bring about fundamental reform in instruction (Ogawa and Malen, 1989, p. 10). It is but one additional small step to treat site-based management as a substitute for districtwide reform initiatives.

Given the substantial expenditures that likely will be necessary to support training, technical assistance, and improvements in curriculum and instruction as part of any serious reform effort (regardless of whether or not the effort involves emphasis on site-based management), district decision makers may be particularly tempted to adopt site-based approaches that can be (wrongly) defined and presented as "low-cost" interventions. (For analyses describing the numerous and sizable central responsibilities that are involved in implementing reform successfully on a districtwide basis, see Cox, French, and Loucks-Horsley [1987], Pajak and Glickman [1989], and Shoemaker [1986]). Beyond financial considerations, site-based management also may be treated as a substitute for the myriad difficult tasks and changes required to improve the basic functioning of school districts as a whole. By way of contrast, much recent analysis of school districts as well as other organizations recognizes that "transformational" changes are required to greatly enhance organizational effectiveness (Goldman, Dunlap, and Conley, 1991). Thus Beckhard (1989) recently reviewed the literature bearing on "transformational change" and identified a set of "nine challenges that must be met any time" such a change is attempted (pp. 264–265). These tasks, which can easily be neglected when site-based management is treated as a substitute for more comprehensive reform throughout the larger organization, are as follows:

- Ensure the commitment of the chief executive officer and key leaders.
- Ensure that adequate resources are allocated.
- Reach an appropriate balance between managing change and managing stability.
- Ensure appropriate use of special roles, temporary systems, study groups, consultants, and transition teams.
- Continually evaluate both the total effort and its parts.
- Establish and maintain continuity of leadership.
- Appropriately allocate rewards and punishment in line with priorities.
- Ensure adequate information flow.
- Constantly monitor to ensure that participants understand their roles and comprehend the total effort.

Related to the probability that site-based management sometimes or even frequently will be treated as a substitute for central reform responsibilities, dependence on waivers of external constraints may itself become an unproductive reform strategy. As we noted above, waiver possibilities should be viewed as constituting a promising strategy to facilitate effective implementation of site-based management, but more may be lost than gained if allowing an occasional waiver becomes the predominant strategy and each school must go through a laborious process of identifying and winning approval for one or another exemption. Instead, districtwide changes should be initiated whenever possible to eliminate or forestall the need for constant exceptions, even though such changes may be controversial and may spark overt conflict.

For example, many teacher association leaders have been issuing eloquent statements regarding the importance of "restructuring" schools and school districts. In our view, one of the key prerequisites for successful restructuring is massive staff development carried out continuously at the school-site level. Unfortunately, teacher association contracts in most school districts of any size currently require equally massive expenditures to pay teachers for participating in this kind of staff development. Central decision makers' insistence that significant pay raises for teachers in the future will be awarded only in return for participation in continuous staff development as part of the basic contract could do far more to facilitate "restructuring," site-based management, and other substantial reforms than would dependence on waivers of constraints worked out on a hit-or-miss basis for a few particularly dedicated and willing faculties.

3. *Substituting of group processing for "authentic" problem solving.* Just as site-based management is likely to fail when participants do not receive technical assistance to develop their skills in working together to identify and solve problems, so, too, the opposite extreme marked by emphasis on group-process skills that are not applied to concrete problems is unlikely to be successful. Provision of a significant discretionary fund, decentralization of school budgeting functions, or encouragement and support to identify and request productive waivers can introduce useful possibilities for focusing site-based management efforts on specific problems to address while project leaders learn to work productively as a group. When central decision makers do not take these or other steps to anchor site-based management in a context that stimulates or even forces participants to address important issues, the entire project frequently degenerates into an unproductive exercise in group process. Goldman, Dunlap, and Conley (1991) called attention to this difference in the following description of "authentic situations" at schools they found were making progress in site-based management:

> Rather than providing training in "problem solving," "consensus building," or "communications skills," these projects provide school staffs with real reasons to solve problems, seek consensus, and communicate. In this environment, when training in group process skills is offered, it can be applied immediately to real situations that have meaning and value to the participants. [P. 23]

4. *Confusion between site-based management and "effective schools" approaches.* As we pointed out at the beginning of this chapter, one of the pluses of the site-based management movement is its emphasis on faculty participation in decision making, which frequently has been cited as an important consideration in school improvement efforts in general and in carrying out projects to improve school effectiveness in particular (i.e., "effective school" projects emphasizing improvement in the characteristics or "correlates" of unusually effective schools). Conversely, successful effective schools projects generally incorporate a central emphasis on development of plans for improvement through the functioning of site-based councils (Levine and Lezotte, 1990; Taylor and Lezotte, 1990).

Perhaps because site planning is such an important part of the effective schools movement, it is easy to confuse site-based management and effective schools approaches. Strictly speaking, site-based management need not involve any particular emphasis on or approach to improvement of instruction; thus many implementations instruct faculties to take more responsibility for decisions but provide little if any guidance or support regarding the types of decisions and problems to be addressed or the interventions to be considered in addressing them. By way of contrast, the term "effective schools approaches" as used in this paper (and widely used in the field) refers to efforts that include emphasis on improvement in instructional leadership, testing, organization and implementation of instructional services, expectations for students' performance, and other aspects of instruction, particularly for students who currently are low achievers. Attention thereby is fixed on both *effectiveness* and *equity* in delivering instruction.

Lacking an effective schools emphasis or some comparable formulation stressing that all students can learn at an adequate level, site-based management easily neglects concerns about *effectiveness* and, even more likely, about *equity* that are likely to involve difficult, time-consuming, and perplexing changes in teachers' behaviors and attitudes. In addition, the effective schools approach, like other fundamental school improvement efforts, draws on several decades of research and experience that can help faculties improve delivery of instruction. Not so the site-based management movement, which is still relatively new and to date has produced relatively little research and knowledge regarding effective implementation.

In this context, pitfalls regarding the temptation to confuse site-based management and school improvement approaches have been identified and discussed by Harrison, Killion, and Mitchell (1989). Based on experience in a school district that defined "site-based management as school improvement," they noted that in some schools in the district, "principals were mistakenly trying to use the school improvement process as the decision-making forum for all decisions about school management and curriculum." In others, school improvement teams were formed and mission statements were developed, but "decisions about budgeting, staffing, and use of facilities continued to be made by the principals with little or no input from teachers. . . . Neither site-based management nor school improvement was having the impact we had hoped for" (p. 56).

CONCLUSION

Innovations in education usually appear as a faddish response to important problems, neglect fundamental prerequisites for success in the schools, and soon are judged as inconsequential and disappear.

Years or decades later they reappear in somewhat altered form as someone's "new," simple answer to complex challenges. Such will be the fate of site-based management if it fails to focus teachers' and administrators' efforts on feasible possibilities for reform of instruction at the school level. In our opinion, school districts should not ignore research-based possibilities for improvement that can be attained through effective schools approaches, while placing a singular emphasis on site-based management. Conversely, site-based management will be more likely to succeed if it is carried out within a larger effective schools framework that provides this focus. If implementors also attend early on and seriously to the problems and issues we described in the first parts of this chapter, site-based management may become a plausible approach for bringing about widespread school reform throughout the 1990s.

REFERENCES

Azumi, Jann E. "Effective Schools Characteristics, School Improvement, and School Outcomes: What Are the Relationships?" Paper presented at the Annual Meeting of the American Educational Research Association, Washington, D.C., 1989.

Beer, Michael; Eisenstat, Russell A.; and Spector, Bert. "Why Change Programs Don't Produce Change," *Harvard Business Review* 68, no. 6 (1990): 158–166.

Beckhard, Richard. "A Model for the Executive Management of Transformational Change." In *The 1989 Annual: Developing Human Resources*, edited by J. William Pfeiffer. San Diego, Calif.: University Associates, 1989. Pp. 255–265.

Brown, Daniel J. *Decentralization and School-Based Management*. London: Falmer, 1990.

Buttram, Joan L., and Kruse, Janice. *Critical Ingredients for School Improvement Efforts*. Philadelphia: Research for Better Schools, 1988.

Carrano, Frank. "Training the Players for Power Sharing," *Education Week* 10, no. 15 (1990): 38–40.

Clune, William H., and White, Paula. *School-Based Management*. New Brunswick, N.J.: Center for Policy Research in Education, Rutgers University, 1988.

Collins, Robert A. *Interim Evaluation Report, School-Based Management/Shared Decision-Making Project*. Miami, Flor.: Dade County Public Schools, 1988.

Collins, Robert A. "Projectwide Impact of School-Based Management on Selected

Indicators over 3 Years." Paper presented at the Annual Meeting of the American Educational Research Association, Chicago, 1991.

Conley, Sharon C. "From School Site Management to 'Participatory School Site Management'." Paper presented at the Annual Meeting of the American Educational Research Association, San Francisco, 1989a.

Conley, Sharon C. "'Who's on First': School Reform, Teacher Participation, and the Decision-Making Process." Unpublished paper, University of Arizona, Educational Administration Program, 1989b.

Conley, Sharon C.; Schmidle, Timothy; and Shedd, Joseph B. "Teacher Participation in the Management of School Systems," *Teachers College Record* 90, no. 2 (1988): 259–280.

Corcoran, Thomas B.; Walker, Lisa J.; and White, J. Lynne. *Working in Urban Schools.* Washington, D.C.: Institute for Educational Leadership, 1988.

Cox, Pat L.; French, Lindsay C.; and Loucks-Horsley, Susan. *Letting the Principal Off the Hot Seat: Configuring Leadership and Support for School Improvement.* Andover, Mass.: Regional Laboratory for Educational Improvement of the Northeast and Islands, 1987.

David, Jane L. *Restructuring in Progress: Lessons from Pioneering Districts.* Washington, D.C.: National Governors' Association, 1989a.

David, Jane L. "Synthesis of Research on School-Based Management," *Educational Leadership* 46, no. 8 (1989b): 45–53.

Duke, Daniel L.; Showers, Beverly K.; and Imber, Michael. "Teachers and Shared Decision Making: The Costs and Benefits of Involvement," *Educational Administration Quarterly* 16 (Winter 1980): 93–106.

Duttweiler, Patricia Cloud. *Organizing for Excellence.* Austin, Tex.: Southwest Educational Development Laboratory, 1988.

Elmore, Richard F. *Early Experience in Restructuring Schools: Voices from the Field.* Washington, D.C.: National Governors' Association, 1988.

Everson, Susan Toft; Scollay, Susan J.; Fabert, Barbara; and Garcia, Mary. "An Effective Schools Program and Its Results: Initial District, School, Teacher, and Student Outcomes in a Participating District," *Journal of Research and Development in Education* 19, no. 3 (1986): 35–49.

Firestone, William A., and Corbett, H. D. "Planned Organizational Change." In *Handbook of Research on Educational Administration,* edited by Norman J. Bogan. New York: Longman, 1988. Pp. 321–338.

Fleming, Douglas S. "The Literature on Teacher Utilization of Research: Implications for the School Reform Movement." Paper presented at the Annual Meeting of the American Educational Research Association, New Orleans, 1988.

Ford, Darryl J. *The School Principal and Chicago School Reform.* Chicago: Chicago Panel on Public School Policy and Finance, 1991.

Fullan, Michael. *The New Meaning of Educational Change.* New York: Teachers College Press, 1991.

Goldman, Paul; Dunlap, Diane M.; and Conley, David T. "Administrative Facilitation and Site-Based School Reform Projects." Paper presented at the Annual Meeting of the American Educational Research Association, Chicago, 1991.

Hackman, J. Richard, and Walton, Richard E. "Leading Groups in Organizations." In *Designing Effective Work Groups,* edited by Paul S. Goodman. San Francisco: Jossey-Bass, 1986. Pp. 72–119.

Hansen, Kenneth H. "Decentralizing Education Decision Making: A Policy Framework." Paper prepared for Chief State School Officers of the Northwest and the Pacific, Northwest Regional Educational Laboratory, Portland, Oregon, 1988.

Harrison, Cynthia R.; Killion, Joellen P.; and Mitchell, James E. "Site-Based Management: The Realities of Implementation," *Educational Leadership* 46, no. 8 (1989): 55–58.

Hart, Ann W., and Murphy, Michael J. "Work Design Where It Happens: Five Comparative Cases of Schools." Paper presented at the Annual Meeting of the American Educational Research Association, San Francisco, 1989.

Heim, Max O.; Flowers, David; and Anderson, Patricia. "School Improvement in Geary County Schools." In *Case Studies in Effective Schools Research*, edited by Lawrence W. Lezotte and Barbara O. Taylor. Okemos, Mich.: National Center for Effective Schools Research and Development, 1989.

Hill, Paul T.; Wise, Arthur E.; and Shapiro, Leslie. *Educational Progress: Cities Mobilize to Improve Their Schools*. Santa Monica, Calif.: Rand, 1989.

Hoerr, John. "The Payoff from Teamwork," *Business Week*, No. 3114 (1988): 56–62.

Johnson-Lewis, Sharon. "Closing the Achievement Gap: Developing and Evaluating Detroit's School Improvement Plans." In *Rising to the Challenge of Differential Performance among Student Ethnic Groups*. Portland, Oreg.: Portland State University/Portland Public Schools, 1988.

Kelly, Tina, and Willner, Robin. *Small Change: The Comprehensive School Improvement Program*. Albany, N.Y.: Educational Priorities Panel, 1988.

Kirby, Peggy C. "Shared Decision Making: Moving from Concerns about Restrooms to Concerns about Classrooms." Paper presented at the Annual Meeting of the American Educational Research Association, Chicago, 1991.

Levine, Daniel U. "Creating Effective Schools: Findings and Implications from Research and Practice," *Phi Delta Kappan* 72, no. 5 (1991): 389–393.

Levine, Daniel U., and Eubanks, Eugene E. "Organizational Arrangements at Effective Secondary Schools." In *Organizing for Learning*, edited by Herbert J. Walberg and John J. Lane. Reston, Va.: National Association of Secondary School Principals, 1989.

Levine, Daniel U., and Lezotte, Lawrence W. *Unusually Effective Schools: A Review and Analysis of Research and Practice*. Madison, Wisc.: National Center for Effective Schools Research and Practice, 1990.

Levine, Daniel U., and Taylor, Barbara O. "Effective Schools Projects and School-Based Management," *Phi Delta Kappan* 72, no. 5 (1991): 394–397.

Louis, Karen S., and Miles, Matt B. *Improving the Urban High School*. New York: Teachers College Press, 1990.

Malen, Betty; Ogawa, Rodney T.; and Kranz, Jennifer, "What Do We Know about School-Based Management?" In *Choice and Control in American Education*, vol. 2, edited by William H. Clune and John F. Witte. London: Falmer, 1990.

Mann, Dale. "It's Time to Trade Red Tape for Accountability in Education," *Executive Educator* 12, no. 1 (1990): 26, 28.

Marburger, Carl L. *One School at a Time*. Columbia, Mary.: National Committee for Citizens in Education, 1985.

Mauriel, John J., and Lindquist, Karin M. "School-Based Management: Doomed to Failure?" Paper presented at the Annual Meeting of the American Educational Research Association, San Francisco, 1989.

New York State Board of Regents Committee on the New York City Schools. *Creating Freedom and Accountability in School Leadership*. Albany, N.Y.: New York State

Department of Education, 1988.

Ogawa, Rodney T., and Malen, Betty. "Site-Based Governance Councils: Mechanisms for Affirming Rather Than Altering Traditional Decision-Making Relations in Schools (A Working Paper)." Paper presented at the Annual Meeting of the American Educational Research Association, San Francisco, 1989.

O'Neill, Kate, and Shoemaker, Joan, eds. *A Conversation between James Comer and Ronald Edmonds.* Okemos, Mich.: National Center for Effective Schools Research and Development, 1989.

Pajak, Edward F., and Glickman, Carl D. "Dimensions of School District Improvement," *Educational Leadership* 46, no. 8 (1989): 61–64.

Purkey, Stewart C., and Smith, Marshall W. "Effective Schools—A Review," *Elementary School Journal* 83 (1983): 427–452.

Richardson, Claiborne T. "School-Based Management Briefing Papers." A report prepared for the Fairfax (Va.) County Public Schools Office of Research and Evaluation. Falls Church, Va.: Fairfax County Public Schools, Office of Research and Evaluation, 1986.

Sagor, Richard. "What Project LEARN Reveals about Collaborative Action Research," *Educational Leadership* 48, no. 6 (1991): 6–7.

Schwab, Donald P., and Cummings, Larry L. "Theories of Performance and Satisfaction: A Review," *Industrial Relations* 9, no. 4 (1970): 408–430.

Shoemaker, Joan. *Research-Based School Improvement Practices.* Hartford: Connecticut State Department of Education, 1984.

Shoemaker, Joan. "Developing Effectiveness in the District, School, and Classroom," *Equity and Choice* 2 (Winter 1986): 1–8.

Short, Paula M., and Greer, John T. "Increasing Teacher Autonomy through Shared Governance: Effects on Policy Making and Student Outcomes." Paper presented at the Annual Meeting of the American Educational Research Association, San Francisco, 1989.

Stringfield, Sam, and Teddlie, Charles. "A Time to Summarize: Six Years and Three Phases of the Louisiana School Effectiveness Study." Paper presented at the Annual Meeting of the American Educational Research Association, Washington, D.C., 1987.

Stringfield, Sam, and Teddlie, Charles. "A Time to Summarize: The Louisiana School Effectiveness Study," *Educational Leadership* 46, no. 2 (1988): 43–49.

Strusinski, Marianne. "The Provision of Technical Support for School-Based Evaluations: The Researcher's Perspective." Paper presented at the Annual Meeting of the American Educational Research Association, San Francisco, 1989.

Tannenbaum, Arnold. *Control in Organizations.* New York: McGraw-Hill, 1968.

Taylor, Barbara A., and Lezotte, Lawrence W., eds. *Case Studies in Effective Schools Research.* Okemos, Mich.: National Center for Effective Schools Research and Development, 1990.

Wagner, John A., III, and Gooding, Richard Z. "Shared Influence and Organizational Behavior: A Meta-Analysis of Situational Variables Expected to Moderate Participation-Outcome Relationships," *Academy of Management Journal* 38, no. 3 (1987): 524–541.

Wohlsetter, Priscilla, and Buffet, Thomas. "School-Based Management in Big-City Districts: Are Dollars Decentralized Too?" Paper presented at the Annual Meeting of the American Educational Research Association, Chicago, 1991.

Part Two
Cases: Perspectives on Restructuring and School-Based Management

CHAPTER 4

A Tale of Two Cities: Radical School Reform in Chicago and London

Bruce S. Cooper

It was the best of times, the worst of times, it was the age of wisdom, it was the age of foolishness, it was the epoch of belief, it was the epoch of incredulity, it was the season of Light, it was the season of Darkness, it was the spring of hope, it was the winter of despair, we had everything before us, we had nothing before us, we were all going direct to Heaven, we were all going the other way—in short, the period was so far like the present period, that some of its noisiest authorities insisted on its being received, for good or for evil, in the superlative degree of comparison only.

> —Charles Dickens, *A Tale of Two Cities*, p. 1.

Charles Dickens captures, as only great novelists can, the sense of fear and optimism, change and continuity, progress and regression, and confusion that often accompany revolution. His words apply today. In fact, he might be describing modern events in two great cities, London and Chicago, where revolutions are taking place in the way schools are organized and governed—revolutions that challenge central beliefs about large urban school systems.

On April 1, 1990, London, England, saw the nation's (perhaps the world's) largest city school system dissolved by government action: the Inner London Education Authority (ILEA), the central agency for elementary and secondary schools in the city, ceased to exist. In a

single act, Parliament reversed 115 years of organizational development. After April 1, 1990, London's thirteen boroughs became separate school authorities, a change that was exciting and disruptive,
even revolutionary in a nation where education had become large,
centralized, unresponsive, and monopolistic.

And on October 11 and 12, 1989, the public schools of Chicago,
Illinois, invited parents to elect representatives to local school councils for all of the city's 540 schools, and handed these councils
significant control over the operation of schools. School elections are
hardly revolutionary in a nation that has had "local control" of
education since the seventeenth century. However, in Chicago, a large
bureaucracy ran the schools, and parents had little or no say in the
education of children. The bureaucracy in Chicago was like those in
London and in hundreds of other cities across the world.

In the Chicago School Reform Act of 1988, the Illinois legislature
"restructured" Chicago's schools by creating at every school site a
local school council (LSC) to consist of six parents, two community
representatives, two teachers, and the principal. These lay-dominated
councils held authority over the hiring and firing of principals and
teachers, and over curriculum and budget—a revolution that Dickens
would appreciate.

Thus, these two cities have tales to tell: of school districts being
decentralized, even broken up; of "central offices" being disbanded
completely (as in the case of the Inner London Education Authority)
or reduced in size and significance (as in Chicago); of parents getting
a much increased voice in how schools are run, by serving on boards
of governors (London) or on local school councils (Chicago); and of
decisions affecting teachers and students being made at the school
level, not higher up in the bureaucracy.

Yet, London and Chicago are vastly different political settings and
are driven by very distinct ideologies. British schools in general and
London schools in particular were restructured as part of a conservative, New Right belief in smaller units, more consumer choice, more
decentralized services (the "devolution revolution"), and even more
"privatization" (Sexton, 1987; Cooper, 1989a; Cooper, 1990; Lieberman, 1989). In contrast, the Chicago reform efforts were started by
more left-wing, liberal politicians and parents interested not so much
in "choice" (in fact, the Chicago School Reform Act specifically
delayed choice as a policy) but rather in a desire to improve all
schools through "parent empowerment." The plan was to strengthen
the hand of parents and communities in their existing schools through

locally elected advisory councils—not to encourage parents to exercise greater mobility through consumer transfer, choice, open enrollment, magnet schools, and the like. The purpose was to improve parental "voice," not to encourage the "exit" option (see Hirschman, 1970).

For Chicago reformers, special schools and open access, and other parental choice plans—so much an interest of the Thatcher government since 1979—were seen as divisive, elitist, and separatist, creating tiers of higher-class, mainly white, academic achieving schools, and a wholly unacceptable group of the worst or "sink" schools for the rest: blacks, Hispanics, the poor (Moore and Davenport, 1990). In fact, Donald Moore (1990), an architect of the Chicago reform plan, had researched magnet schools in a number of American cities and found them elite and segregating—"a new kind of sorting machine" in his terms. Thus, the Chicago reforms were based on a different set of assumptions than those in London, providing interesting contrasts for comparing these nations.

This chapter compares reforms in the governance of the London and Chicago school systems, and the effects of major change on schools, educators, and parents. In particular, we examine the effects in Chicago schools and in one particular London borough, Wandsworth (a local borough council controlled by the Conservative party), where the elimination of ILEA has encouraged real experimentation, change, and renewal.

Comparative case studies, particularly international ones, are useful—they force clearer definitions, categories, and cautious conclusions. Yet, the parallels in London and Chicago are striking: (1) common criticism about failure of current schools; (2) legislation diminishing or dissolving central authority, (3) devolution to local schools, which (4) democratically select their own governors, who in turn (5) make key decisions about school heads and staff—that is, policies, programs, and funding.

Yet, differences between cities are also extensive: dissimilar political structures, school organizations, and very different political ideologies are at work. Reform in the London schools was nationally imposed, while Chicago insiders prevailed on the Illinois legislature and governor to reorganize the city's school system. The Chicago School Reform Act was sponsored by Democratic legislators in the General Assembly, with no obvious help from the Republican Reagan administration, while the Tory party was very much behind the breakup of ILEA and the support of reform in Wandsworth. Thus, it is in the effort both to compare and contrast these recent cases that generalizations can be made, as the United States and Great Britain pursue their own school reforms.

SIMILAR BACKGROUND, SIMILAR CRITIQUES

Both Britain and the United States had studied their education services and found them wanting (see National Commission on Excellence in Education, 1983; National Governors' Association, 1986; Cox and Boyson, 1977). Report after report documented poor achievement, loss of national and international standing, and the failure of schools to prepare children for life, work, and further education. At-risk children, attending poor schools in urban areas, had put the "nation at risk," or so the arguments went in both nations.

Chicago's Schools

Glass (1989) wondered, "Are the Chicago schools the 'worst in America' as claimed by former Secretary of Education William J. Bennett and others? And can they be reformed?" (p. 1. See also Walberg, Bakalis, Bast, and Baer, 1988, 1989; Chicago *Tribune*, 1988). In 1987, prior to the recent reform, the indications were that the Chicago schools were indeed in deep trouble. Even among the many other ailing urban systems in the United States, Chicago's schools stood out as needing immediate reform. This fact was so strong, so pervasive, that a coalition of parents, community groups, and politicians, and even the usually reluctant-to-change Chicago teachers' union, helped to lobby the Illinois state legislature to restructure school governance, funding, staffing, and organization. Chicago's school reform legislation will perhaps be the most dramatic change in education in the United States in the twentieth century.

Chicago schools suffered from a rigid educational system that denied autonomy and crippled reform. Bullough (1974) reminds us, however, that large bureaucracies were the great innovation of the late nineteenth century. He writes:

> Schools in American cities may yet be paying the price for the success of turn-of-the-century reform. The highly structured educational system which

emerged from that period remains essentially intact, increasing the difficulty of evolving programs and institutions relevant to the demands and needs of a constantly changing urban society and frequently impeding the flow of communications between the schools themselves and the public they serve. [P. 112]

Chicago's school problems are not unique. Corcoran, Walker, and White (1988) had found that many big city school systems suffered substandard buildings, lack of basic resources, poor supervision, inadequacy of help from the "downtown" or central offices, large classes (between twenty-five and thirty pupils), loss of control over curriculum, and so on. Most significantly, the researchers found that many urban schools were inhospitable places for teachers to work. They concluded:

> The findings paint a bleak picture of conditions of urban teaching. These findings are consistent with national and state teacher surveys, but urban conditions are worse. . . . Unsupportive leadership, lack of respect, low participation in policymaking, limited opportunities for collegiality, lack of recognition, and inadequate professional development seem to be the norms of teaching rather than the exception. In urban areas, however, these issues take on a different and debilitating scale given the resource problems, the bureaucracy, and the special needs of students. [Corcoran, Walker, and White, 1988, p. 127]

The shortcomings of Chicago schools, then, included the litany of urban problems: student dropouts, truancy, poor achievement, teacher turnover, and racial and social isolation. Importantly, the "system" was not organized to handle these problems, as the central board attempted to run things "from the top." Rev. Kenneth B. Smith (1990), past president of the Chicago Board of Education, commented on the difficulty of changing a city system:

> First, a word or two about time. We should not expect a dramatic change in achievement scores in a year, or three years, or five years. Because this first step in reform emphasizes governance, we must still confront the more compelling task of developing education programs that work for all children. [P. 19]

The problems of the Chicago schools earned it the appellation, the "worst in America," an assertion documented by Walberg and colleagues (1988). These researchers found that "centralization of the Chicago Public Schools has closed off many avenues for parental involvement in the schools. . . . Principals have little say in hiring and firing of teachers, how the budget for their school is set, and how their building is used" (p. 63). Attempts at reform foundered because the system itself was not working, and the quality of education had continued to decline.

Interestingly, this worsening reputation made radical reform possible, and the argument was: Things are so bad now, they can only get better. Reformers, then, could argue for radical restructuring of the Chicago public schools, which they did successfully.

London's Schools

In Britain, the Inner London Education Authority (ILEA) had much the same reputation as Chicago had in the United States. The school authority was expensive, ailing, and overly bureaucratic; further, many Tory politicians saw ILEA as a "hotbed" of left-wing control, a center of what was disparagingly called "the loony Left." Brent, a borough of London, was particularly despised by the Thatcher government as a council that pressed a socialist ideology and was impervious to pressure by the national government. While Chicago reform was basically an "inside job," with Chicago people leading the charge, the London reform was mainly accomplished by the Tory national government through Parliamentary action that abolished the Inner London Education Authority. While political action in the two situations was different, criticisms of schools in Chicago and London were similar:

1. *Inefficient bureaucracies.* Both cities suffered from massive overhead, built up over the years to manage hundreds of schools and scores of national, regional, and local programs. People within the system came to recognize that the sheer scale of these systems, their layers of bureaucracy and mounds of red tape, their inability to respond creatively to changing conditions, and their unresponsiveness to consumer demands required strong action.

2. *Falling quality.* National attention was focused on the apparent lack of achievement in both cities. In some Chicago schools, 60 percent of their students did not graduate; in London schools, 90 percent of the students were not continuing their education beyond age sixteen (the legal age at which British children can leave school, although they often do so without a diploma or passing the key examination, the General Certificate of Secondary Education [GCSE]).

The *Economist* puts the crisis in British education as follows: "In Britain, 60 percent of children [in urban schools, percentages are even higher] abandon full-time education at sixteen, compared with only 10 percent in West Germany and America and 4 percent in Japan." And the article laments:

> But if Britain continues to leave the mass of its sixteen- to eighteen-year-olds poorly educated, it will be trapped between high-skill economies such as Germany and low-wage economies such as Portugal or the nearly liberated countries of Eastern Europe. If Britain cannot afford education, it cannot afford a modern economy. [1990, p. 18]

3. *Disenfranchisement of participants.* Both cities saw teachers and parents complaining that the system was insensitive to their needs. In Chicago, for example, poor parents found their schools neglected by the central office. While the Board of Education absorbed enormous resources, it tended to treat all schools alike, being unresponsive to difficulties in each setting. Teachers, too, were treated as "employees" in a heavily overadministered, bureaucratic, "top-down" system. The Chicago Federation of Teachers (Local #1, American Federation of Teachers, AFL-CIO) had responded in kind, tending to take the "hard line" to protect its members.

4. *Stand-off and inaction.* Glass (1989) described conditions in Chicago prior to the passage of the Chicago School Reform Act as a "logjam," as the state government tried to force reform and the city representatives worked to free state funds and support local schools. In London the role of the Inner London Education Authority became an issue for the national government and the source of struggle between local Labour leaders and a Conservative-controlled Parliament.

POLITICAL ACTION

Going Outside to Change Inside

In both cities, the key players went "outside" to change the schools inside. In Chicago, reformers appealed to the Illinois legislature and governor and successfully lobbied for a law to restructure the governance of the city's schools. In Britain, reform came from Parliament (Britain has no states) as part of the most sweeping school reform effort since World War II. Rather than attempting reform with more incremental, organizational change (through new regulations and programs), schools in London and Chicago were restructured through a political process.

The reform laws in Britain and Chicago pressed for major school restructuring from opposite ends of the political spectrum, however. Chicago's reform was the end result of years of local, 1960s-style "community organization." In the city of Saul Alinsky (a well-known community organizer in the 1950s and 1960s) where grassroots mobilization was developed and raised to a high art, Chicago reformers knew, in the words of community organizer Michael Bennett, "that power is never given, that it must be taken away." He continues, "The very process of confronting and winning was seen as a way to enhance the self-esteem of rank-and-file citizens and provide them opportunities to expand their potential as leaders and participants in a democratic society" (Bennett, 1990, p. 12).

The ideology of the Chicago School Reform Act of 1988 is pure 1960s—left-wing, Democratic, and empowering. It sought to shift control from the school bureaucrats and the local political machine, which dominated Chicago politics for generations, to the local, grassroots, school-site, parental level. Aware of the shortcomings of "community control" in the 1960s, where the school itself got lost in open warfare over control, the Chicago experiment put the *school* (its parents, staff, and students) at the center of the reforms. The plan avoided, for example, electing regional boards to run the schools (minibureaucracies), as had been the case in the New York City decentralization plan of 1968 (see Rogers, 1984; LaNoue and Smith, 1973).

Instead, schools were central, as the Chicago School Reform Act (Public Act 85-1418) spells out in no uncertain terms:

> The General Assembly intends to make the individual local school the essential unit for educational governance and improvement and to establish a process for placing the primary responsibility . . . in the hands of parents, community residents, teachers, and the school principal at the school level. [Sect. 34-1.01, p. 26]

This section reads like a magna carta for schools and their constituents, an all-out limitation on central control, external political manipulation, and even the "market." On the last matter, the law deferred choice and open enrollment considerations—at the center of the British reform effort—until 1990, at which time such plans were to be reconsidered.

The British Education Reform Act of 1988, of which the dissolution of the Inner London Education Authority was one part, is the most comprehensive school reform bill in Britain's recent history. It was the work of the right-wing Tory leadership interested in "privatizing" education as much as possible. Its purpose was to break up the system and empower parents and school staff (much as Chicago's plan did), but also to introduce stronger choice incentives and greater diversity in the marketplace. Two (now three) new kinds of schools were created, which gave families even greater choice. In effect, the British law, which disbanded London's central system of school governance, sought also to strengthen regional and local education markets. As Stuart Sexton (1987), one of the architects of this school reform, explained:

> The only choice left is to devolve the system to the schools themselves, and to create a direct relationship between suppliers of education, the schools, the teachers, and the consumers, the parents and their children. It is to create, as near as practicable, a "free market" in education. To use a popular word, it is in some sense to "privatize" the State education system. [P. 10]

Thus, in both Britain and the United States, in London and Chicago, the legislative arm of government intervened directly in the inner workings of their largest city school systems, and took action that ran counter to the operating norms of the authority. In choosing to focus on parents rather than on school management, Parliament determined that parents would compose half of the members of school governing boards, that London's district would devolve to its borough councils, and that parents would gain access for their children to greater numbers and types of schools, some old and others newly created.

In Illinois, the state legislature decided that each school would be self-governing and that parents would voice their preference through their lay representation on each of the 540 local school councils. In both cases, radical (even revolutionary) changes such as these came about mainly because the consensus was that large, rigid, centrally managed, monopolistic structures had not worked.

New Policies, New Programs

Examination of the Chicago School Reform Act and the British Education Reform Act points out some interesting similarities. Both bills constrain the "producers" or the "supply side" of the equation.

Taking power from the top of the system, the legislation shifts resources and authority to school sites, to building educators (administrators and teachers), and to parents by placing a majority of parents on local school councils (Chicago) or governing boards (London), thus extending greater control to "consumers."

A few items illustrate the similarities between the British and Illinois laws:

1. *Parents on local school governing boards.* The laws in both Britain and Illinois are very clear on this issue: Parents will have the majority vote on school councils. The British law for new kinds of local schools, called "grant maintained" schools, specifies "five parent governors, at least one but not more than two teacher governors; the head teacher [principal] as ex-officio governor, and two others selected by the foundation" that created the school (see Education Reform Act, Chapter IV, Section 38, p. 34). In fact, all schools in Britain have a board of governors, and by law, at least half of its members are to be parents elected by the parent body.

The Chicago School Reform Act also provides for a majority of parents on local school councils:

> Each local school council shall consist of the principal and ten elected members, six of whom shall be parents of the students currently enrolled at the attendance center [school], two of whom shall be community residents residing within the attendance area . . . and two of whom shall be teachers employed at the attendance center elected by the entire school staff; . . . and in each secondary [school] one full-time student shall be elected annually by the students as a non-voting student member of the local school council. [Chicago School Reform Act, Ch. 122, Section 34-2.1, p. 29]

2. *Staffing decisions at the local school site.* The British act specifies that "the governing body of a school shall have power to appoint, suspend and dismiss staff as they think fit" (Ch. III, Section 34 (3), p. 30), though British school governors have long had greater discretion in hiring than have their United States counterparts. Thus, the Chicago School Reform Act is quite revolutionary, giving the local school council tremendous power to evaluate the principal, "to determine whether the performance contract of the principal shall be renewed, and to directly select a new principal—without submitting any list of candidates for that position to the sub-district superintendents" (Section 34-2.3, p. 35). Within two years, in fact, all Chicago school principals must resign. The local council can either rehire them or

replace them, which gives parents and community enormous control over school direction and leadership.

The principal then hires teachers, though recommendations can be made by the council:

> To evaluate the allocation of teaching resources, . . . to determine whether such allocation is consistent with the instructional objectives and school program; and to make recommendations to the board, the sub-district superintendent and the principal concerning any reallocation of teaching resources when the Council determines that any such reallocation is appropriate because the qualifications of any existing staff do not adequately match or support instructional objectives of school programs. [Section 34-8., pp. 40–41]

Thus, both the Illinois and British reform agendas provided for greater lay power over schools, thus diminishing control by the hierarchy. In fact, the Chicago reform law specifies a narrower management role for a reduced central office staff, clearly with the intent of putting schools at the center of reform.

The Chicago School Reform Act states: "Within thirty days after the effective date of this Act of 1988, the terms of all members of the board holding office are abolished and the Mayor shall appoint a seven-member Interim Board" (Ch. 122, par. 34-3, p. 51), which indicates a reduced role for the board and a greater emphasis on school-site control. Hence, between local school councils firing and hiring or rehiring all new principals over a two-year period, and by replacing the citywide Board of Education, the power of professional administrators was significantly reduced and the governance of Chicago's schools was changed. Or as one commentator explained, control was "returned to 'civilian control'—a domestic *coup d'etat* almost as stunning as recent developments in Eastern Europe" (Finn, 1990, p. 65).

3. *Fiscal control at the school site.* The laws controlling schools in London and Chicago were very specific on budgeting and fiscal management. Reformers on both sides of the Atlantic Ocean realized that unless schools and their leaders gained access to the finances of the school, school-site governance was not really possible. Large city systems are accustomed to central budgeting, with schools receiving allotments from the board for staff, program, equipment, and so on. Many systems are so rigid that principals and teachers cannot even move funds from one budget "line" to another, to adapt to local needs.

The British Education Reform Act goes to great pains to help local schools gain their fair share of resources:

> The scheme shall provide for (a) the determination in respect of each financial year of the authority of the share to be appropriated for that school . . . which is available for allocation to individual schools, and (b) the delegation by the authority of the management of a school's budget share for any year to the governing body of the school. [Ch. III, 33, p. 29]

To increase the opportunity for parents, principals, and teachers to influence the program in their schools, the Chicago School Reform Act specifies that the central board

> shall allocate a lump sum amount to each local school based upon the school enrollment and the special needs of the student body. The local school principal shall develop an expenditure plan in consultation with the local school council, the professional personnel, and other school personnel which reflects the priorities and activities as described in the school's local school improvement plan. . . . [Section 34-2.3, p. 36]

Thus, in both London and Chicago, school-site management goes hand in hand with school-site budgeting.

4. *Program control at the school site.* Finally, the policies in the two cities attempt to encourage individual schools to make key decisions about program planning. Local school councils in Chicago are required to formulate an improvement plan that includes goals, objectives, activities, staff, and evaluation. The Chicago School Reform Act gives the local school council some control over selecting textbooks, setting student disciplinary policies, and forming school improvement plans—all key to making schools better. British schools too have received some freedom to select their own program, usually formulated by the headteacher and approved by the school's board of governors.

LOOKING AT CHICAGO AND LONDON . . .
AFTER THE "REVOLUTION"

Thus, the intent of the school revolution in Chicago and London was much the same: to empower parents, heads, and teachers, and to reduce the bureaucratic and political control of the local education authorities. Dissolving the Inner London Education Authority moved power to the thirteen boroughs. We shall examine here the response of one such jurisdiction, the Borough of Wandsworth, an interesting community southwest of the Thames River, where the new education director (superintendent), Donald Naismith, has taken over for the ILEA and is making radical change that was unthinkable under the central control of the London authority.

But as Dickens warns us, these are the best and worst of times. We have, in the language of policy analysts, "intended" and "unintended" outcomes. What happened as a result of the radical reform? What were some of the opportunities and constraints of these changes? What can we learn about school revolution versus evolution? What new problems replace old ones, sometimes as a result of innovations?

Impact of School Reforms

In both Britain and Chicago, reforms were intended to upset the status quo and to revolutionize the way schools operate. Yet, both efforts are very recent. For example, on February 28, 1990, newly elected local school councils in Chicago had to tell the central board whether they planned to keep their current principals or begin replacing them. And in London on April 1, 1990, ILEA was dissolved, though some borough superintendents (called "education officers" or "directors") had been hired six months previously to begin organizing the thirteen new borough education authorities.

Some interesting results may already be noted:

1. *Release of energy.* Revolutions energize and engage people in the act of reform. Chicagoans were amazed at the level of activity during local school council elections. Suddenly, democracy came home to each and every school in the city. Parents who had long given up on schools became active in campaigning for office or supporting candidates. Joravsky (1990) found that "corporate money and aggressive community organizing . . . thrust some schools in impoverished black and Hispanic neighborhoods ahead of several largely white schools, reversing traditional voting patterns" (p. 12). In fact, estimates are that a quarter million voters turned out to elect candidates to the 5,400 places on school councils. About 115,000 voters were parents supporting the parental candidates on the councils (six per council), while 97,000 "community residents" voted for their two members on

each council; and 35,000 teachers voted for their choices for the two "teacher slots." One observer talked about "high-octane" campaigns, with community organizations, corporations, teacher groups, and other coalitions (e.g., United Neighborhood Organization) involved.

But perhaps Joseph Reed, a member of the Chicago Interim Board of Education (the central body), expressed it best:

> A high turnout sends a signal that parents want to get involved in their schools. We have to convince black, white, and Hispanic parents that this is a vehicle for taking control of their schools. We had a lot of impediments this [election] time that we won't have next time. We made some mistakes, but we learned a lot. Now we have to get better. [In Joravsky, 1990, p. 15]

Suddenly, Chicago had almost six thousand newly elected advocates (council members) to argue, lobby, and support its schools. Outsiders, too, were energized to help the schools. For example, some ninety certified public accountants offered to help schools set their budgets, a proposal that few schools can refuse.

The effects of the British Education Reform Act in London were more subdued. The closing of ILEA was announced months before, staff were hired at the borough halls, and the transition was more gradual. However, the Wandsworth borough, for one, was awake, active, and exciting. It had to be, since the education director, Donald Naismith, was hired by a borough council composed of forty-one Tories and forty Labourites, in a constituency that was traditionally blue-collar Socialist (before the south Thames area became "gentrified" by white-collar workers who came from fashionable Chelsea, just north of the river).

Naismith had been hired by the conservatives and was putting together a conservative-style program of magnet schools, choice, transfers, and by far the two most interesting new high schools in Britain: a City Technology College, privately run and started up by industry, but publicly supported; and a totally new genre of school, a voluntary aided technical high school, funded with government help, run by an independent trust, but fully part of the Wandsworth Local Education Authority. (Many church schools operate that way, as part of the public or "maintained" sector with full public funding but more autonomy, since the church or synagogue provides some independent authority and resources.)

The prime minister and the secretary of state for education and science had both praised Naismith for his initiative in introducing choice, competition, and variety into a borough authority. Then, suddenly, a Tory councillor died, leaving the education director (Naismith) with a 40–40 split in the borough council. In a much publicized election, with eyes on Wandsworth for signs of Prime Minister Thatcher's loss of popularity, the Tory candidate won, and Naismith and his program survived until May 6, 1990, when all the local councillors stood for election with Mrs. Thatcher's popular support at a record low.

Nevertheless, the British school reform agenda clearly opened an opportunity for change and restructuring in London, particularly in Wandsworth, not seen in Britain since 1944. Clearly, a whole new set of actors (parents, heads, teachers) got into the act, and new schools, programs, and governance emerged. As intended, the "devolution revolution" in Chicago and London unleashed new energy not seen in decades, with new actors, new ideas, new programs, and even new schools that were run in new and exciting ways.

2. *New politics, new power.* Revolutions often have ideologies that contrast with those of the regimes they replace. In Britain, the British Education Reform Act and the programs in Wandsworth were highly ideological, putting politics squarely into the schoolhouse in ways not seen since the 1960s, when Prime Minister Harold Wilson and the Socialists had sought to shut down (or merge) the "elite" grammar schools with the proletarian "secondary modern schools" to form the new Labour ideal—the "comprehensive" school for all students.

The hard Right in Britain sought to empower the consumer, both as governors and as consumers. The government attempted to privatize the "supply side" of education by breaking up monopolies, aiding state and private schools (children of the poor could attend elite independent schools under the Assisted Places Scheme), and placing a majority of parents on all school governing boards. Simultaneously, the reform act also tried to extend choice on the "demand side," using open enrollment and extending access by eliminating school catchment areas, offering a greater variety of schools, and building an all-out competitive, market approach (Elmore, 1991).

Wandsworth was an exemplar of this ideological revolution. It was run by a Tory school director, under a Tory-run council—a situation unheard of in London schools, which under ILEA had been mostly left-wing. The Wandsworth school authority—noting that 25 percent of its students transferred to Surrey, the next suburban county, for secondary school—sought to compete head-on by offering parents attractive choices in their home borough. This entrepreneurial spirit saw a redesign of a number of schools, including a City Technology College (CTC), a new voluntary aided CTC, and a magnet technology school within the local authority, giving parents much more choice than ever before and sending a strong message to the other schools in the area that they had to fight, compete, and recruit, or lose patrons.

Chicago's reform ideology could not have been more different from Britain's, nor from the prevailing beliefs of the Chicago Board of Education. Resembling a community organization, the Chicago reform effort avoided issues of exclusivity, choice, and competition, and worked to empower and politicize all the schools. Local elections, local school councils, and local hiring, funding, and programming of schools all combined to make real the "power to the people" view.

In many ways, the Chicago revolution was the best of the 1960s come true. The voice of the people was heard; the poor rose up, gained power, and made schools accountable. All the traditional enemies of reform—machine politicians, big bureaucracy, unresponsive "professionals," red tape, a sense of helplessness and hopelessness—were banished by a law that gave greater authority to parents and children, rather than to politicians and managers. But the stonewalling so common to big systems was present in Chicago, right up to the election of the new council members. As one observer found, "I had to keep kicking to get administrators to do anything. They'd look me in the face and tell me something was getting done, and then wouldn't do it. We were going to have an election and the public didn't know it" (Joravsky, 1990, p. 14).

Yet the revolutions in London and in Chicago had much in common. Both recognized the failure of large, unresponsive bureaucracies, and sought to break them up—by dismantling the largest school system in Britain or by devolving control to school sites in Chicago and in London.

3. *New constituents, new leaders.* The results of these reforms are informative as well. When the heady days of passing new laws and changing policies end, the process of implementation begins. Now the problem becomes one of translating intent into action and concepts into practices.

Chicago. One reformer in Chicago explained, "God is in the details, now." Getting 540 new elected bodies in place and educated; reviewing and hiring 540 principals; writing and approving 540 school improvement plans, new budgets, staff arrangements, curricula, and textbooks, as well as running the system in often dilapidated buildings—all these activities must occur if the school revolution is to work.

The election of local school councils went off amazingly well, given the cynicism in the city about public services. Next came the painful process of reviewing the principals and determining whether to fire or rehire them (half in the first year, half in the next year), not to mention screening new applicants for the job. Again, the process went reasonably well, though councils lacked any experience in personnel review and selection.

By March 1990, 216 school councils had voted to keep the incumbents and 43 had fired their principals. The principals who lost their jobs could either apply for another principalship or try to find a teaching job in the system. Another sixteen principals simply retired and a few schools had no principal at all.

But predictably, about eight well-publicized cases got messy, and some made press headlines across the country. For example, at Wells High, the white principal faced eight Hispanic council members (six parent and two community representatives):

> One principal won back a job he had lost by ousting an opponent from his council. David Peterson of Wells High School fell one vote short of retention, in part because of a "no" vote by a teacher the council had selected to replace another teacher who had resigned. At his comeback meeting, Peterson joined his five supporters in ruling that the meeting at which the replacement was chosen violated the Open Meetings Act. These members then seated a teacher who gave him the sixth vote (out of ten) he needed to hang on to his job. The [central] School Board was investigating. [Gorov, 1990, p. 2]

At Kelly High School, another predominantly Hispanic school, the council fired the interim principal, who was Hispanic, and replaced her with another Hispanic, at which time the former administrator filed a law suit (one of two) claiming violation of "due process." In another case, Naomi Nickerson, an African-American principal, was dismissed from Cameron Elementary School. She filed a $1 million federal discrimination suit on the grounds that Myra Perez, the local school council chair, discriminated against Nickerson in favor of Hispanic candidates. Cameron School is 53 percent Hispanic, 45 percent black.

Finding replacements is not always so easy. Can a council offer the post to a candidate from "outside the system," as some wish to do? How much can they pay a newly hired principal from another state (applications have come from as far away as Alaska)? As Gorov (1990) explained, "Even confident, smoothly running councils have questions. For example, must they abide by a long standing Board rule that puts principals who are new to the system at the *bottom* of the salary schedule?" (p. 2). And is it legal to require new candidates to live in the city of Chicago once hired? Must they have traditional administrators' licenses?

Once principals are in place, another set of questions arises. How will these administrators balance the demands of their lay-run councils with the needs of their teachers? Will principals be under the gun to produce results, without the resources to produce the outcomes demanded? Certainly, principals cannot eliminate problems of youth unemployment, student mobility, drugs, disease, and gang violence. Principals and councils, too, are not sure how much real support they will receive from the central board. Some schools are complaining already that the personnel office has refused to forward resumes of strong outside candidates; even advertising jobs was slowed by the "approval" procedure at the central office.

Hence, radical decentralization of school governance pressures the central board to change its behavior, a ripple effect of the devolution revolution in Chicago.

London. Thirteen new borough authorities must now operate, replacing the functions of the defunct Inner London Education Authority. New plans, staff, schools, and ideas are possible. Suddenly, since the passage of the British Education Reform Act of 1988, British schools have enormous options, as demonstrated by the reaction of the Wandsworth leadership. The new school authority (district) has produced new schools, new programs, and more choice for parents—in a flat-out attempt to make the district more competitive with the fancier schools in Surrey, the suburban county southwest of Wandsworth. The system also faces internal challenges, such as competition from the St. Paul's School, a famous independent "public" boarding school located in the Wandsworth school authority.

But as in Chicago, the implementation of the new law in London is complex. Already, we see principals overloaded with work as they try to handle the complexities of the British Education Reform Act of 1988. Schools must be self-managing; the local management of schools shifts resources and responsibility to school governors and headteachers. So on top of having new bosses in the London boroughs, schools there must assume greater control over their own budgets and programs. Second, heads are responsible for implementation of the extensive new National Curriculum just being written (with testing for all pupils ages seven, nine, eleven, and thirteen, with examinations already in place at ages sixteen and eighteen).

Third, schools now have the choice of "opting out" of their local education authority (district) and becoming "grant maintained." The school may seek to leave the district, become independently run, and receive its budget directly from the national government (avoiding the local district authorities altogether). Applications for grant-maintained status go directly to the secretary of state for education and science. So while reviews are going on in the national government—a long and complex process—the headteacher must "still work amicably with officials of the local authority, just in case the request to 'opt out' is denied" (Cooper, 1989a, p. 56).

Needless to say, revolutions are not for the weak at heart. The pressure on school leaders, many of whom were trained for tamer times when the system "took care of its own," has increased in both Chicago and London. Administrators complain about mounds of paper, new forms, tests, reports, planning documents, budget justifications, evaluation reports, personnel reports, and reports to the council or governors, to the central office, and to the government. Principals find that with greater authority comes greater accountability and demands. Fourteen-hour days are not uncommon—as parents, teachers, and administrators take on the functions that bureaucracies had supposedly performed, but in many cases never really accomplished.

In sum, massive changes have occurred in two nations. New philosophies of government, radically different, supported new roles for top, middle-level, and school-site leadership, and for parents in the schools. London offered parents the chance to serve on the governing body of their children's school, and also allowed them wide latitude in selecting a school. Chicago's reform focused mainly on giving parents a stronger voice through voting and membership on local councils. Schools, caught between a changing political environment and newly empowered families, have yet to work out their role, a task particularly difficult for the school principal.

LESSONS TO BE LEARNED

Comparisons teach interesting lessons about revolutions in education. We know that the process of change continues, and will always remain dynamic, as each new reform calls for others. Take the following lessons from London and Chicago as examples:

1. *Things get worse before they can get better.*   In both Britain and the United States, the 1980s was a period of intense criticism, as schools were evaluated as never before. Hardly a year went by without major commissions and studies condemning schools as mediocre, uninspiring, and unproductive. Global economies demanded world-class education, and both Britain and the United States found serious shortcomings: drop-outs, illiteracy, lack of occupational skills, unemployability, poor work habits.

Mrs. Thatcher had come to office dedicated to "turning Britain around"—to overcoming a weakened economy, low productivity, and a strike-prone work force—and in effect, to finding a cure for the "British disease," as the sluggish economy was called. President Reagan and his second secretary of education, William J. Bennett, had a similar vision: a strong, tough, academic education system, dedicated to "choice, competition, and character" and able to help the United States compete successfully with West Germany and Japan.

Desperation bred innovation, as education achievement continued to decline. Revolutions often occur when problems get worse and expectations and demands for improvement rise. Education reform in Britain and Illinois had reached that point.

2. *Real organizational change comes from "outside" the system, rarely from "inside."*   In Britain and in Chicago, reforms were imposed from outside the system: Parliament and the Illinois Assembly changed laws for London and Chicago, respectively. Both sets of reformers realized that attempts to improve schools by incremental changes made *within* by the local authorities are difficult to accomplish, since few insiders are willing or able to close and open schools, change incentive systems, and shift power and authority from managers and administrators to parents and teachers (Duax, 1990). Asking inside leaders to commit a form of "organizational suicide" is impractical, which helps to explain why reformers went to outside legislative bodies.

3. *Change in one area involves changes in others.*   As the local schools

and systems began to implement the laws in both London and Chicago, it became obvious that innovations in governance required changes in budgeting, staffing, and program, too. Governors of local British schools, now with a majority of parents on the board, found themselves implementing local management of schools, a national curriculum and testing scheme, and in some cases having to decide whether to "opt out" of the system as a grant maintained school or become a new voluntary aided city technology college or a magnet school (as in Wandsworth). Chicago participants found themselves electing new leadership, changing administrators, and redoing plans and budgets—all highly interrelated reform activities.

4. *Revolutions overload systems and confound participants.* The increased demands to run the school, improve it, change its management and control, and oversee its planning, budgeting, and controls all fall on busy people previously used to being "managed" from above. Changing obedient bureaucrats (or beaten innovators) into independent operatives is the greatest problem for major change, though revolutions also energize people, awakening them to the potential of their positions, opportunities, futures.

For example, one laywoman in Chicago, Pamela Price, a twenty-seven-year-old parent of three, after an arduous political campaign, was elected as president of Piccolo School's brand new Local School Council. She worked long days at the school, with her two-year-old on her hip, sharing the burden of planning, making lists of needed school repairs, visiting other schools, attending workshops, and just meeting with her council to make key decisions—like whether to rehire the principal (Casten, 1990).

5. *Revolutions contain contradictions that confound and even deny their purpose.* Britain's reform act appears confusing, even contradictory, as the government attempts to privatize education (more markets, more choice, more diversity, more decentralization) while also politicizing it and controlling the teaching and learning as never before. The national curriculum may be among the most restrictive in the Western world, with eleven "foundation subjects" all required to be taught and tested. If schools in Britain all teach the same syllabus, what use are parents' choice and the local management of schools?

Chicago's reform bill, too, is a bit confusing, since it empowers parents to do everything but switch to schools in other neighborhoods. What happens, too, when the system needs to open a new school in a mostly minority neighborhood and white parents have no access or incentive to attend? Will not the Chicago schools under the new reform law simply produce greater racial and social isolation, unless some opportunity is available to allow and entice parents to send children to schools in other racially diverse neighborhoods?

This chapter argues that a revolution of sorts occurred in Chicago and London. Perhaps these changes in education signal that many other urban school systems are not working and need overhauls. For both revolutions attacked the "one best system" (Tyack, 1974), the centralized, urban school system, and the assumptions that organizations are more important than the people in them, that bigger is better, that "top-down" control is preferable to "bottom-up decision making (Cooper, 1989b), and that standard practices take precedence over clients' needs and demands.

These revolutions were ratified not by education decision makers within the system but by legislatures outside the organization. The changes were thus imposed, though the Chicago plan came from local leaders, parents, businesses, and communities, who pressured school district authorities and won.

And these laws came from opposite ends of the political spectrum. Britain saw a right-wing, Tory government attack the London authority (ILEA) through devolution and privatization—a decidedly *free market* approach. In contrast, Chicago was a triumph of the left-thinking, 1960s-type protesters, lobbying a law through a traditional "down-state" Illinois legislature for the right to turn all schools, including ghetto schools, over to the parents and the community. And parents and other citizens control eight out of eleven votes on local school councils—a kind of *radical democratic* revolution.

Somehow, Left met Right in a similar attack on the school "system" as unmanageable, inefficient (wasteful), ineffective (unproductive), and frustrating. While Chicago worked to build a compact between family and school, London thrust schools into a competitive market (though parents do sit on school governing boards by law in Britain). For all these differences between the two cities, lessons can be learned.

London can discover much from the Chicago experience: that diverse racial and cultural groups can and should run schools in their communities, and come to share in local management of schools. Chicago shows the involvement, dedication, and resources of poor black, Hispanic, and Asian families in dedicating themselves to their children's education. Britain is starting to build leadership like this in the minority community. Seats on governing boards and positions as

professionals in schools are there for Asians and blacks to fill.

Chicago can also learn much from London about choice and openness; though Chicago already has some magnet schools, it needs more. Parental choice is a powerful tool that drives reform in some boroughs of London. There parents not only are voters and council members, but are also consumers of education. As long as most children can choose, not just the elite, smart, or whites, then London-style reform has a future in cities like Chicago.

These are the best of times, and they can be an "age of wisdom," an "epoch of belief." For if political cultures as radically different as London and Chicago can agree to let parents have back their children and their schools, then perhaps this revolution will be a "spring of hope," as Dickens described.

REFERENCES

Bennett, Michael. "A Prediction: Chicago Won't Go Way of New York," *Catalyst* 1 no. 2 (March 1990): 12–13.

Bullough, William. *Cities and Schools in the Gilded Age*. Port Washington, N.Y.: Kennikat Press, 1974.

Casten, Liane Clorfene. "One Building, Two Councils, Many Problems at Piccolo," *Catalyst* 1, no. 1 (February 1990): 6–8.

Chicago *Tribune*. "Chicago's Schools: Worst in America," 21 November 1988, p. 11.

Cooper, Bruce S. "Education Reform in Britain," *Education Week*, 8 November 1989a, p. 56.

Cooper, Bruce S. "Bottom-up Authority in School Organization: Implications for the School Administrator," *Education and Urban Society* 21, no. 4 (Fall 1989b): 380–393.

Cooper, Bruce S. "Privatization in Education." In *International Encyclopedia of Education, Supplement*. London: Pergamon Press, 1990.

Corcoran, Thomas B.; Walker, Lisa J.; and White, J. Lynne. *Working in Urban Schools*. Washington, D.C.: Institute for Educational Leadership, 1988.

Cox, Caroline R., and Boyson, Royce, eds. *Black Papers, 1977*. London: Temple Smith, 1977.

Duax, Timothy. "The British Method for Community Control of Schools: A Possible Model for American Schools," *Metropolitan Schools* 11, no. 4 (1989):

Economist. "Teach, Don't Train," *Economist* 314, no. 7848 (March 31, 1990): 17–18.

Elmore, Richard F. "Working Models of Choice in Education." In *Privatization and Its Alternatives*, edited by William T. Gormley, Jr. Madison: University of Wisconsin Press, 1991.

Finn, Chester E., Jr. "The Radicalization of School Reform," *Wall Street Journal*, 2 February 1990, p. 65.

Glass, Thomas. "Chicago's Schools 'Worst in America': Can They Be Reformed?"

Paper presented to the British Education Management and Administration Society, University of Leicester, September 12, 1989.

Gorov, Lynda. "Muddling Through Principal Selection," *Catalyst* 1, no. 2 (March 1990): 1–3.

Hirschman, Albert O. *Exist, Voice, and Loyalty: Responses to Decline in Firms, Organizations, and States*. Cambridge, Mass.: Harvard University Press, 1970.

Joravsky, Ben. "Money Made Difference in Voter Turnout," *Catalyst* 1, no. 1 (February 1990): 12–15.

LaNoue, George R., and Smith, Bruce L. R. *The Politics of School Decentralization*. Lexington, Mass.: Lexington Books, 1973.

Lieberman, Myron. *Privatization and Educational Choice*. New York: St. Martin's Press, 1989.

Moore, Donald R. *A New Kind of "Sorting Machine."* Chicago: Designs for Change, 1990.

Moore, Donald R., and Davenport, Suzanne. "School Choice: The New Improved Sorting Machine." In *Choice in Education: Potential and Problems*, edited by William L. Boyd and Herbert J. Walberg. Berkeley, Calif.: McCutchan Publishing Corporation, 1990.

National Commission on Excellence in Education. *A Nation at Risk: The Imperative for Educational Reform*. Washington, D.C.: U. S. Department of Education, 1983.

National Governors' Association. *Time for Results: The Governors' 1991 Report on Education*. Washington, D.C.: National Governors' Association, 1986.

Rogers, David. *110 Livingston Street Revisited*. New York: Basic Books, 1984.

Sexton, Stuart. *Our Schools: A Radical Proposal*. London: Institute of Economic Affairs, Education Unit, 1987.

Smith, Kenneth B. "Give School System Time, Helping Hand, a Break," *Catalyst* 1, no. 1 (February 1990): 18–20.

Tyack, David B. *The One Best System: A History of American Urban Education*. Cambridge, Mass.: Harvard University Press, 1974.

Walberg, Herbert J.; Bakalis, Michael J.; Bast, Joseph L.; and Baer, Steven. *We Can Rescue Our Children: The Cure for Chicago's Public School Crisis, with Lessons for the Rest of America*. Chicago: Heartland Institute, 1988.

Walberg, Herbert J.; Bakalis, Michael J.; Bast, Joseph L.; and Baer, Steven. "Restructuring the Nation's Worst Schools," *Phi Delta Kappan* 70, no. 10 (1989): 802–806.

Impressions of School-Based Management: The Cincinnati Story

John C. Daresh

In the fall of 1983, the central administration of the Cincinnati Public Schools announced that it was going to proceed with a plan that would call for the establishment of strategies to be used in the implementation of a new school-based management program in the city. The plan called for the program to be introduced gradually in the system, with only a handful of schools being designated as "Site-Based Management Schools" for the first three years of the project. In fact, while more than thirty schools would be involved in the project by creating local school advisory committees, only half of the original pilot sites would have fully operational site-based budgeting activities.

The original plan in Cincinnati was compatible in design and philosophy with the recommendation for school-based management made by Roland Barth in *Run School Run* in 1980. In that work, Barth proposed that a central feature of more effective schools must be the ability for those affected by decisions to have a direct voice in how those decisions would be made. While this idea for more decentralized school management could hardly be referred to as "innovative," it represented a voice not often heard in large city school systems. District leaders in Cincinnati had long recognized that their schools were losing touch with the community that they purportedly served, and that strategies such as school-based management were acceptable ways of dealing with a situation that could soon cause tremendous harm to the city's educational system. In short, the district was attempting to follow a path that would link the schools more directly to those whom it served. It was expected that such a practice would eventually enable the system to improve the quality of its programs in general.

The purpose of this chapter is not to provide a chronicle of the site-based management program in the Cincinnati Public Schools during the 1980s. The project has witnessed tremendous changes in the past few years, and it is likely that present practices will be modified many times in the future. Instead, this chapter represents a collection of one witness's reactions to the initial stages of the experiment as it initially unfolded. From 1983 until 1985, I participated in the Cincinnati program not as a faculty member and researcher from the University of Cincinnati, but rather as a practitioner of school-based management. For nearly two years, I served as the president of the local school advisory committee for one elementary school in the city. It is from that vantage that I prepare the following collection of impressions recalled from my days as a lay community member involved with the management of a school. This is neither precise documentation nor tight evaluation of a program. Rather, it is an effort to recall the "feeling" of what it was like to be involved with something that was designed to improve schooling in at least one urban setting.

THE PROGRAM AND MY ROLE

As I noted earlier, there were alternative versions of school-based management that were practiced in Cincinnati when the program first began. In one approach, local groups were given great control over making all decisions related to the individual school. Included were decisions concerning the budget—how much money should be spent for what at the local level. In other schools, the local school advisory groups worked on efforts to serve and influence the daily operation of a single school, but did not have authority related to the school's budget. Here, the advisory group was to work with the school principal in reviewing curricular and staffing decisions; it worked with the staff in whatever ways possible so that the educational program could be made more effective. The type of activity in which I was involved was the latter, and the school in which I was able to work was the Douglass Elementary School, located on the east side of the city.

The Douglass Local School Advisory Committee was composed of three parents, three residents-at-large from the surrounding attendance area, a representative of Taft Broadcasting, Inc., of Cincinnati (the school's "Educational Partner" for that period of time), three teachers, three classified staff members, and a university faculty member. I served in that last category. Our primary responsibility was to meet at least once each month with the principal and assistant principal, and to provide input to the decision-making processes of the school. Soon after our first meeting, the council decided that it was appropriate to select a president to direct its activities. I was elected by the group to serve in that capacity during my tenure with the council.

In general, we represented a very compatible group of people who enjoyed meeting and discussing matters of mutual interest from time to time. However, at least three aspects of the description that I just provided served as problematic areas for our work. And, I suspect that many of these same issues might serve as the basis for problems that might emerge as part of similar school-based management schemes that are now the vogue across the nation. The areas in which I believe unavoidable problems arose were related to the mission of the council, its membership, and its operational pattern. I will review each of these areas a bit further in the sections that follow.

COUNCIL MISSION

As I noted earlier, the primary duty of the council was to provide input to the school's decision-making processes. This was certainly a commendable goal, but most of our time together was spent trying to determine the ways in which this could be done. During the first few meetings of our group, we discussed such issues as the ways in which volunteers might be used effectively in the school, behavior of students at bus stops, and the likelihood that a new reading program would be more effective. In short, we engaged in many interesting discussions, but our primary concern was that we were constantly searching for a legitimate focus for our energy. The principal was helpful as a facilitator to our discussion, but like the rest of us, he was constantly searching for our place to settle. In short, we suffered from a lack of a true description of our duties.

The consequences of this lack of focus were many. First, attendance at council meetings was often quite disappointing. When issues discussed were of a technical nature (e.g., proposed changes in the reading program), parent members of the council tended to avoid meetings, presumably because they felt that the material to be discussed was "above them." In other cases, the discussions were related to more mundane concerns such as the need for another stop sign on a residential street near the school. At those times, only the parents were active participants in discussions. Attendance suffered over time.

A second consequence of the lack of specified mission was that council members often used the sessions as opportunities to bring up very personal concerns about the nature of the ways in which things were done in the school. Often these concerns were based on unfounded rumor about the activities of one teacher or staff member. Council members would sit and listen to lengthy discussions between the principal and one or another council representative concerning "What Mrs. X did in my child's class the other day." Again, there is little doubt that such issues were important and deserved attention. However, the concern that I had was whether or not the use of the Local School Advisory Council meeting was an appropriate time for such discussions.

As I reflected on the problems present in council sessions that were the result of the clear lack of mission for our group, I thought about a number of strategies that might have served to help in future iterations of the program. No doubt, the first suggested change would have been to be much more prescriptive about the precise charge of the Local School Advisory Committees in general. For example, it was not clear if they were to be groups that responded to concerns and issues raised within the school, or whether they should be more proactive with regard to the design of action agendas. If they did engage in the formulation of action plans, what difference would there be in the activities suggested by the Local School Advisory Council and the Douglass Parent-Teachers' Organization? The exact nature of the kinds of issues that could be viewed as the purview of the Local School Advisory Committees was never very clear.

Two strategies might help to alleviate future problems. First, the school system might be well-advised to articulate very precisely the nature of the activities in which advisory councils might be involved.

In our case, a major issue arose toward the end of my participation when the principal left the school for a position in the central office. We were told that the Local School Advisory Council would have a major role in the selection of a new principal for the school. Because the individual who left was extremely competent and popular, we assumed that we would be quite occupied with the process of recruiting, identifying, and selecting a replacement who would be well received in the school. After a brief instructional session by a representative of the school system, we found that our role would be limited almost exclusively to interviewing two or three final candidates who had already been screened by the district's central personnel office. We were told that if we found none of the finalists acceptable, it was our duty to explain our reservations. If our concerns were accepted by the central office, another group of two or three prescreened candidates would be forwarded for our review. In all cases, candidates for the principalship were transfers from other positions in the city. Although the process could have been followed far enough so that we could have pushed for candidates to be considered from outside the district, we had neither the time nor the energy to pursue that route. We agreed to accept someone from another building within the city of Cincinnati.

Our problem in this case was not that we did not find a suitable replacement for the former principal. Instead, we were frustrated by the process because we did not believe that we had a very significant part in the selection process. We felt as if our role was to ratify decisions made at another level. Perhaps this is a reasonable way to approach the use of a Local School Advisory Council, or school-based management in general. It was unfortunate, however, that we were unaware of the true scope of our authority in this and many other cases.

A second recommendation for the improvement of such practices is found in the role that I played in this situation. I was simply not an extremely directive leader of the council. I felt that my role was more of a discussion facilitator or group convenor, at best. Perhaps if the president's role were more exactly defined as one where more assertive behavior would be viewed as appropriate, some of the lack of a sense of mission would have been absent.

COUNCIL MEMBERSHIP

A second broad category of problems that we experienced pertained to the membership of the group. As I have already described, there were precise specifications that were to be followed in the development of the council. Parents, teachers, community members, and "significant others" were all to be included in the group, with the assumed expectation that the identified parties would all have an interest in what was going on in the school. Further, it was an implicit expectation that no single member, or group represented by individual members, would take control over the deliberations of the council.

Both of these assumptions proved to be somewhat flawed. First, while all members of the council gladly served and, to a large extent, were flattered to be included, there was a considerable lack of balance regarding the extent to which people were truly interested in all discussions each month. A few of the members of the council—the representative of the local corporate sponsor and at least two of the at-large members—seemed interested in serving mostly in a ceremonial capacity. There was a realization that it made apparent good sense to include these people in the group, but participation was more of a goodwill gesture rather than one of great commitment and substance. Not surprisingly, council members who represented this category tended to come to the monthly sessions only sporadically. When they did come, they arrived late, said little, and left early. I can recall participating in several meetings where I felt as if I had returned to the days of token involvement in schoolwide decision-making when such groups as "Principals' Cabinets," "Instructional Improvement Committees," or "Program Improvement Councils" were fashionable across the country. In those settings, teachers often came to weekly meetings and simply stared at the clock to see when the session would be concluded. They felt little true involvement in the proceedings.

A second problem with the ways in which Local School Advisory Councils were constituted concerned the belief that there would be some type of parity among group members. No individual or subgroup was supposed to dominate discussions. Again, this proved to be a design error. It became quite apparent during the course of the first few meetings that each gathering of the council would be dominated by those who had suggested the topic for discussion at that meeting. For example, when the parent members wanted to consider a new stop sign for a side street near the school, they were virtually the only participants in the discussion. Teachers and other council members did not engage in talk that was related to "nonschool" concerns. In a similar vein, when the agenda centered on possible changes in the reading program for the school, it seemed like the only persons involved were the teachers, the administrators, and me. In fact, the majority of discussions taking place each month were dominated by those individuals traditionally involved with all other forms of school advisory groups: teachers, parents, administrators, and local university faculty. The goal of the site-based management program to get wider participation from a broader segment of the local community did not appear to be very successful. Instead, traditional patterns of influence in school decision making remained clear and unchanged. When the issues being considered dealt with in-school matters, only the professional educators had much to say. "Noneducators" deferred to the judgment of those whom they perceived to be experts. At the same time, when the issues on the table were related to matters outside the normal boundaries of school property or the time frame for the school day, the professional educators demonstrated little concern. Although the experiment was designed to increase opportunities for involvement in decisions across the range of school-related topics, people seemed to cling to other well-established patterns of behavior.

ORGANIZATIONAL STRUCTURE

The third area in which I noticed some problems with our approach to school-based management was related to the overall organizational structure of the program. Two specific issues seemed particularly relevant here. First, the range of true decisions that were permitted to us as a council was greatly limited. Second, and most important, we never fully understood what our responsibilities were supposed to be.

The first issue—that we really had little control over matters of importance—became an increasing source of frustration as we met. Our first sessions were full of considerable enthusiasm regarding the ways in which we could have an impact on "our school." We were led to believe that Douglass would truly become an institution that reflected our wishes, our interests, and our sense of values and mission. We could shape the future of Douglass by making important decisions concerning staffing patterns, curricular programs, instructional materials, and the ways in which resources could be allocated within the school. In each of these areas, we soon found that we had little true control. Staffing patterns, for example, were largely determined as a consequence of the district's negotiated agreement, a document that did not recognize our experiment in grassroots school governance known as school-based management. If we suggested the rearrangement of students into larger groups from time to time, we quickly learned of the limitations on class sizes at the elementary school level. When suggestions were made about offering special programs before or after the normal school day, we quickly acquired an appreciation of the mandated definition of "school day" for classroom teachers. In a similar vein, we soon began to realize the legal restrictions placed on the curricular programs of schools by state minimal standards. It mattered little if mathematics scores were very low and the Local School Advisory Council suggested that more time should be spent on instruction in that area. We learned about minimal required minutes of classroom instruction each week in all curricular areas. When we wanted to look into the choice of certain instructional materials and texts, we learned that such things were normally dealt with at the central administration level, and that other district committees were charged with responsibilities for such issues. Finally, many of our other suggestions and plans were greatly limited by the fact that, at least for the version of school-based management in which we were participating, control over budget was not part of our duty. Even if it were, nearly 85 percent of the operating costs for any school was predetermined as a result of personnel costs.

The second general area where the structure of the Cincinnati approach to school-based management tended to frustrate us at the individual building level was perhaps the single most important factor of all. Simply stated, we were never provided with any training prior to or during the time we worked together as a Local School Advisory Council. Our "preparation" for service consisted of agreeing to serve on the council when invited to do so by the principal of the school. Each person was glad to assist a very talented young principal do what he could to improve an excellent program at a school already acknowledged to be one of the best in the city. Further, each of us was convinced that the Cincinnati Schools were headed in the right direction by seeking the involvement of people throughout the community. Unfortunately, we soon learned that all of our best wishes, confidence, and caring attitudes were not enough to make our council function effectively. We did not truly understand what we had gotten ourselves into by agreeing to participate in the site-based management project. Our only official orientation came during our first meeting, when the school principal led us in introductions along with a statement regarding the system's philosophy concerning school-based management. We were also told that we needed to select a council president, and that we needed to meet at least once each month.

We proceeded through our first year reasonably well. Each session involved a period of time when we engaged in a search for the topics to be discussed at our next meeting. However, we generally agreed on issues that seemed to be relevant to a majority of group members in attendance. Our discussions moved along quite smoothly for the most part. Most council members had some experience in working on similar committees, so our work had a degree of sophistication. Nevertheless, we often found ourselves "stretching" to find out what we could do, what we were supposed to do, how we were to do it, and what we were to do after we did something. As the year progressed, all council members expressed the concern that the year could have been much more profitable had we been provided with some type of orientation and support from the school system.

Our frustrations became more pronounced during the second year, when our principal announced that he had accepted a position in the district central office and that he would be leaving Douglass in just a few weeks. It was our assumption that in the case of the departure of the principal, the Local School Advisory Council would have an extremely critical role to play in the process of selecting a replacement. We were told that we were a key group in the process of shaping the path for our school, and that we should think of ourselves as a type of "mini school board" when it came to important issues such as selecting the continuing leadership for the school. We soon found that our assumptions were not accurate.

Soon after the principal announced his decision to leave, we were brought together for a meeting with one of the city's area directors for elementary schools. At that session, we were informed of the process that was to be followed during our deliberations. In effect, we were told that our duty would not be to recruit or screen candidates for the principalship in the way that a school board might seek appropriate applicants for an open superintendency. Rather, our job was to visit with and interview individuals who applied to the central personnel office and who were found to fit the qualifications for the Douglass principalship. In essence, our job was to approve the decision made at the central office. Even more frustrating was the fact that little or no true recruitment was to take place for the opening. Instead, currently active principals and assistant principals from across the city were notified of the opening so that they could apply for a transfer to our school. We had a type of veto power if we found that none of the transfer applicants met our standards. However, we would then be asked to review further applicants who came from within the system. Given the fact that the replacement of the principal was taking place in mid-year, we felt under a great deal of pressure to move quickly so that the school's educational program could proceed. This was difficult because we had no access to the personnel files of applicants, and we were quite happy with the performance of the departing principal. In short, we knew what kind of person we wanted, but we had little data to review about the approved finalists.

Eventually, we were able to interview four finalists for the principalship. Each of these group sessions was marked by a certain awkwardness. A representative of the district was present in all cases to make certain that we did not violate any standards concerning employment interviews. After our fourth session, we concluded that none of the candidates fully met our expectations that had been formed as a result of our work with the former principal. However, we realized that the school needed a leader, and we presented our recommendation to the district personnel office. We received our recommendation back almost immediately with an explanation that such a statement was inappropriate. After all, it was not our duty to select a new principal. Rather, we were directed to review the strengths and weaknesses of the four finalists and present that statement to the district office, without a stated preference for the new principal.

Five members of the Douglass Local School Advisory Council, including myself, resigned shortly after the new principal was selected. Part of that was based on our frustration with the process that had been followed during the search. However, the most compelling reason for our departure was based on the belief that the new principal had the right to select her own council members. Neither the new principal nor the central office did anything to change our minds.

SO, WHAT WAS LEARNED?

It might be tempting to declare that because of the problems I have noted here, the school-based management program in which I participated in Cincinnati was a failure. After all, our Local School Advisory Council did not get involved with many very important issues, and when we did, our degrees of freedom were greatly limited. On the other hand, I believe that most of us who served in those first experimental years of the program did so gladly, and we would be eager to join a similar future effort if invited to do so. I have a number of suggestions to improve the program.

First, considerably more detail concerning the program goals, objectives, and intended design must be provided to people before they are invited to serve. All members of the Local School Advisory Council in which I was involved agreed to participate because we were deeply committed to the school principal, and we believed in the quality of Douglass Elementary School. We joined without knowing much more about the path that we were going to take. In future versions of the same program, such "blind faith" involvement cannot reasonably be expected. We needed to know what "site-based management" was, particularly as it was to be defined in the city of Cincinnati. Incidentally, this observation might also have considerable value on a broader basis as many other systems endeavor to implement similar programs. Recent reviews of school-based management (David, 1989; Guthrie, 1986) have also pointed to the need for clarity regarding the goals of any effort to develop site-based leadership capabilities. Further, such goals must reflect local system priorities. What is appropriate in Cincinnati may not work in Columbus, Chicago, or Denver. Finally, the true goals of a program must be communicated openly to those who will participate.

A second suggested area for improvement in the implementation of a school-based management program is that considerable effort must be given to training the individuals who will serve as partners in the process. This is true for those who serve internally to each school as well as for those who represent constituencies outside the school. There is often an implicit assumption that people who are professional educators will know how to engage in the types of discussions and shared decision making needed to support successful school-based management practices. That is as false as the corresponding belief that parents and community members know nothing about and have no experience with small-group work. One of the community members in our council had years of experience as a consultant to small businesses throughout Ohio. In that capacity, she had acquired a great deal of expertise that she shared with our group.

Third, I believe that ongoing in-service support is needed for school-based management teams, in addition to the type of preservice training noted above. Someone with skill in observing and providing process feedback to small groups would have been very helpful as a periodic visitor to our sessions. In addition, we needed someone to keep us on track to avoid what appeared to be an almost nonstop tendency to speak only from our "official" perspectives. Parents tended to speak only as parents, and teachers represented only the "teachers' point of view" on subjects discussed by the council. As a result, teachers said nothing about stop signs and parents kept quiet about reading texts. This was truly unfortunate because we never had the opportunity to engage in the type of open dialogue that could have made the whole project very useful and interesting.

The final recommendation concerns the need for districts that adopt school-based management schemes to "play by the rules" once the rules have been adopted, and once programs have begun. Our frustration over the principal selection procedure had little to do with the outcome of the process. Those of us who left the council did not do so because we disapproved of the person finally named as the new principal. To the contrary, we felt that she was a qualified administrator who would keep Douglass on the move. Our concern came from the fact that we felt as if our role in the overall selection process was that of a rubber stamp to the decisions made at another level of the school system. We were told that we had a critical job in assisting our school to succeed. However, when we got close to engaging in one of the most important decisions that could possibly be made in any school—the selection of a principal—we were asked to step back and assume a very responsive mode as choices were clearly being made at the central office. In short, many of us felt that our time had been wasted as part of a gesture that contained little substance and support from the school district. If we were truly critical actors, we needed to have that fact affirmed by the system's behavior. If there were to be restrictions on our work, we also needed to know that, but well in advance of the time when we came together to choose a new principal.

SUMMARY

Several years have passed since my involvement with the Cincinnati site-based management program. The city schools are now directed by a new superintendent, with a new cabinet, and a different school board. As I look at the city now, I see that the entire system has adopted the concept of site-based management for all schools. More important, the various suggestions for improvement that I have noted here have been incorporated into the present program. In short, the activities in Cincinnati are moving along in a very positive direction. A good effort at an early experiment has resulted in an excellent program.

My greatest single recollection about my involvement in school-based management was that I was excited and very enthusiastic about the extent to which it would afford an opportunity for people to work together to improve a school. Although I reviewed here many of the shortcomings of our particular work, I have not given up hope that school-based programs will in fact still be able to reach their full potential. If I were asked to serve on the council again, my response at this moment is that I would do so.

REFERENCES

Barth, Roland. *Run School Run*. Cambridge, Mass.: Harvard University Press, 1980.

David, Jane L. "Synthesis of Research on School-Based Management," *Educational Leadership* 46, no. 8 (1989): 45–53.

Guthrie, James W. "School-Based Management: The Next Needed Education Reform," *Phi Delta Kappan* 68 (December, 1986): 305–309.

CHAPTER 6

School-Based Management in South Carolina: Balancing State-Directed Reform with Local Decision Making

Kenneth R. Stevenson and
Leonard O. Pellicer

INTRODUCTION

As a result of the combined efforts of the public and private sectors, the South Carolina General Assembly passed the comprehensive Educational Improvement Act of 1984. This legislation required that school systems throughout the state improve instructional productivity. The state of South Carolina increased the sales tax by one cent to generate revenue to fund the improvement programs. Subsequently, student test scores improved, more businesses chose to locate in the state, and South Carolina became recognized nationally as a leader in educational reform. However, questions have begun to arise about the substantive nature of the changes, the long-term commitment to the reform, and the locus of control for decision making.

The reasons questions have emerged regarding the educational reform movement in South Carolina are the same as in other states that have instituted reform programs. More and more, educational reform is being recognized for what it is in most states—a top-down model wherein state policymakers determine the improvements to be made, the measures to be used to determine progress, and the penalties to be paid for lack of productivity. As Timar and Kirp (1989) pointed out in a recent analysis of what states have learned as a result of educational reform, "The school reform movement has created a whole new body of rules governing the activities of teachers, students, and administrators" (p. 506).

Educational reform in South Carolina typifies in many respects the top-down pattern with accompanying highly centralized control. As part of its reform package, among other things, the state of South Carolina prescribes instructional time (in minutes) to be allocated to various subjects, the number and types of credits to be taken to graduate, promotion and retention standards, remediation criteria, when field trips are appropriate, minimum requirements for extracurricular participation, how state funds will be spent, and even the composition of local school input committees.

The nationwide movement toward greater state control of public education has been a reaction to a growing dissatisfaction with schools in general and academic productivity in particular. As Guthrie (1986) pointed out, those who control educational funding became increasingly disenchanted with the "permissiveness and laissez-faire ethos" that carried from the 1960s and 1970s into the early 1980s (p. 306). With test scores continuing to decline, with dropout rates increasing, and with discipline becoming more lax, concern was transformed into action. Guthrie has summarized this trend:

> A new and not-very-subtle understanding evolved between state-level policymakers and professional educators: no more new money would be forthcoming from the states except in exchange for local school reform. Since schools had just endured a decade of economic turmoil, many local educators would quite willingly have traded their pedagogical souls to Mephistopheles himself for more funds. School reform in return for state money seemed pure, by comparison. [P. 306]

Interestingly, during the period when South Carolina and other states were initiating public educational reform through imposition of statewide, top-down mandates, blue chip organizations in the private sector were doing just the opposite. Large corporations had found that centralization of control was not profitable, that employees were disenchanted, and the public was disgruntled with the lack of both quality products and responsiveness to consumer problems and needs. The work of researchers such as Peters and Waterman (1982) had convinced hard-nosed business leaders that organizations profited most when there was shared decision making, mutually agreed upon goals, two-way communication between management and worker, encouragement of new and innovative approaches to problems and tasks, and flexibility to use resources in varying ways as job assignments changed.

State-mandated educational reform of the 1980s, with its highly prescriptive rules, regulations, and procedures, was taking a course that was in direct opposition to that occurring in the business world. Prasch (1984) may have said it best when he stated, "At the same time that industry is dismantling its top-down structure to achieve truly participatory management, schools are being pushed into greater degrees of centralization" (pp. 27–29).

As a result, many believe the educational reform movement of the 1980s has been a dismal failure. Orlich (1989) has said, "The nation has wasted billions of dollars on poorly conceived but politically popular reform movements that have sapped the energies of school people" (p. 517). Others such as Guthrie (1986), while believing that preliminary data indicate that "reform efforts are having a positive effect," fear that the movement will not reach its potential because sustained educational reform requires "the active involvement of educators at the building level" (p. 306). Guthrie surmised:

> Unless policies are identified that unleash productive local initiatives, the reform movement seems likely to lose its momentum. And the loss of momentum will end virtually all short-term prospects for sustaining citizens' confidence in the schools and for generating additional public resources for them. [P. 306]

On the other hand, many feel that educational reform must balance the need for greater local initiative with continued state control. As Pipho (1986) pointed out in his special report on the educational reform movement, "If anything is clear since 1983, it is that the interest of state policy leaders in education is not waning" (p. K7). Guthrie (1986) reinforced the need for state involvement in educational improvement. He stated:

> Greater empowerment for local schools, while eliciting professional commitment and organizational involvement, is insufficient by itself to sustain reform.

Without a well-developed "feedback loop," school districts and individual schools run the risk of lapsing back into isolation and letting standards slide. Educators and local officials need to know—and state policymakers and the public deserve to know—how the schools are performing. [P. 309]

South Carolina, according to some, has been more successful in balancing the demand for state oversight with the need for local initiative. In describing successful delivery models for educational reform, Timar and Kirp (1989) expressed the view that "South Carolina . . . treads a path somewhere between the highly centralized policies of Texas and the decentralized policies of California" and has achieved meaningful educational reform "by fostering institutional competence through state action, not by miring schools in a regulatory swamp" (p. 509).

According to others, however, educators in South Carolina are literally suffering as a result of educational reform. Because of a lack of opportunities to be independent and creative, increased centralized state control, little appreciation from others of their effort, and massive paperwork, a majority of South Carolina teachers have exhibited major symptoms of burnout (Ginsberg, 1989). In addition, recent surveys by Craven (1989) and Pawlas (1989) revealed that almost all elementary and secondary principals and teachers intend to leave the profession as soon as they reach retirement age.

Perhaps the question for South Carolina as an educational reform state becomes, "Does the state really provide a balance between state control and local initiative?" While there is no easy way to determine if this balance has been achieved, one indicator would be the extent to which schools and school districts feel that they have been given local control. What follows is a summary of a study of local school control as reported by principals and superintendents in South Carolina. The study assessed the degree to which schools have been given decision-making power, based on responses by district superintendents and principals to the following questions:

1. Have schools in this state been formally given some local control to bring about instructional improvement through institution of school-based management?
2. What form has such local control taken when it has been provided to individual schools?
3. Has school-based management been successful?

4. What, if anything, has hindered the implementation of school-based management?
5. Is local decision making through school-based management a growing phenomenon in this state?

Before we present the analysis of the data, however, we will clarify the definition of school-based management used for this study. One of the problems faced by educators in South Carolina, as well as in other places, is lack of a mutually agreed upon definition of school-based management. To some, school-based management is merely the delegating of prescribed district-defined tasks to individual schools. For others, it means virtual autonomy to determine the program and almost unrestricted control of fiscal resources.

For the purpose of analyzing the presence or absence of school-based management in South Carolina, a relatively broad definition was used so that any movement, even slight, toward local control could be identified. School-based management, therefore, was defined as formally providing to individual schools some amount of primary decision-making power and authority over the educational process. This definition is very similar to that provided by the American Association of School Administrators, the National Association of Elementary School Principals, and the National Association of Secondary School Principals in the recent publication *School-Based Management: A Strategy for Better Learning* (American Association of School Administrators, 1988). In this document, school-based management is described as "a process that involves the individuals responsible for implementing decisions in actually making those decisions. In general, under school-based management, decisions are made at the level closest to the issue being addressed" (p. 5).

CONDUCT OF THE STUDY

Each of the ninety-one public school superintendents in South Carolina was sent a questionnaire regarding the status of school-based management in his or her respective school district. Sixty-one superintendents, or 67 percent of the total population, responded. In addition, a questionnaire was sent to a random sample of 10 percent (110) of the K-12 public school principals in the state to determine their perceptions of the status of school-based management in South Carolina. Slightly less than 40 percent of that sample, forty principals, responded. The responses of superintendents were analyzed to determine the extent to which they believed school-based management had been adopted in South Carolina. The questionnaires received from principals were analyzed in a similar manner to determine the extent to which those working at the school building level agreed with the superintendents' views.

STATUS OF SCHOOL-BASED MANAGEMENT IN SOUTH CAROLINA

The Superintendents' Perspective

Fifty-seven percent of the superintendents responding to the survey indicated that their school districts were formally using some type of school-based management. Of those, 89 percent indicated that school-based management was being practiced at all schools in the district. Only one superintendent indicated that school-based management was being pilot tested at certain schools. Interestingly, school district size had some impact on the extent to which school-based management was being practiced. Responses from superintendents in districts serving less than 2,500 students revealed that only 45 percent were practicing school-based management. On the other hand, 67 percent of the superintendents of districts serving from 2,500 to 7,500 students indicated that school-based management was in place. Fifty-five percent of those districts with over 7,500 hundred students were also using school-based management.

The Principals' Perspective

Though there was no great discrepancy between the responses of principals and superintendents, slightly less than half (48 percent) of the principals responding indicated that school-based management was being practiced in their respective school districts. No significant variations resulting from school size or district size were noted. However, one interesting difference emerged. While approximately half of the elementary and high school principals reported that school-based management was being practiced, less than 40 percent of the middle/junior high principals indicated that school-based management was being used in their school systems.

A PROFILE OF SCHOOL-BASED MANAGEMENT IN SOUTH CAROLINA

The Superintendents' Perspective

Superintendents who reported that school-based management was formally being used in their school districts were asked to indicate the type and degree of decision making being practiced at the school level. Table 6-1 presents in rank order the task areas for which superintendents indicated schools had major or complete responsibility.

Table 6-1.
Tasks for Which Schools Had Major or Complete Responsibility

Management Task	Percentage of Superintendents Indicating Major or Complete School Responsibility
Setting instructional priorities	78
Determining grouping patterns	61
Textbook/material selection	58
Managing/controlling support services	55
Assessing school productivity	53
Determining how funds are allocated	53
Designing/determining course offerings and sequence	47
Setting teacher/pupil ratios	25
Establishing employee evaluation criteria and procedures	25

Generally, superintendents indicated that most schools had considerable responsibility to set instructional priorities and determine student grouping patterns (i.e., homogeneous or heterogeneous grouping). About half of the superintendents reported that their schools were given major or complete responsibility for selecting textbooks and materials, controlling support services (custodial, food service, and maintenance), assessing their own productivity, determining how funds would be allocated within the school, and designing and determining course offerings and sequence. Only 25 percent of the school districts implementing school-based management allowed schools major or complete responsibility for establishing teacher-pupil ratios or employee evaluation criteria and procedures.

Analysis of the management tasks assigned to schools revealed significant differences based on the size of the school district. Table 6-2 provides the rank order of management tasks based on the percentage of superintendents from small, medium, and large districts indicating that their schools had major or complete responsibility. The number "1" in the table indicates the task most often identified as a major or complete school-based responsibility. The number "9" indicates the task least often identified as a major or complete school-based responsibility.

Table 6-2.

Rank Order of Management Tasks Based on Percentage of Superintendents Indicating That Schools Had Major or Complete Responsibility

| Management Task | Rank Order | | |
	Small Schools	Medium Schools	Large Schools
Setting instructional priorities	1	1	1
Determining grouping patterns	4	4	4
Textbook/material selection	2	6	6
Managing/controlling support services	5	5	3
Assessing school productivity	8	2	5
Determining how funds are allocated	9	3	2
Designing/determining course offerings and sequence	3	7	7
Setting teacher-pupil ratios	7	9	9
Establishing employee evaluation criteria and procedures	6	8	8

Superintendents from districts with less than 2,500 pupils indicated that their schools had the greatest control over areas dealing with instruction. The three tasks most often listed as major or complete responsibilities of schools in small districts included setting instructional priorities, selecting textbook and instructional materials, and designing/determining course offerings and sequence. On the other hand, superintendents from districts serving from 2,500 to 7,500 students provided another ordering of the top three tasks over which schools had major or complete responsibility. These were setting instructional priorities, assessing productivity of the school, and determining how funds are allocated. Superintendents of large districts, those serving over 7,500 students, also ranked setting instructional priorities as the management task for which schools were most often given major or complete control. However, for large districts, determining how funds would be allocated and managing/controlling support services (custodial, food service, and maintenance) ranked two and three, respectively.

Based on the data, it appears that superintendents in small school districts tended to leave management of instructional activities to schools while maintaining control of resources and support functions. Medium- and large-size districts tended to give schools authority over instructional priorities and to delegate management of local resources. However, schools in medium and large districts have been given little control over teacher-pupil ratios, textbook and material selection, or design of course offerings and course sequence. This may be a factor directly related to size. As districts increase in size, there are more central office personnel on hand to manage the instructional program across the district. In smaller districts, schools may manage the instructional program by default, since there are few, if any, central office professionals available to provide assistance with this function.

The Principals' Perspective

Principals who reported that school-based management was being used in their school districts were also asked to indicate the type and degree of local decision making being practiced at the school level. Table 6-3 presents in rank order these management tasks based on the percentage of principals indicating that schools had major or complete responsibility. For purposes of comparison, Table 6-3 also provides the percentage of superintendents who responded to the same items.

Table 6-3.

Percentage of Principals and Superintendents Indicating that Nine Management Tasks Were Major or Complete School-based Responsibilities

Management Task	Percentage of Principals	Percentage of Superintendents
Setting instructional priorities	95	78
Determining grouping patterns	79	61
Textbook/material selection	32	58
Managing/controlling support services	52	55
Assessing school productivity	53	53
Determining how funds are allocated	42	53
Designing/determining course offerings and sequence	43	47
Setting teacher-pupil ratios	16	25
Establishing employee evaluation criteria and procedures	11	25

Except for textbook and material selection, principals' responses were quite similar to the responses of superintendents regarding the functions for which schools are given major or complete responsibility. Less than one-third of the principals felt that their schools had a major role in textbook and material selection, while over one-half of the superintendents responded that schools in their districts were given substantial responsibility in this area.

Perhaps of more interest were the differences between principals and superintendents in the "intensity" of their responses. While both groups ranked setting instructional priorities as the task most often assigned to a school, almost all principals (95 percent) compared to a little over three-fourths (78 percent) of the superintendents stated that schools had major or complete responsibility in this area. On the other hand, while over one-half (53 percent) of the superintendents reported that schools had major or complete control over allocation of funds within the school, only 42 percent of the principals indicated major or complete control in this area.

In general, however, principals and superintendents responded very similarly as to the functions being assigned to schools in South Carolina using school-based management. Schools were most likely to be responsible for establishing instructional priorities and determining student grouping patterns. They were much less likely to have major or complete responsibility for establishing employee evaluation systems or for setting teacher-pupil ratios.

PROBLEMS IN IMPLEMENTING A SCHOOL-BASED MANAGEMENT SYSTEM

The Superintendents' Perspective

Superintendents who indicated their school districts were using school-based management were asked to stipulate problems in establishing the system. Only five areas were identified by as many as one-third of the superintendents as problems in implementing school-based management. In rank order, the five problem areas were (1) training principals, teachers, and community members to manage the school (37 percent); (2) the South Carolina Education Finance Act (36 percent), which mandates basic criteria for receiving state funding; (3) the South Carolina Education Improvement Act of 1984 (34 percent), which is a statewide educational reform act mandating school improvement; (4) fiscal management and accounting (34 percent); and (5) defining "school-based management" (33 percent). Included in parentheses are the percentages of superintendents who indicated that a problem was substantial or major.

Interestingly, the superintendents who had *not* implemented school-based management in their districts responded very similarly when asked what problems they might anticipate if they did institute such a system. In rank order, with the percentage of these superintendents specifying the areas as a major or substantial problem, the concerns were (1) training principals, teachers and community to manage a school (70 percent); (2) fiscal management and accounting (69 percent); (3) defining "school-based management" (57 percent); (4) logistical services such as custodial, food service, and maintenance (54 percent); and (5) policies and regulations (50 percent).

The major difference between the responses of the superintendents who were currently using school-based management and those who were not was again "intensity." A majority of school superintendents in districts without school-based management felt that they would face substantial or major problems in the area specified above. Only about one-third of the school superintendents in districts with school-based management had actually experienced substantial or major problems in any of the areas identified. Apparently, the anticipation of problems with school-based management is greater than what is actually experienced when the system is put in place.

The Principals' Perspective

While principals in schools with school-based management generally agreed with superintendents on what the problems were, they ranked the problems in a different order. Principals felt that dealing with logistical services (custodial, food service, maintenance) was the biggest problem, followed by fiscal management/accounting, district office support, the South Carolina Finance Act, and, finally, state rules and regulations. Principals operating school-based management systems appeared to experience more problems with noninstructional functions than superintendents apparently did.

Principals who were not in a district using school-based management expected to face a different set of problems. These principals most often cited defining "school-based management" as a substantial or major problem to be faced if such a system were to be implemented in their districts. Other problems were district office support, managing logistical services, school board support, and state/local policies and regulations. In general, the responses from principals in districts without school-based management seemed to indicate that these principals did not believe the district supported the concept. They seemed to feel that there would be trouble defining school-based management, compounded by problems of district office and school board commitment and support.

The notion that school-based management has not been implemented in some districts because of lack of central office support can be inferred given the difference in "intensity" between responses of superintendents and principals. In no case did more than 43 percent of the non-school-based management principals sampled indicate that any factor would be a substantial or major problem. On the other hand, from 50 to 70 percent of superintendents of non-school-based management districts considered five factors to be at least a substantial problem.

THE RELATIONSHIP OF STATE REFORM TO SCHOOL-BASED MANAGEMENT IN SOUTH CAROLINA

The Superintendents' Perspective

School superintendents using school-based management were asked if state mandates for educational reform in South Carolina have helped or hindered the school-based management movement. Over half (58 percent) indicated that the school-based management movement had in fact been hindered rather than helped. Superintendents from school systems without school-based management supported this contention. Sixty-two percent of these superintendents stated that the mandates of state educational reform and accompanying rules and regulations had decreased the likelihood of successful implementation of school-based management in their school systems.

Nonetheless, 56 percent of the superintendents now using school-based management intended to increase the amount of decision making at the school level in years to come, while 25 percent of the superintendents not now using school-based management indicated that they probably or definitely would do so in the next five years. Generally, it appears that while state reform has hindered school-based management, superintendents still want to implement it or expand its use.

The Principals' Perspective

Principals viewed South Carolina's educational reform movement differently from superintendents. Only 37 percent of the principals in schools with school-based management felt that such reform had hindered the movement. However, only about half (47 percent) thought that their districts were likely to provide an increasing amount of decision-making responsibility at the school level in years to come.

Principals in schools without school-based management responded similarly to their colleagues. Only 36 percent felt that South Carolina's statewide educational reform movement had hindered the movement. Thirty-five percent indicated that they expected school-based management to probably or definitely be implemented in their school systems during the next five years.

SUCCESS OF SCHOOL-BASED MANAGEMENT IN SOUTH CAROLINA

Fifty percent of the superintendents with school-based management in their school systems indicated that it had been very successful. The remainder indicated that school-based management had been somewhat successful. No superintendent rated school-based management "not successful." Principals in districts with school-based management were even more positive in their evaluation. Sixty-eight percent rated school-based management very successful while the remainder considered it somewhat successful. Again, no principal indicated that school-based management had been unsuccessful.

The results of the survey of superintendents and principals regarding the interrelationship between statewide educational reform and school-based management seem to indicate that many school systems in South Carolina have concurred with Timar and Kirp (1989), who said, "Policies designed to reform education are no better than the schools that implement them" (p. 511). At least 50 percent of the school districts have recognized the importance of individual school initiative and have implemented some form of school-based management giving principals and staff greater autonomy in decision making, innovation, and creativity. Many other school systems foresee moving to school-based management in the next five years. Over one-half of the superintendents and two-thirds of the principals engaged in school-based management in South Carolina have judged it very successful, with the remainder finding it somewhat successful.

This does not mean that school-based management is without problems. First, most superintendents believe that state mandated and directed educational reform has hindered dispersion of authority, responsibility, and resources to individual schools. Some principals agree. Second, many superintendents are not sure school principals and faculties are adequately trained to manage schools with any independence. Some principals agree. Third, responsibility is not always accompanied by resources. Most principals and superintendents in South Carolina who practice school-based management indicated that individual schools have major or complete responsibility for the instructional program. Most also agreed, however, that decentralization of the financial management function has not occurred to any great extent. Principals and schools are being given more responsibility, but freedom to control resources has not been forthcoming.

SUMMARY

Organizational approaches such as school-based management are not intrinsically at odds with state-level educational reform. In fact, the benefits of local control, such as creativity, commitment, and initiative, may well be the most important tools to bring about the lasting changes most desired by state policymakers. Unfortunately, what is often lacking is the meaningful involvement of those who must carry out change in determining the form and substance of such change. Without such involvement, change is perceived as a "top-down" process, misunderstood and often resented by those charged with implementation.

In the best of all possible worlds, policymakers using input from a variety of sources, including local educators, determine the expectations of schools and schooling. Then, principals, teachers, staff, and community representatives most knowledgeable of local conditions are given the authority, resources, and responsibility to meet those expectations.

In supporting their contention that educational reform has been successful in South Carolina, Timar and Kirp (1989) indicate that this kind of relationship already exists:

> State-level policymakers, local school officials, teachers, administrators, and professional organizations figure significantly in creating and maintaining the uneasy tensions among state, local, and professional interests. Those tensions are requisite elements for creating an organizational culture that promotes educational excellence. South Carolina's reform strategy shows the reform can succeed if disparate—and often competing—interests can be combined to foster schools that are organizationally purposive and have the flexibility and competence to allocate and use resources in accordance with their defined mission. [P. 509]

Our survey data regarding the status of school-based management showed that only about half the school systems in South Carolina have begun to decentralize decision making. Even in districts with school-based management, power delegated to individual schools was narrowly defined, often limited to fairly innocuous management activities such as "goal setting." Few districts provided principals with meaningful authority to allocate resources or determine personnel matters.

We, therefore, are not as sure as Timar and Kirp that schools in South Carolina have been given sufficient local authority over resources to be successful. In fact, evidence from our survey suggests that South Carolina principals face the same dilemma as their peers in other reform states—they have responsibility for bringing about state-mandated educational improvement without local flexibility to allocate resources. Generally, much of the educational decision-making process continues to be top-down in South Carolina.

Since the passage of the Education Improvement Act of 1984, South Carolina students have made significant academic gains. How permanent these gains ultimately will be may rest on the willingness of teachers and principals at the local level to continue to implement the mandates of the legislation. We believe that commitment to institutionalization of reform will come only to the extent to which such individuals feel ownership in and some sense of control over the direction of education.

The fact that half the school systems in South Carolina have begun to empower schools gives some hope that principals and teachers are becoming more involved in decision making. If such is the case, the prospects of continued improvement of public education in South Carolina are very positive. However, without local empowerment, school reform in South Carolina may eventually be recorded as another educational fad that, like a meteor, shone brightly for a while but was extinguished in a growing atmosphere of resistance.

REFERENCES

American Association of School Administrators. *School-Based Management: A Strategy for Better Learning.* Reston, Va.: American Association for School Administrators, 1986.

Craven, L. L. "Supply and Demand Trends for Secondary School Administrators in South Carolina from 1977 through 2002." Doctoral dissertation, University of South Carolina, Columbia, 1969.

Ginsberg, R. *Teaching in South Carolina: A Retirement Initiative.* Columbia: South Carolina Educational Policy Center, University of South Carolina, 1989.

Guthrie, James W. "School-Based Management: The Next Needed Education Reform," *Phi Delta Kappan* 68 (December 1986): 305–309.

Orlich, Donald C. "Education Reforms: Mistakes, Misconceptions, Miscues," *Phi Delta Kappan* 70 (March 1989): 512–517.

Pawlas, G. E. "Supply and Demand Trends for Elementary School Administrators in South Carolina from 1977 through 2002." Doctoral dissertation, University of South Carolina, Columbia, 1969.

Peters, T. J., and Waterman, R. H. *In Search of Excellence.* New York: Harper and Row, 1982.

Pipho, Chris. "Kappan Special Report: States Move Reform Closer to Reality," *Phi Delta Kappan* 68 (December 1986): K1–K8.

Prasch, John C. "Reversing the Trend Toward Centralization," *Educational Leadership* 42, no. 2 (1984): 27–29.

Timar, Thomas B., and Kirp, David L. "Education Reform in the 1980s: Lessons from the States," *Phi Delta Kappan* 70 (1989): 504–511.

Part Three
Policy Perspectives: Restructuring and School-Based Management

CHAPTER 7

School–Based Management: Implications for Minority Parents

Edgar G. Epps

In this chapter, school-based management is examined from the standpoint of minority parents and communities. The first section provides a brief history of the community control movement. This is followed by a discussion of the role of parental involvement in the education of minority children during the past three decades. The final section raises questions about the effect of school-based management on parental involvement, using the Chicago reform model as a case study.

THE COMMUNITY CONTROL MOVEMENT

During the mid 1960s, community control gained wide appeal in New York City and elsewhere in conjunction with the black power movement and other efforts to improve educational opportunities and general conditions of living for low-income minority groups (Rogers and Chung, 1983): "Blacks, in particular, resented the fact that the system had failed to improve the quality of education for them, either through compensatory programs or through desegregation" (p. 1).

Citizen groups agreed with Clark (1965), who placed much of the responsibility for the academic problems of African-American children squarely on the teachers and school administrators. There was general agreement among African-American educators and community leaders that school personnel used terms such as "culturally deprived" and "culturally disadvantaged" as excuses for educational neglect. Thus, Clark contended, a key factor leading to the academic failure of African-American children was that generally their teachers did not expect them to learn, and considered custodial care and discipline their function as educators. The prevailing view among educators was that parents were primarily responsible for their children's early learning and, therefore, subsequent educability. Preschool programs such as Project Head Start were partly designed to compensate for the presumed absence of appropriate parental input (Slaughter and Epps, 1987). Today, the discourse continues, only the labels have changed. "At first they were deprived (1960s); then, they were curiously different in language, skills, attitudes, and overall culture (1970s); and more recently, they have been understood as passively reproduced, put through the mills of inequality, and . . . marked only by cross generational failure (1980s)" (McDermott, 1987, p. 362). Current labels include "marginal students" and "students at risk." What all these explanations have in common is that they blame the victims for their own failure rather than examine the system that institutionalizes failure.

Through the community control movement, the representatives of low-income minority students were expressing their belief that professional educators had failed; despite their (sincere?) efforts, the schools continued to decline in quality. The minority communities now demanded the chance to solve their own educational problems. Reed (1973) argued that the push for community control of public schools was essentially a political movement whose objective was to wrest power from traditional boards of education and shift it to local communities. It was assumed that such a shift in power would make schools more responsive to the needs of minority children and communities and decrease alienation between school and community. Advocates also expected community control to result in improved student achievement because teachers and administrators would be accountable to the parents and the community.

In New York City, the movement's "main goal was to decentralize the . . . school system into a series of smaller community school districts. . . . Each district would be governed by an elected community school board that would hold the educators . . . accountable and would have significant power over *budget, staffing*, and *program decisions*" (Rogers and Chung, 1983, p. 2, emphasis added). Community control advocates identified the following potential benefits of decentralization:

> (1) more *accountability* of the educators to their school and district constituencies; (2) more parent and community *participation* in educational decision making; (3) increasing educational *innovation*; (4) a more *organic relation of schools to communities* in curriculum and staffing and in program *linkages* to outside agencies; (5) more *jobs* within the school system for district residents; (6) *the development of more local-level leadership*; (7) improved *legitimacy* of the schools; and, ultimately, (8) *improved student performance*. [Rogers and Chung, 1983, pp. 2–3]

Community control was strongly resisted by professional educators and their supporters. For example, Albert Shanker, head of the American Federation of Teachers, in an interview published in 1968, professed the belief that decentralization has no educational value at all, and that parental participation in the politics of education has no effect on the educational achievement of children. He referred to the community control movement as the politics of giving local people satisfaction (Lederer, 1968). After much conflict, the New York legislature passed the Decentralization Act of 1969. Thirty-two community school districts, ranging in size from 36,000 to 11,000 students, were created in New York City with elected school boards that had the power to appoint district superintendents. However, "the powers that were transferred from headquarters to the districts were limited, ambiguous, and hemmed in by many concurrent powers that remained with the chancellor" (Rogers and Chung, 1983, p. xvi). New York City school districts were also hampered by declining resources during the 1970s and 1980s. According to Schiff (1976):

> Five years after the inception of decentralization in New York, its results were decidedly negative:
> (1) The city was Balkanized into thirty-two school districts, many of whose leaders were financially irresponsible, educationally incompetent, and patronage-oriented.
> (2) These were largely segregated districts, thereby curbing integration efforts in the early formative years of childhood.
> (3) Districts were often taken over by strident and militant elements who encouraged violence and chaos. [P. 426]

Schiff concluded that "even the goal of significantly increasing public participation in school affairs by decentralization and community control has not been achieved" (p. 423).

Not all observers were quite so harsh in their evaluation of the New York City decentralization effort. Rogers and Chung (1983) reported that while there remain many unsolved problems, several positive developments occurred under decentralization. Among the positive outcomes are (1) schools and districts have a greater legitimacy than they had in the 1960s, particularly in minority areas; (2) the fit between the schools and the community is much better than it was in the past; (3) district superintendents are clearly community-oriented; (4) principals exhibit much greater sensitivity to the community and concern under decentralization; and (5) new educational programs and program linkages with outside agencies have been developed "that seem to be a direct result of the greater flexibility and openness of the system under decentralization" (p. 215). Rogers and Chung conclude that "decentralization is working in many places and could work in many others, if given needed support" (p. 215). District 4 in East Harlem is frequently cited as an example of a local district that has developed innovative and effective programs (e.g., Arias, 1991). Rogers and Chung acknowledge, however, that "one of the greatest disappointments of decentralization has been the limited participation of parents in school affairs" (p. 221).

Decentralized school boards were also established in Detroit by the Michigan state legislature (Foley, 1976). Limited forms of decentralization were implemented in other cities. For example, in Chicago, the Woodlawn Experimental Schools Project (WESP) was established as an Elementary and Secondary Education Act, Title III government-funded project (Sizemore, 1974). The district included three schools: an elementary school, an upper-grade center, and a high school. According to Sizemore:

> The primary objective of the WESP [was] to restructure the social system through a mutuality of effort by subsequent interventions which [had] two focuses: (1) to change the roles and relationships in the school and (2) to change the roles and relationships in the community. The project [was] not only interested in who works together, but how. To the degree that the mutuality of effort effects a restructuring of the social system, the following secondary objectives [were] to be achieved: (1) elevation of achievement scores, (2) an improvement in self-concept, (3) a reduction in alienation, and (4) a sense of power over one's destiny. [P. 101]

The mutuality of effort was to be achieved through a collaborative decision-making structure consisting of community representatives, administrators, principals, teachers, and students (CAPTS). The project had limited success because it was resisted vigorously by the central administration, the high school principal, and some school board members. More important, the local district superintendent (project director) had almost no control over *budget, personnel,* or *curriculum.* The experiment was not extended beyond the end of federal funding. Opponents of the project were pleased with its failure to achieve its goal of providing quality education for African-American children through community empowerment. A more accurate assessment of the project suggests that it was never given an opportunity to implement community control because too much power was retained in the central office.

The community control movement attempted to move decision making from a centralized and unresponsive bureaucracy to local schools or local districts. The political response to community control was *decentralization.* Decentralization defused the community control movement by shifting limited decision-making powers to local school districts. However, powerful interest groups such as the American Federation of Teachers were successful in defending their constituencies by assuring that personnel and budget decisions remained largely centralized. Negative publicity in New York City (Schiff, 1976), and the failure of the Chicago experiment dampened the enthusiasm for both decentralization and community control. Despite the vigorous advocacy of Superintendent Mark Shedd in Philadelphia, decentralization was never implemented in that city (Foley, 1976). Decentralization is still very much alive in New York City, with some notable successes and failures (Rogers and Chung, 1983). However, until the recent movement toward school-based management in the 1980s, there was little national interest in community control or decentralization.

PERSPECTIVES ON PARENTAL INVOLVEMENT

Why do so many poor and minority children perform poorly, cause discipline problems, and drop out of school? Davies (1987, pp. 3–4) states that educators and citizens tend to define the problem by placing the blame on someone else. If schools are failing, it is "the teachers' fault," "the students' fault," "the parents' fault," "the bureaucracy's fault," or "the community's fault." Comer (1980) has developed a theory of urban education that focuses on problem solving, not blame fixing. Davies (1987) correctly emphasized the fact that: "children are a part of, and are influenced by, several institutions: the families, neighborhoods, racial and ethnic communities; churches, schools, health and social agencies; and the city and state in which they live" (p. 5).

Comer (1980) and Coleman and Hoffer (1987) contend that the absence of communal bonds between poor minority communities and public schools is one of the major reasons these institutions fail to provide quality education for minority children. Comer (1988) believes that most of the educational problems of poor minority children stem from a lack of understanding between homes and schools. In order for schools to become effective educational and socialization agencies, an atmosphere of trust must be developed. Increasing communication and trust between schools and parents is crucial to restructuring schools in ways that will empower both teachers and parents.

One of the most widely accepted beliefs about parental involvement in education is that it has positive effects on children by encouraging their cognitive and affective development (Slaughter and Kuehne, 1989). It is believed that parental involvement in the schools can produce a collaborative effort among educators and families to improve the academic achievement and school experience of students by producing changes in the way schools are operated as well as changes in the educational environment of the home. While the research evidence is inconclusive, effective schools advocates consider high levels of parental involvement to be an important characteristic of effective schools (Edmonds, 1979).

Although parental involvement is considered an important aspect of school reform, achieving this goal is extremely difficult, especially in schools serving low-income minority students. Studies generally report that parents in middle-class communities are very involved and supportive, while lower-class parents are less involved and less supportive (Lareau, 1987). Slaughter and Kuehne (1989) identified three barriers to successful development of parental involvement: professionals (principals, teachers, etc.), the bureaucracy, and parental power (or the lack of power).

Teachers see the parental role as minimally supportive and traditional, if not somewhat passive, in relation to the school and children's learning in school. The role of parents is [viewed as] primarily home-based. Parents, however, express interest in being co-learners with their children, functioning as their advocates and participating in decision making. [Slaughter and Kuehne, 1989, p. 69]

Silvestri (1991) observed that an important lesson learned from "the experience of legislatively mandated school-based management programs in Florida, South Carolina, and California—as well as . . . attempts to include parents in school governance in New Jersey—was that *parent education* [emphasis added] was one necessary precondition for parent involvement" (p. 24). Parents need to acquire the skills needed to become better involved in their children's education. The Public Policy and Public Schools Program in New Jersey has developed a course for low-income parents that is offered in twelve cities. "Sessions are designed to enable urban parents to understand the administration, curriculum, and organization of public schooling" (Silvestri, 1991, p. 24).

Minority parents have often failed to participate in the schooling of their children because they have been unable to understand bureaucratic regulations, or have failed to obtain responses to their requests for information from school system personnel. In addition, many minority parents avoid the school because they feel rejected by school staff (Comer, 1988; Lightfoot, 1978). "Black families have historically been particularly vulnerable to shifting ideological trends and perspectives on the roles of parent involvement because of racial oppression and because disproportionate numbers of black families are also impoverished" (Slaughter and Kuehne, 1989, p. 72). Slaughter and Kuehne recommend an ecological perspective that views the child, the family, the school, and the broader community as mutually interdependent socialization systems. Such a perspective has the potential to affirm the social and cultural integrity of both the school and the family as primary socialization institutions. For Comer (1988), the key to academic progress for minority children lies in changing the way all the people involved in the educational process (parents, teachers, administrators, staff, and students) think about the school and its relationship to the community. Positive social relationships based on mutual respect and trust are necessary for students to develop positive attitudes and to improve achievement.

Epstein (1986) reported that her research found that teachers and principals control and manage parental involvement; parents tend to react to school policies and practices. Comer (1990) also found that schools, more than parents, are in a position to create the conditions needed to overcome difficult relationship barriers. School personnel must change their attitudes and practices if desirable home-school relationships are to become part of the school climate. Institutionalization of attitudes and practices that promote student growth, high achievement, and positive attitudes toward school is a challenge that too few schools meet. The strategies developed by Comer and his associates provide a model that is currently being implemented in other settings, including Chicago (Payne, 1991).

Two widely cited models of parental involvement have been developed independently by Epstein (1987) and by Comer (1980). Each of these models describes different levels of parental involvement including *broad-based participation* designed to include most or all of the parent body (attendance at school performances, general meetings, potluck suppers, report card conferences, workshops, or other programs for their own education or training), *participation in day-to-day school affairs* (serving as classroom assistants, tutors, clerical workers, or cafeteria aides), and *parental involvement in school governance* (becoming members of the school's regular governing body, serving on planning committees and monitoring bodies), which is the most sophisticated level of participation, and requires the greatest commitment of time and resources.

The area of parental involvement that has received least attention in urban schools is *home-school partnerships in learning activities*. According to Epstein and Becker (1982), parental supervision of learning activities at home is likely to have the greatest impact on student achievement and attitudes toward school and learning. What is needed are well-planned systematic efforts to involve principals, professional staff, and parent organizations in the development of programs that will encourage teachers to enlist parents as partners in the education of their own children. This will require teachers and other staff to plan activities that will encourage parents to engage in learning activities at home with their children. Such activities may include reading to children, listening to children read, becoming familiar with children's school subjects, learning school policies and rules concerning discipline and other responsibilities of students, and monitoring homework assignments. Linkages with universities or other community agencies could help schools provide staff development for both professional and nonprofessional staff and parents on home-school learning practices that have been successful in other settings.

An example of a well-designed, research-based, parental involvement program is the Baltimore School and Family Connections

Project. This program, based on the work of Joyce Epstein, involves eight schools in a three-year effort to develop projects that increase teachers' practices of parental involvement, contribute to a more comprehensive program of connections between school and family, and increase students' success in school (Epstein and Herrick, 1990).

The project seeks to address five levels (types) of parental involvement identified by Epstein in her earlier work (Brandt, 1989): (1) *Home conditions to support learning* are strengthened by providing families with information concerning child development, discipline, and behavior. (2) *Communications from school to home* are encouraged through newsletters, family nights, home visits, conferences, computerized message systems, informational report cards, and information about course and program choices. (3) *Volunteering at school* is promoted through such practices as redefining volunteer opportunities, an increase in volunteer training, and the creation of a parent clubroom. (4) *Learning activities at home* are improved through the distribution of homework packets, which require parent-child interaction in reading, language arts, and mathematics activities and are accompanied by concrete suggestions on how parents can help improve their children's writing. (5) *Parental influence on school decision making* is increased by encouraging and training parent leaders and lobbyists (Epstein and Herrick, 1990).

Successful programs of parental involvement require careful planning and organization and institutional support. A study of promising parental involvement programs found seven characteristics present in all programs: (1) written policies describing the program of parental involvement; (2) administrative support (including funding, resources, and people; (3) training for parents and staff; (4) a partnership approach (which involves joint planning and the establishment of joint goals); (5) two-way communications on a regular basis; (6) networking with other successful programs to learn about effective strategies; and (7) program evaluation at regular intervals (Williams and Chavkin, 1989).

Although teachers differ individually in the degree to which they involve parents (Epstein, 1986), a school-based effort is vital. Most teachers lack the resources to initiate a schoolwide parental involvement program. Not only is the classroom teacher too busy with other responsibilities to design and implement single-handedly such a program; the impact on families is obviously greater if the program has the strong support of the principal and parent-teacher groups. Parental involvement is most effective when it is comprehensive, long lasting, and well planned (Henderson, 1988).

CHICAGO SCHOOL REFORM: IMPLICATIONS
FOR PARENTAL INVOLVEMENT

The reforms of the 1980s can be characterized as a movement in three waves. The first wave emphasized the increasing influence of the states in determining curricula, monitoring achievement, evaluating and certifying teachers, and setting goals and standards. The second wave used the language of school restructuring, with an emphasis on reducing the isolation of teachers, increasing the role of teachers in formulating and implementing school policy, sharing decision making at the local school level, and devolving authority from the central bureaucracy to the local school. The third wave, which is still a minor ripple on the broad surface of reform, emphasizes empowering the major actors at the school site—teachers, principals, and *parents and community*. The Chicago reform movement exemplifies what I mean by the third wave of reform. The Chicago School Reform Act of 1988 (P.A. 85-1418) has a strong emphasis on parental and community empowerment. Nationally recognized scholars Michael Katz, Michelle Fine, and Elaine Simon (1991), in an article in the *Chicago Tribune*, referred to Chicago's school reform as "radical," "a social movement," "historic." The law stripped principals of tenure, placing them on four-year contracts renewable by the local school councils (LSCs). Since the councils consist of six parents (one of whom *must* be an LSC chair), two community representatives, and only two teachers (plus the principal), it is clear that power has shifted formally from the professionals to the lay members of the LSC. Cochran (1987) defines empowerment as

> an interactive process involving mutual respect and critical reflection through which both people and controlling institutions are changed in ways which provide those people with greater influence over individuals and institutions which are in some way impeding their efforts to achieve equal status in society, for themselves and those they care about. [P. 11]

The Chicago School Reform Act, implemented during the 1988–1989 school year, provides *legal empowerment* for parents and communities. Whether "mutual respect" and "critical reflection" will emanate from the interaction processes initiated by the new legal status is open to question. These local school boards, consisting of a majority of parents and community representatives, have the power to hire or fire the principal, to negotiate a performance contract with the principal, to evaluate the performance of the principal, to approve the school's budget, to help develop and approve a school improvement plan, and to make decisions about curriculum, facilities, and other matters that affect the operation of the school. Public Act 85-1418 clearly legitimized parental power in Chicago schools. For the first time in the history of the Chicago Public Schools, principals and teachers in schools that serve economically disadvantaged minority children are legally accountable to parents and communities. Peterson (1990) has observed that empowerment of local school councils has meant a drastic change in the way principals view their work. Rather than attending primarily to central office or subdistrict demands as in the past, principals must now negotiate daily with LSCs about every aspect of school policy and procedure. Principals must now exercise leadership in an atmosphere of shared authority and power. This is one of the primary goals of school-based management.

Whether this "radical" empowerment of parents and communities will have long-term positive effects on schools cannot be determined until systematic research and evaluation of the reform has been undertaken. Both national and local observers of the implementation of reform in Chicago are optimistic about its potential for improving the quality of education, especially in schools serving minority children (Clements and Forsaith, 1991; Katz, Fine, and Simon, 1991). However, as Payne (1991) noted, some principals will try to create the appearance of collaborative decision making while retaining real power in their own hands.

> They will create committees they can manipulate, influence decision making by controlling the flow of information, judiciously use rewards and punishments to influence teacher members of the LSCs, curry favor with parent members, and so on—the familiar catalogue of techniques by which executives maintain democratic forms without democratic substance. [P. 20]

Payne also points out that, unlike the Comer model, the Chicago reform process has taken place in an atmosphere of political conflict, and that while the Illinois legislature gave "power to the people, [it] saw no need to give them any significant new funding" (p. 16).

During October 1989, the first year of Chicago's school reform, elections for LSCs were held in 540 schools. The law required one-half of the schools to decide to retain their principals or to select new ones. LSCs were also required to approve the school budget and the school improvement plan. All of this was undertaken with little training and little assistance from the central office. Outside agencies, including universities and nonprofit organizations that supported the reform movement, attempted to fill the void, but most councils reported that they had not received the amount or type of training needed for them to operate effectively under the pressure of "unreasonable" deadlines.

Despite the haphazard way in which reform was implemented, interviews with seven hundred LSC members conducted in October 1990, one year after the beginning of reform implementation, indicate that most council members believe their schools are operating better than they were a year earlier (Leadership for Quality Education, 1990). Parents (especially black parents) were more likely than teachers or principals to say that their schools had gotten better in such areas as safety and discipline, interaction between parents and school personnel, and planning the learning process. Overall, all constituencies expressed optimism about school improvement in 1990–1991. Two-thirds of the respondents said that volunteer and parental involvement in the school had improved. It appears that this survey supports the opinion of Albert Shanker (Lederer, 1968), that decentralization and community control are programs designed to produce parental and community *satisfaction*. At least LSC members appear to be more satisfied with their schools now that they feel empowered. We do not know how other parents and community residents feel about the effects of reform. To this observer, very little improvement in overall parental and community participation has taken place in most schools. Nearly all schools listed "improving parent involvement" as a goal to be accomplished in their school improvement plans for the spring of 1990.

Observations of seventy-four local school council meetings in twelve schools by staff of the Chicago Panel on Public School Policy and School Finance (Easton et al., 1990) indicated that average attendance at meetings for LSC members was 70 percent in elementary schools (8 of 11) and 78 percent in high schools (about 8.5 of 11). Principals (97 percent), teachers (88 percent), and LSC chairpersons (88 percent) had the highest attendance rates. Community members (67 percent) and parent members (62 percent) had lower attendance rates. A similar pattern emerged for participation in discussions during LSC meetings. Absence of members was a concern in at least two of the councils observed. Payne (1991) estimates that there has been a possible 30 percent dropout rate among those elected to councils in 1989. Some schools are unable to attract substantial numbers of parents to LSC meetings, and some have difficulty obtaining a quorum of LSC members to conduct business at scheduled meetings (Obejas, 1991). It is difficult to know how many councils are functioning well and how many are experiencing difficulties. Also, it is not possible after two years to determine how many councils are operating collaboratively and how many are dominated by the principal or have been ineffectual because of political, ethnic, or personality conflicts. The Consortium on Chicago School Research, which includes representatives of Chicago area universities, advocacy agencies, and the Chicago Public Schools, is planning to monitor the progress of school reform and its impact on schools and children (Bryk and Sebring, 1990). However, the outcomes of these monitoring efforts will not be available for some time.

BRINGING THE COMER MODEL TO CHICAGO

Youth Guidance, a social service agency in Chicago, in a project funded by the Chicago Community Trust, Citibank, and the MacArthur Foundation, is attempting to implement the Comer School Development Program (SDP) in Chicago (Youth Guidance, 1990). In 1990, four elementary schools on Chicago's near westside were chosen as pilot programs for the SDP. Selected schools were among the lowest in the city in academic achievement and had principals eager for change and open to sharing power. By the third year of the program, all fourteen elementary schools in the community will be added to the program.

Principals of the pilot schools, their key staff, and Youth Guidance staff spent two weeks at Yale University in an intensive orientation to the SDP. They observed the SDP in operation in New Haven Schools, and talked with parents, teachers, and children involved in the process. They learned what worked for those involved, what did not, and the "growing pains" associated with social change. A two-day retreat is planned for other members of the Chicago school teams so that those who visited Yale can share their experiences. Parents at the pilot schools have expressed enthusiasm for the program and a willingness to become involved in the process.

The core element of the SDP, *the governance team*, is charged with the goal of creating a good climate in the school. Representatives of all stakeholders should have a voice on the team (administrators, parents, the principal, union representatives, curriculum specialists, and coun-selors). Decisions of the governance team are made by *consensus* to avoid a winner/loser situation. The team must learn to work cooper-atively on the problems common to the school. Its major task is to formulate a comprehensive school plan aimed at developing social and academic skills.

Creating governance teams in the pilot schools was surprisingly easy. Comer originally suggested that the LSC serve as the proxy for the governance team in order to avoid conflict. The four schools, however, chose to create their own teams, entitled School Manage-ment and Planning Teams (SMPTs). The rationale given by all four was that the LSC *disproportionately* represents the interests of parents, and that the SMPT should represent all of the stakeholders equitably. Members of the LSC are on the SMPT at each school, but the LSC itself is not involved in the day-to-day management of the schools. The schools are currently working to establish parent programs and mental health teams. Youth Guidance has been joined in the project by two local universities. DePaul University's Center for Urban Education will provide staff development for curriculum improvement and parental involvement. Two members of the Urban Teacher Corps from DePaul will be based at each school, with experienced teachers at each of the four schools acting as mentors.

The SPD will be evaluated by a team of researchers from North-western University. The evaluation will examine both the process and the outcome. The process evaluation will focus on the functioning of the three teams at each school in order to observe the decision-making process and quality of participation. In addition, changes in school climate and parent-teacher relations will be examined.

Whether the SDP will be successful in Chicago depends on the ability of the school teams, Youth Guidance, and the affiliated univer-sities to create climates at each school that meet the criteria of the Comer model. Vivian Loseth, Assistant Director of Youth Guidance, points out that there are some difficulties in Chicago that Comer did not face in New Haven (Gardiner, 1991). First, the Chicago school administration has not provided any assistance to the project. A specific problem area involves the mental health teams. Whereas the New Haven board made an attempt to make sure social workers and psychologists were a part of the process, their counterparts in Chicago have voiced resistance to participation in the process. They prefer to continue to perform their traditional functions of individual assess-ments and counseling or therapy. In addition, social workers and psychologists visit schools only once each month, and each person is responsible for serving several schools. According to Loseth, "There is an overwhelming resistance toward working in collaboration with a team to provide services that benefit the whole school as opposed to focusing on a categorical problem like special education. [It] is very difficult to get them to think differently about schools and providing services" (Gardiner, 1991). An alternative approach would be for each school to use discretionary funds from their local budgets to hire social workers, psychologists, counselors, and school nurses or other specialists needed for the mental health team.

If the problems cited above and the conflictual nature of Chicago's school reform (Payne, 1991) cannot be resolved, the SDP will have a difficult time in Chicago. However, I would caution against forming quick conclusions about the effectiveness of the program in Chicago. It took nearly ten years for the New Haven program to demonstrate its value to the satisfaction of the skeptics. It may take several years for the management teams to learn how to work together consensually and to develop ways of obtaining resources and cooperation from the Chicago central administration as well as from other agencies.

CONCLUSION

Grant (1985) concludes: "Schooling experience, for the most part, seems to contribute to socialization of each race-gender group in a manner consistent with prevailing societal norms about appropriate roles for adults of each ascribed-status group" (p. 73). Teachers continue to express concern about the quality of the home environments of urban minority children. Thus, teachers frequently express concerns about educational disadvantages of their pupils, the perceived lack of support for education among parents, and what they perceive to be lack of ambition among students. They express excuses for failure that "blame the victim" rather than seek to examine the policies and practices of the schools that victimize economically disadvantaged minority children. Brookover and Lezotte (1979) found that teachers in low-achieving schools tended to have higher job satisfaction scores than teachers in improving schools. This seeming anomaly is explained by the low expectations of teachers in low-achieving schools and the comparatively higher scores of teachers in improving schools on a measure of perceived pupil improvability.

Another example of the effect of teacher attitudes on African-American students' achievement and attitudes is reported by Massey and colleagues (1975). The researchers found that African-American students maintain generally high self-conceptions despite their relatively low achievement in school. (Hare and Castenell [1985] report similar results.) According to Massey and colleagues (1975), inner-city children have generally high educational aspirations and report that their parents place great value on education. For the most part, they perceived teachers as warm and responsive. But the teachers did not communicate high expectations of effort to these students and did not provide sufficiently challenging academic work. Thus, the students were allowed to have greatly inflated notions about the quality of their academic work and had little awareness of their low levels of performance. Interestingly, low achievers reported receiving more praise from teachers than did high achievers. It appears that teachers expected little from students and provided little encouragement for them to improve their achievement. One might conclude from this research that paternalism had replaced overt racism among teachers, but with equally negative results.

For the past two decades, some educators and policymakers have advocated cultural pluralism in American education. However, in spite of efforts in urban school systems to respond to diversity in a positive manner, American education remains generally wedded to a traditional view of education that stresses a single universal school program. The typical curriculum is still very much Eurocentric rather than pluralistic. This applies to the curricula of teachers' colleges and other institutions of higher education. Thus, few teachers are knowledgeable about the history and cultural traditions of African Americans, Native Americans, or Hispanic Americans. Educators and policymakers who seek to reform urban education through improving the quality of the teaching force almost exclusively focus on increasing the arts and sciences content of the programs of prospective teachers without giving consideration to the narrowness of the typical college's conception of "art," "humanities," or "science." The result of this approach has been a focus on requiring higher SAT or ACT scores for prospective teachers and increasing subject matter competence. If Shade (1986) and others (Cummins, 1986; McDermott, 1987) are correct in observing that disadvantaged minority students, because of their different cultural experiences, respond more favorably to teachers with excellent interpersonal skills, the emphasis on arts and sciences will do little to improve the classroom environment in schools serving such populations. Perhaps Comer's SDP program, with its focus on social relationships, is consistent with the notion of culturally compatible schools and instruction techniques.

The most optimistic outlook for school-based management as it concerns minority families and schools is that if implemented carefully with appropriate attention to social relationships and high academic standards, every school could become a magnet school (the example of District 4 in New York is often cited; e.g., Arias, 1991). How much of the difference in achievement between children attending magnet schools and neighborhood schools can be attributed to superior teachers and teaching and how much to other factors such as selective admission is not clear. However, research comparing private schools and public schools serving similar populations (Coleman and Hoffer, 1987) suggests that one factor favoring these schools is social integration. The idea is that teachers, administrators, parents, and students share a commitment to common goals that makes it possible for all involved to be integrated into a single community of values. The teachers in these schools expect the students to learn; there is no "slow" track or "fast" track. All students are expected to master the same academic program with no watered-down curriculum for low-income minority children. The climate of expectations is that teachers teach and children learn. While there are good reasons that public schools cannot adopt all features of private schools (e.g., selectivity), some aspects of the private school model can be used to advantage. For example, Comer, Haynes, and Hamilton-Lee (1989) also stress the importance of social integration in their school improvement model. Effective schools encourage children to raise their aspiration levels as well as their academic achievement. The performance standards considered acceptable by the school and the community should be reviewed constantly by teams of parents and teachers to make sure that children are being challenged and that the level of performance required is appropriate for age and grade level.

The most effective way to strengthen the school is to improve interpersonal relationships among teachers, parents, and students. In effective schools, personnel value children as they are. However, they believe that children can grow, and that they, as professionals working with parents and other responsible adults, can help them to grow in positive and productive directions. They also have faith in their students' ability to learn and achieve at a high level of proficiency and they communicate this belief to the children and their parents. Recognition and respect are hallmarks of good teacher-student relationships. Schools should be restructured to facilitate and enhance the development of the child, integrating the school community so that children can be sure they *belong*. This is especially true for disadvantaged minority children who have been found to be oriented more to social relationships than to instrumental skills. Finally, a well-functioning school leadership team recognizes and focuses on strengths and assets and uses the resources of the school and the community to energize the instructional program in developing socially and emotionally competent children.

Effective schools may be viewed in terms of *outcomes* (on performance measures, self-attitudes, etc.), in terms of *processes* (how school staff, parents, and students interact), or in terms of the relationship of processes to outcomes. I agree with Comer that effective schools are characterized by interpersonal relationships, among pupils, parents, and school staff, based on mutual respect, and by a communality of goals and objectives. Effective teaching involves "getting through" to children and letting them get through to you. Interactions between pupils and teachers must be based on a willingness to accept each other as persons; to be interested in each other as unique individuals. This type of relationship is impossible to develop and maintain in a climate of mistrust and racial stereotypes. Much more needs to be done in schools of education and in school systems to help educate the public and policymakers to the importance of developing trusting school climates and good interpersonal relations in schools.

Effective schools recognize cultural differences, but accept them as legitimate forms of group experience that can be used to foster talent development, creativity, self-confidence, and group pride and identification. African-American children want to express themselves and develop their talents as much as anyone else. Effective schools encourage them to do this without insisting that they develop according to someone else's prescription. In effective schools, teachers expect children to work hard and they expect them to learn. They encourage every child to develop a desire to achieve competence. Most of all, they show the children that they care about them by striving to help them become effective learners. As long as racial, gender, and class beliefs continue to infect the minds of educators and policymakers, many children, including a large proportion of low-income minority children, will not be able to experience school as a positive learning environment.

REFERENCES

Arias, M. Beatriz. "Choice in Chicago: Thinking through the Issue." In *Chicago School Reform: National Perspectives and Local Responses*. Proceedings of a conference sponsored by the Educational Excellence Network and the Joyce Foundation, Chicago, November 19, 1990. Washington, D.C.: Educational Excellence Network, Vanderbilt University Institute for Public Policy Studies, 1991. Pp. 19–24.

Brandt, Ron. "On Parents and Schools: A Conversation with Joyce Epstein," *Educational Leadership* 47, no. 2 (1989): 24–28.

Brookover, Wilbur, and Lezotte, Lawrence. *Changes in School Characteristics Coincident with Changes in Student Achievement*. East Lansing: Michigan State University Press, 1979.

Bryk, Anthony S., and Sebring, Penny A. *Commentary and Recommendations on the Indicators for Assessing Reform in the Chicago Public Schools Systemwide Plan*. Chicago: Consortium on Chicago School Research, 1990.

Clark, Kenneth. *Dark Ghetto*. New York: Harper, 1965.

Clements, Stephen K., and Forsaith, Andrew C., eds. *Chicago School Reform: National Perspectives and Local Responses*. Proceedings of a Conference sponsored by the Educational Excellence Network and the Joyce Foundation, Chicago, November 19, 1990. Washington, D.C.: Educational Excellence Network, Vanderbilt University Institute for Public Policy Studies, 1991.

Cochran, Moncrief. "The Parental Empowerment Process: Building on Family Strengths," *Equity and Choice* 4, no. 1 (1987): 9–23.

Coleman, James S., and Hoffer, Thomas. *Public and Private High Schools: The Impact of Communities*. New York: Basic Books, 1987.

Comer, James P. *School Power*. New York: Free Press, 1980.

Comer, James P. "Educating Poor Minority Children," *Scientific American* 295, no. 5 (1988): 42–48.

Comer, James P. "Home, School, and Academic Learning." In *Access to Knowledge: An Agenda for Our Nation's Schools*, edited by John I. Goodlad and Pamela Keating. New York: College Entrance Examination Board, 1990. Pp. 23–42.

Comer, James P.; Haynes, Norris M.; and Hamilton-Lee, Muriel. "School Power: A Model for Improving Black Student Achievement." In *Black Education: A Quest for Excellence*, edited by Willy D. Smith and Eva W. Chunn. New Brunswick, N.J.: Transaction Publishers, 1989. Pp. 187–200.

Cummins, Jim. "Empowering Minority Students: A Framework for Intervention," *Harvard Educational Review* 56, no. 1 (1986): 18–36.

Davies, Don. "Looking for an Ecological Solution: Planning to Improve the Education of Disadvantaged Children," *Equity and Choice* 4, no. 1 (1987): 3–7.

Easton, John Q.; Storey, Sandra; Johnson, Cheryl; Qualls, Jesse; and Ford, Darryl. *Local School Council Meetings during the First Year of School Reform*. Chicago: Chicago Panel on Public School Policy and Finance, 1990.

Edmonds, Ron. "Effective Schools for the Urban Poor," *Educational Leadership* 37 (October 1979): 15–24.

Epstein, Joyce L. "Parents' Reactions to Teacher Practices of Parent Involvement," *Elementary School Journal* 86, no. 5 (1986): 277–294.

Epstein, Joyce L. *Teachers Manual: Teachers Involve Parents in Schoolwork (TIPS) Process.*
     Baltimore, Mary.: Center for Research on Elementary and Middle Schools, 1987.
Epstein, Joyce L., and Becker, Henry J. "Teachers' Reported Practices of Parent
     Involvement: Problems and Possibilities," *Elementary School Journal* 83, no. 2
     (1982): 103–113.
Epstein, Joyce L., and Herrick, Susan C. *Written Description of Baltimore School and
     Family Connections Project.* Baltimore, Mary.: Center for Research on Effective
     Schooling for Disadvantaged Students, 1990.
Foley, Fred, Jr. "The Failure of Reform: Community Control and the Philadelphia
     Public Schools," *Urban Education* 10, no. 4 (1976): 389–414.
Gardiner, Karen. "Interview of Vivian Loseth, Assistant Director, Youth Guidance,
     May 23, 1991." Cited in Karen Gardiner, "Family Background and Education:
     Bringing the Comer Model to Chicago." Unpublished research paper for a
     seminar on Race and Urban Education, University of Chicago, 1991.
Grant, Linda. "Uneasy Alliances: Black Males, Teachers, and Peers in Desegregated
     Classrooms." Paper presented at the Annual Meeting of the American Educa-
     tional Research Association, Chicago, 1985.
Hare, Bruce R., and Castenell, Louis A., Jr. "No Place to Run, No Place to Hide:
     Comparative Status and Future Prospects of Black Boys." In *Beginnings: The Social
     and Affective Development of Black Children*, edited by Margaret B. Spencer, Geraldine
     K. Brookins, and Walter R. Allen. Hillside, N.J.: Lawrence Erlbaum Associates,
     1985. Pp. 201–214.
Henderson, Anne T. "Good News: An Ecologically Balanced Approach to Academic
     Improvement," *Educational Horizons* 66 (Winter 1988): 61–62.
Katz, Michael B.; Fine, Michelle; and Simon, Elaine. "School Reform: A View from
     Outside," *Chicago Tribune*, 7 March 1991.
Lareau, Annette. "Social Class Differences in Family-School Relationships," *Sociology
     of Education* 60 (April 1987): 73–75.
Leadership for Quality Education. *A Survey of Members of Chicago Local School Councils.*
     Chicago: Richard Day Research, October 25, 1990.
Lederer, Joseph. "Interview with Albert Shanker," *Urban Review* 3 (November 1968):
     23–27.
Lightfoot, Sara L. *Worlds Apart: Relationships between Families and Schools.* New York:
     Basic Books, 1978.
McDermott, R. D. "The Explanation of Minority School Failure, Again," *Anthropol-
     ogy and Education Quarterly* 18, no. 4 (1987): 361–364.
Massey, Grace C.; Scott, Mona V.; and Dornbusch, Sanford M. "Racism without
     Racists: Institutional Racism in Urban Schools," *Black Scholar* 7, no. 3 (November
     1975): 2–11.
Obejas, Archy. "Getting Down to Business: Councils Chalk up Small Gains," *Catalyst*
     2, no. 6 (1991): 13–15.
Payne, Charles. "The Comer Intervention Model and School Reform in Chicago:
     Implications of Two Models of Change," *Urban Education* 26, no. 1 (1991): 8–24.
Peterson, Kent D. "The New Politics of the Principalship: School Reform and
     Change in Chicago." In *Chicago School Reform: National Perspectives and Local
     Responses.* Proceedings of a conference sponsored by the Educational Excellence
     Network and the Joyce Foundation, Chicago, November 19, 1990. Washington,

D.C.: Educational Excellence Network, Vanderbilt University Institute for Public Policy Studies, 1991. Pp. 1–9.

Reed, Rodney J. "The Community School Board," *School Review* 81 (May 1973): 357–363.

Rogers, David, and Chung, Norman H. *110 Livingston Street Revisited: Decentralization in Action.* New York: New York University Press, 1983.

Schiff, Martin. "Community Control of Inner-City Schools and Educational Achievement," *Urban Education* 10, no. 4 (1976): 415–428.

Shade, Barbara. "Cultural Diversity and the School Environment," *Journal of Humanistic Education and Development* 25, no. 2 (1986): 80–87.

Silvestri, Kenneth. "Parent Involvement Goes to School: New Jersey's Public Policy and Public Schools Program," *Equity and Choice* 7, no. 1 (1991): 22–27.

Sizemore, Barbara. "Making the Schools a Vehicle for Cultural Pluralism." In *Cultural Pluralism*, edited by Edgar G. Epps. Berkeley, Calif.: McCutchan Publishing Corp., 1974. Pp. 93–105.

Slaughter, Diana T., and Epps, Edgar G. "The Home Environment and Academic Achievement of Black American Children and Youth: An Overview," *Journal of Negro Education* 56 (Winter 1987): 3–20.

Slaughter, Diana T., and Kuehne, Valerie S. "Improving Black Education: Perspectives on Parent Involvement." In *Black Education: A Quest for Equity and Excellence*, edited by Willy D. Smith and Eva W. Chunn. New Brunswick, N.J.: Transaction Publishers, 1989. Pp. 59–75.

Williams, David L., Jr., and Chavkin, Nancy F. "Essential Elements of Strong Parent Involvement Programs," *Educational Leadership* 47 (October 1989): 18–20.

Youth Guidance. "Near Westside Elementary School Development Program." Unpublished grant proposal. Chicago: Youth Guidance, 1990.

CHAPTER 8

Public Schools of Choice: School Reform in the Desegregating Urban Districts of Massachusetts

Evans Clinchy

The first remarkable thing about the revolution of choice in American public education is that it has not occurred because those of us in the public school establishment wanted it to happen or actively assisted in its birth. It has, rather, risen from the grass roots, from the search for genuine educational equity for poor and minority children and the need to desegregate the public schools.

Since the Supreme Court's decision outlawing segregated schools in *Brown vs. Board of Education* in 1954, school desegregation has gradually become a fact of life in American public education. The earliest desegregation remedies, beginning with those in Southern states and gradually moving northward, required school systems to achieve educational equity through the arbitrary assignment of minority and nonminority children to schools in order to achieve a numerical racial balance.

While this early "forced busing" approach to remedying the ills of segregation did, in most cases, achieve the desired legal result of eliminating segregated schools, it also led to massive resistance to such desegregation orders from many white parents and even some

African-American parents, not only in the South but in the North as well.

The rallying cry of "No forced busing!" was followed by middle-class "flight," the exodus of many urban white middle-class parents and an increasing number of middle-class African-American parents and their children, either to the suburbs or to the private and parochial schools. Many of our large urban school districts—such as Atlanta, Memphis, and Detroit—are now almost entirely populated by African-American and other minority children (most of them living in or close to poverty) and thus are essentially resegregated.

Whatever the drawbacks of this mandatory "no choice" approach may have been, the great achievement of desegregation during this period was to establish the possibility of genuine equity for all African-American and other minority children. This was accomplished by detaching where any such child goes to school not only from that child's color, ethnic background, or sex but also from where that child happens to live.

Thus this form of desegregation did, at the very least, establish the legal fact that poor and minority children could no longer be kept in separate and unequal ghetto schools while their nonminority (and generally better off) counterparts were able to attend schools inhabited largely by other nonminority (and generally middle-class) children.

As desegregation continued into the late 1960s and 1970s, however, it became clear that mandatory or "forced" busing remedies were becoming increasingly counterproductive. By driving middle-class white *and minority* parents out of the public schools and thus lending support to the push for educational vouchers and tuition tax credits for nonpublic school students, these desegregation remedies were edging the country once again toward two separate and unequal school systems: (1) a mixed suburban public and private system for middle-class and predominantly white students; and (2) a largely urban public school system serving almost entirely poor and minority students.

To try to remedy this situation, educational planners—building in no small measure on the "alternative" schools created during the educational ferment of the 1960s—were forced to develop the idea of "magnet" schools, whose specialized educational programs would voluntarily attract a desegregated student population. These magnets were created to give both minority and nonminority parents the opportunity to choose the particular and distinctive kinds of voluntarily integrated schooling their children would receive. Magnets also introduced another surprising idea: that teachers and principals should also be empowered to create and choose schools that embodied *their* ideas about how public education should be practiced.

Educators were thus gradually compelled to face up to something we had really known all along: neither parents nor the educational profession itself agree on a single, standardized, incontestably correct and only way to educate the enormously diverse range of our children and young people. Some parents and educators (those belonging to what might be called the Bloom/Bennett/Hirsch camp) believe that a return to the classical curriculum and the venerable, highly structured way of teaching are the right ways to achieve educational excellence for all children. Other parents and educators (those belonging to what might be called the Dewey/Piaget/Bruner camp) believe this is precisely the wrong way to go, that what we need is more innovation and experimentation, leading to forms of schooling that are more congruent with what we know about how children actually develop.

Given the opportunity to choose, parents and professional practitioners came up with a wide range of differing approaches to educating the young. The array of magnet schools that parents and professionals have so far created runs from very traditional back-to-basics approaches to untraditional approaches such as Montessori, "open" or developmental education, and microsociety schooling. The range also includes schools that specialize in particular aspects of the conventional curriculum—the fine and performing arts, the humanities, and science and technology, to name just a few.

Thus what magnet schooling introduced into the desegregation process—and therefore into American public schooling in general—was the idea of educational diversity and both parent and professional choice. Magnet schooling also began to bring about the demise of the "neighborhood" school as the sole method of assigning children to schools. Whatever the virtues of the neighborhood school may or may not be—and there is much to be said in favor of having a school close to home—the inequities inflicted on poor and minority students by a student assignment process based solely on the inequalities of residential geography have rendered this practice in most of our urban centers morally and legally impossible.

And it is not just poor and minority students and parents who have felt imprisoned in their neighborhood public schools. Many middle-class, nonminority parents, even in situations where desegregation is not involved, have also bitterly resented the lack of options and choices that resulted from student assignment policies that forced them to send their children to only neighborhood schools, whether they as parents approved of the education offered in those schools or not. Indeed, in a Gallup poll conducted in 1987, 76 percent of the public school parents in this country said that they wished to be able to choose the public schools their children would attend, even if desegregation was not involved (Gallup and Clark, 1987).

As our desegregation efforts progressed into the early 1970s, parental choice through magnet schools gradually became *the* primary means of achieving peaceful desegregation in this country. Educators in our desegregating school systems came to believe that they should offer both minority and nonminority parents a range of different kinds of nonselective schools from which they could choose the integrated schools they thought would be best for their children. Since each of these magnets would have to be numerically desegregated, seats in each school were set aside for children of the various races and ethnic groups, thereby *controlling* the admissions to all such magnet schools.

The last major desegregation plan that did *not* rely heavily on magnet schools and thus failed to offer a large degree of parent choice was the Boston remedy, a plan first devised by the state (Phase I) and ordered by the federal court in 1974 and then devised by court-appointed experts (Phase II) and ordered by the court in 1975. This remedy included ten magnet schools out of some 150 schools, but was essentially a mandatory assignment plan. Both phases of this plan resulted in the dramatic television pictures of riots outside South Boston High School. With those pictures very much in mind, one year later the U.S. District Court in Buffalo, N.Y., put into effect a systemwide plan based almost entirely on magnets and both parent and professional choice.

Since then, every major desegregation remedy ordered by the courts, including those in St. Louis, Kansas City, San Jose (Calif.), Seattle (Wash.), and Yonkers (N.Y.), has been essentially a "magnet school/parent choice" plan. Indeed, the chances are now very good that any systemwide desegregation remedy *not* based primarily on choice and magnet schools would fail to win the approval of any federal court.

THE PROBLEMS CREATED BY MAGNET SCHOOLS

In almost all of these cases, however, the introduction of magnet schools created at least two major problems. First, many of the magnets were "selective" in their admissions policies. Students could be admitted only if they displayed either certain levels of academic talent or achievement (the Boston Latin School approach) or demonstrated talent in the school's curricular specialty—perhaps science and technology (the Bronx High School of Science approach) or the fine and performing arts (the High School of Performing Arts or *Fame* approach). Such selectivity, of course, has always created problems for those students (and their parents) who are not selected for attendance.

Even the nonselective magnet schools, however, caused problems. While a few schools in these desegregating school systems became magnets, the large majority of schools were left "unmagnetized," without any special or distinctive kind of educational program that would attract parents and students.

This limited "choice" approach through magnet schools proved immensely popular and successful in its initial form (including parents sometimes camping out on school grounds a week ahead of time in order to get their children enrolled). Those few schools selected to become magnets often received more money than the other schools and certainly got more publicity and civic attention. Parents and other people in the community (including teachers and principals) quickly identified these magnets as the school system's "first-class" schools, while the nonmagnet schools rapidly came to be seen as the system's "second-class" schools.

The parents and educators in those nonmagnet schools saw this arrangement as creating a "two-tiered" and inequitable school system. The magnets, many critics said, "skim off" not only the best and brightest nonminority students but the best *minority* students as well and always seem to end up with low minority enrollments. And many such schools—including, especially, schools that specialize in traditionally "male" fields such as science and mathematics—have ended up with predominantly male enrollments. Meanwhile, so the critics said, the needs of the students in the nonselective, nonmagnet, heavily minority and thus still segregated schools remain largely ignored and unmet.

As these resentments grew, many local educators were compelled to respond with the idea that *all* public schools in their systems should become magnets. Instead of a few highly attractive magnets and many ordinary and unattractive schools, *every* school in the system would become a "school of choice," offering a distinctive educational program desired by parents and students, with all such choices carefully limited and "controlled" to ensure both desegregation and guaranteed access for all poor and minority students, for special needs students, and for female students. Thus has been born the concept of "controlled choice" of *all* schools in a public school system and the new nomenclature of "public schools of choice."

The idea of parent and student choice of schools *within* a school district (*intra*district choice) has now been expanded to include the idea of students' being able to choose schools in *other* school districts (*inter*district choice). The state of Minnesota has pioneered interdistrict choice and also the idea that high school students should be able as well to choose to take courses at public colleges and universities.

THE PROGRESS OF EQUITY AND SCHOOL REFORM THROUGH CHOICE IN ONE STATE: MASSACHUSETTS

The idea of systemwide, intradistrict controlled choice, in which *every* school in the system would become a magnet or "school of choice" was first put forward in Massachusetts in 1971 in a desegregation plan prepared by myself and some of my colleagues for the city of Springfield. The School Committee of Springfield, however, rejected that plan and had to settle later for a court-ordered mandatory busing remedy with a handful of magnet schools.

Indeed, the first successful implementation of a controlled choice desegregation plan took place not in Massachusetts but in Minneapolis, Minnesota, under the leadership of Superintendent John B. Davis, Jr. Starting in the southeast section of the city in 1971, a trial implementation of controlled choice, called the Southeast Alternatives Project, gave parents and teachers a choice of four different kinds of schools—a traditional school, a modified "open" school, a continuous progress school, and a K-12 "free" school. Admissions to all schools were carefully controlled to ensure that the majority/minority mix in each school reflected the majority/minority mix of the school system as a whole. By 1976, this approach to desegregation had proved so popular and so successful that it was adopted by the Minneapolis school board as the city's systemwide desegregation remedy.

Back in Massachusetts, however, the Springfield plan resurfaced in 1974 in the Boston school system following the imposition of the disastrous Phase I state plan that provoked the first riots outside South Boston High School. That fall, the school system and its Educational Planning Center (EPC) were given six weeks by the federal court to come up with their own desegregation remedy. The plan put together by the EPC was essentially a clone of the Springfield systemwide "controlled choice" remedy, but it was called the Program Preference Plan. It contained the addition of an adventurous voluntary two-way urban/suburban component.

This plan was rejected by the Boston School Committee, but it was submitted to the court anyway by the school system's lawyers. The court, however, for reasons that remain mysterious, also rejected this plan and appointed its own set of desegregation "masters" and its own academic experts who proceeded to devise the essentially "forced busing" remedy that the court ordered in 1975 with the expectably unfortunate results.

Thus controlled choice in Massachusetts had to wait almost a decade to achieve actual implementation in Cambridge, Lowell, and Fall River, and now in Boston itself, which is in the process essentially of reviving and implementing the 1975 Program Preference Plan. In all of these Massachusetts cases, the planning and implementation was and has continued to be supported and encouraged by the Massachusetts State Department of Education's Bureau of Educational Equity, headed by Dr. Charles Glenn and Dr. Michael Alves. Indeed, Dr. Alves and Dr. Charles V. Willie of the Harvard Graduate School of Education were the chief planners of the new Boston controlled-choice remedy.

CHOICE AS A MEANS OF ACHIEVING BOTH DESEGREGATION AND SCHOOL REFORM

We will look at the oldest Massachusetts example first, Cambridge. This city of some 95,000 people is separated only by the Charles River from neighboring Boston (sometimes referred to as "suburban Cambridge"). The city has thirteen K-8 elementary schools and a single high school; all fourteen schools house some 7,500 students. As of the 1987–88 school year, 49.9 percent of those students were minority and 50.1 percent majority. The system serves a widely diverse population encompassing forty-seven different language groups.

Cambridge began its desegregation process in 1979 and at first attempted to solve its racial imbalance problem through simple and straightforward redistricting and, in at least one case, the pairing of two schools (combining their enrollments and assigning all students in certain grades to each school). These approaches worked in the sense that numerical desegregation was essentially achieved, but they also caused considerable unhappiness among parents and thus failed to work well. The school system then, in an effort both to maintain the desegregation already achieved and to devise a desegregation remedy that would satisfy parents and provide a permanent solution to the imbalance problem, moved in 1981 to establish the state's first systemwide "controlled choice" plan.

This essentially meant that all neighborhood district attendance zones for the system's thirteen elementary schools were abolished. Instead of geographic attendance lines, each school now has minority/majority and male/female quotas (no school may have less than a 30 percent minority enrollment or more than 50 percent, and each school must have a 50/50 male/female enrollment).

Students are now assigned to schools through parents' choosing the schools they wish their children to attend. The parents of all entering kindergarten students, the parents of all students entering the system for the first time, and all parents who wish to transfer their child from one school to another must go to the central Parent Information Center where they learn of the variety of choices available to them. They then list their first, second, and third choices of schools—and, of course, one of the those choices can be the school that is closest to home—what would previously have been called their "neighborhood" school.

In addition to providing parent information specialists, the Parent Information Center also houses the school system's official student assignment officer. As parents make their choices, those choices are immediately put into the student assignment officer's computer to determine whether the assignment of that child to the requested schools falls within the desegregation guidelines and whether there is space available at the student's grade level.

If these requirements are met at the school of first choice, the assignment officer is empowered immediately to make the assignment to that school. If not, then the assignment can be made to the parents' second-choice school or perhaps to the third choice. In 95 percent of the cases in Cambridge, parents get their first- or second-choice school. As a result of this "controlled choice" approach in Cambridge, all of the system's schools are desegregated, with 63.4 percent of the parents choosing a school other than their "neighborhood" school.

The Cambridge plan has had another interesting result. In the days before desegregation and controlled choice, more than half of the school-age children (mostly nonminority) in Cambridge attended nonpublic schools; indeed, there were more nonpublic schools in Cambridge than public schools. In the past school year, 84.8 percent of Cambridge's school-age children attended the public schools. The increased attractiveness of the public system (especially for nonminority parents) is due, according to the Cambridge school people, in no small measure to providing *all* parents with choice, thus clearly making the task of desegregation in Cambridge much easier.

Although Cambridge did not initially desegregate its schools by means of educational diversity and controlled choice, the introduction of both desegregation and now choice has spurred the growth of educational diversity in the system. Before desegregation, there was a small degree of diversity in the schools (including one of the country's early and most successful "open education" alternative schools, what is now the Graham and Parks School). Over the past several years, however, individual Cambridge schools have been encouraged and assisted by the system's central administration to develop increasingly distinctive and unique educational programs, including both very traditional schools and more "open" schools and even a "School of the Future" devoted to exploring and implementing the most advanced educational technologies, with a special emphasis on computers.

DESEGREGATION AND CONTROLLED CHOICE IN LOWELL

The city of Lowell is a former mill town with a unique history. It began in 1820 as the nation's first planned industrial community, based on utopian models developed in England. It claims as well the distinction of being the birthplace of the American Industrial Revolution, with its elaborate canal system supplying water power for the operation of its huge textile mills. Lowell fell on hard times when the textile mills moved South in the 1920s but has recently undergone a remarkable economic and cultural renaissance as high-technology industries have moved into the city's restored and converted mill buildings. This renaissance has also brought a wave of new immigrants, mostly Hispanic and Southeast Asian, to a city that had already been home in the past to waves of Irish, Greek, and Portuguese immigrants.

Lowell thus has had a severe desegregation problem, which it began to address in 1981 through the adoption of the Springfield systemwide choice model. The establishment of this model was contained in Lowell's original 1981 plan, but its implementation progressed very slowly in a series of stages, beginning with the establishment of a network of seven magnet schools. These magnet schools were created by means of a unique communitywide planning process involving the creation of a citywide parent planning council, surveys of all public school parents, and the establishment of the educational choices or options parents asked for in those surveys.

As the minority population grew, these seven magnets proved insufficient to handle the desegregation or "minority isolation" problem. So during the 1987–88 school year, with the strong encouragement of the state's Bureau of Educational Equity, Lowell moved to implement fully its original systemwide "controlled choice" plan. Now every school in Lowell is a school of choice, with every school going through a school-based planning process to develop the systemwide educational diversity necessary to make choice a reality.

What is particularly interesting about Lowell's experience is that the city's parents, in the first systemwide parent survey conducted in 1982, named two quite unusual schools as their first and second choices. The first choice of the parents was a K-8 "microsociety" school (now called the City Magnet School) in which the students design and operate their own democratic, free market society in school. Second-place honor went to a K-8 school devoted to the fine and performing arts (the Arts Magnet School). These schools were created as nonselective citywide magnets (they are open to any child in the city of Lowell) and are now flourishing as fully integrated schools (40 percent minority and 60 percent majority under the system's strict admissions controls). They are now housed together in downtown Lowell in newly rehabilitated facilities specifically designed for their unique educational programs.

CHOICE AND SYSTEMWIDE SCHOOL
IMPROVEMENT IN FALL RIVER

Fall River is a middle-sized, semi-industrial, and relatively poor city in southeastern Massachusetts that has a total public school population of roughly 12,000 students housed in twenty-seven elementary schools, four middle schools, and a single high school.

The minority population of the school system by Office of Civil Rights standards (African-American, Hispanic, Asian, and Native American) is quite small—around 2 percent. However, the city has a large Portuguese immigrant population, with more new arrivals coming in each year from both mainland Portugal and the Azores. Many of these children are understandably unable to speak English.

By agreement with the state's Bureau of Educational Equity and the State Board of Education, Fall River has become perhaps the first school system in the nation voluntarily—and in Fall River's case eagerly—to declare any child whose first language in the home is not English to be a "linguistic minority" child. This has allowed many of Fall River's Portuguese immigrant children to be classified as minority, which has led Fall River to become subject to the state's integration requirements. It has also made the city eligible for state financial assistance for both desegregation and school improvement purposes.

This means that during the 1986–87 school year, roughly 36 percent of the system's elementary school population suddenly became "minority." It also meant that fourteen of the system's twenty-seven elementary schools suddenly became "minority isolated" (having a minority population over 50 percent) and that nine schools were then "majority isolated" (having a minority population of less than 30 percent—at least one school had only a 6 percent minority population). The four middle schools and the single high school turned out to be "balanced," having minority populations between 30 and 50 percent.

It thus became the job of the school system's superintendent, John Correiro, and the system's desegregation planners to adopt and implement a remedy that would move all of the system's elementary schools into the proper range of balance—between 30 and 50 percent minority—and with roughly equal numbers of male and female students.

Fall River proceeded to adapt the Springfield/Cambridge

"controlled choice" approach to its own situation. The planners divided the city into four zones, each with six to eight elementary schools and one middle school. In order to reduce the need for busing, parent choice is, for the most part, limited to the zone in which the parents and students live. A parent information center has been set up in each zone to handle the centralized registration process.

Under Fall River's controlled admissions and transfer policy aimed at the gradual achievement of desegregation, all students presently in the system are for the time being "grandfathered" in their present schools; that is, they can remain in their present schools unless their parents wish to choose another school for them. The parents of all entering kindergartners and all students entering the system for the first time (and all parents who wish to choose another school for their child), however, must register at the Parent Information Center in their zone. There these parents are advised of two things.

First (for kindergarten parents), is the systemwide desegregation requirement that all kindergarten classes must fall within the desired minority/majority guidelines of no more than 50 percent and no less that 30 percent minority and roughly 50/50 male and female students. The second (for all parents) is that they can choose to ask that their child or children be enrolled in any school in their zone, subject to space being available in the school of their choice and, again, the requirements of the overall minority and sex balance guidelines.

The programmatic choices available in their zone are described to all of these parents, including the possibility that one of those choices can be that they can request that their children be assigned to their "neighborhood" school. The guidelines requiring the 30 to 50 percent minority population and gender balance in all schools, while limited during the first year to kindergartners, will be extended year by year up through the grades, so that within six years, all elementary schools (and thus all Fall River schools) will have the proper minority/nonminority balance.

THE EVIDENCE FOR CHOICE: IMPROVING EDUCATIONAL QUALITY

While educational diversity and both parent and professional choice were introduced into public education in this country primarily as a means to achieve peaceful desegregation, they have in recent years come to be seen by many educators and parents as one of the most powerful means we have to achieve significant changes and improvements in the *quality* of the education offered in our public schools.

While the introduction of diversity and choice does not, of course, in itself solve all of our educational problems (such as the need for higher teacher salaries or for vastly increased funding of our urban public schools or for the provision of decent school facilities), both research and experience in the field have supported the idea that diversity and choice can be a major step forward in empowering individual school communities to become the primary instruments for achieving educational improvement.

Hard evidence is sparse, because little research has been done in this field. Indeed, we do not at the present time even know how many magnets or schools of choice exist in this country. And, of course, it is often difficult to separate out how much of an individual school's improvement—or a school system's overall improvement—can be attributed to the introduction of diversity and choice and how much to other changes that have occurred at the same times.

Several research studies, however (Blank et al., 1983; Blank, 1984a, 1984b; New York State Education Department, 1985), provide data indicating that the scores on reading and mathematics tests of students in nonselective magnet schools are higher than the district averages. In the Blank study, 80 percent of the magnet schools in the sample had reading and mathematics test scores that were significantly higher (by ten or more points) than their district averages.

The New York State study indicates that the academic performance of schools as a whole improved after they became magnet schools, even in cases where the pupil population changed to include more minority and low-income students. These same studies indicate as well that magnet schools experienced significantly higher attendance rates, fewer behavioral problems, and lower suspension rates than comparable nonmagnet schools. Three-quarters of the magnet schools in the New York study had dropout rates below their district averages. In that same study, the average levels of achievement in magnet schools with high minority enrollments were equal to other schools in their district that had low levels of minority enrollment.

Thus, insofar as improvements in test scores can intelligently and legitimately be used as one (and only one) measure of "success" or "excellence," we certainly have instances where children attending nonselective schools of choice (e.g., the City Magnet School in

Lowell) have done remarkably well on basic skills tests in reading and mathematics in comparison with similar children in nonchoice schools in the same school system with similar student populations.

Virtually every magnet or school of choice, almost by definition and of necessity, also exhibits the basic requirements that the research on "effective schools" says a high-quality, "effective" school must have: a principal who is the true educational leader of the school; a teaching staff imbued with the belief that all children—and especially poor and minority children—can learn; a stable, calm, and well-disciplined school environment; and an emphasis on basic skills development.

I believe, too, that diversity and choice provide individual schools with two further attributes that clearly must promote "excellence": (1) educational continuity for the school's student population and (2) the empowerment of individual school communities largely to determine their individual school's educational philosophy, curriculum, and school organization.

Educational Continuity

In many school systems, especially urban systems that operate on the neighborhood school principle, student mobility and thus student turnover is one of the major problems that makes educating children not just difficult but well nigh impossible. In these systems, whenever children move out of any school's allotted geographic district, they must switch to the school that serves their new neighborhood. Given the degree of mobility of many urban children, many schools experience a student turnover rate that can be 100 percent in the course of a school year. This means that no student who is enrolled at the beginning of the school year is there at the end of the year and, conversely, that no student who is there at the end of the year was there at the start. This constant movement of students in and out of a teacher's classroom and in and out of the school means that many children have no educational continuity at all. Some students may end up attending three or four schools in the course of a single academic year. Given such turnover, teachers have no chance to get to know the children and provide them with a continuous learning experience.

Under a system of controlled choice without neighborhood attendance zones, however, once a child's parents have chosen a school, that child can continue to attend that school no matter where within the district the parents may move, starting in kindergarten and remaining in that school until graduation. This assures educational stability for every child.

The Shared Sense of Mission

Diversity and choice also are much more congruent with what we know about children and about both our parent and teacher populations. We all know in our bones—and our grandmothers always knew—that children are not alike in their talents, interests, and educational needs, that there is no single kind of schooling that can adequately serve the broad diversity of such talents, interests, and educational needs.

And, as I said earlier, we have also known for years that all parents do not share a single vision of how the education of their children should be conducted and that therefore all parents cannot and do not agree on a single kind of schooling that they all want for their children. Similarly, we also know that public school educators— teachers and principals—do not all agree on a single kind of schooling that they believe is the best and only way to educate all children and therefore do not agree on a single brand of schooling that they all wish to practice.

Our traditional way of organizing and operating our public school systems, however, has ignored the large differences in children and the large areas of disagreement among parents and educators. Rather than providing a diversity of schools to match the diverse needs of students and the diverse philosophies of parents and educators, most school systems have concentrated on providing a standardized curriculum taught in schools that are—or try to be—roughly similar to each other.

Our public school systems have historically organized themselves around the concept of that standardized "neighborhood" school to which all children in the school's district must go. Teachers are most often assigned to these neighborhood schools wherever a vacancy happens to occur and in most cases from a list governed mainly by seniority rather than suitability. Under these circumstances, many observers say, there is no way on earth that such a diverse collection of parents, students, teachers, and a principal, all assigned by administrative fiat to an individual school, could possibly all agree on what constitutes an "excellent" public education. That being the case, they will also have difficulty in joining together enthusiastically to put the school's program into practice.

In marked contrast to this situation, a system based on diversity and choice makes it possible for those parents and students who want a particular kind of education to choose to band together with teachers and administrators who want to practice the same kind of schooling. Thus everyone in the school, since they are all there by choice, can have a clear and shared agreement as to precisely what the school's educational mission is, what *kind* of education the school will offer. Consequently these schools, according to both the Blank and New York State studies, tend to be places where a large segment of the parent population is highly satisfied—and even strongly enthusiastic— about the education offered its children and a large segment of the professional staff feels professionally satisfied and rewarded.

Given such a "shared sense of mission," all members of the school's community can concentrate their energies on fulfilling that mission rather than on spending time and energy on resolving disputes and disagreements. Both the objective evidence and a massive amount of anecdotal evidence suggest that such a sharing of each individual school's mission can have remarkable effects on a school's climate and on overall student performance. Indeed, a study conducted by Chubb and Moe (1988) claims that in schools with the organizational auton- omy to establish and practice their own philosophy, curriculum, and school organization, even when all other factors such as school population, family income, financial resources, and the like are con- trolled, there can be full year's difference in achievement on stan- dardized tests.

This empowerment of each individual school community largely to determine its own philosophy and its own curriculum and school organization, and thus in a sense to control and determine its own destiny, is a clear implementation as well of the major recommenda- tions put forward for the achievement of educational excellence by the National Governors' Association in their report, *Time for Results* (1986), and by the Carnegie Task Force on Teaching as a Profession (1986) in its report, *A Nation Prepared: Teachers for the 21st Century.*

THE SHAPE OF THE NEW SYSTEM

In 1984, the desegregating urban school systems of Massachusetts held a two-day conference in Worcester, jointly sponsored by the school systems and the state's Bureau of Educational Equity with the assistance of the Institute for Responsive Education. The purpose of the conference was to give the two hundred participants, half of whom were teachers, principals, and other schoolpeople and half of whom were parents, a chance to sit down together, to pool their experience and to sketch out the new public school system they wanted to see implemented in their cities.

The executive summary of that conference (Worcester Conference on Equity and Choice, 1984) lays out in clear form the basic principles on which such a new system of public schooling should be based:

- The heart of the matter and the primary arena for improvement and excellence is *the individual school*, its staff, its parent body, its students.
- There is no single kind of schooling, no uniform, standardized curriculum, that is equally suitable for every child and equally satisfying to every parent and teacher.
- Parents must therefore be able to specify the different kinds of schools they wish their public school system to provide and then to choose the individual school or schools their children will attend, insofar as such choice promotes desegregation and educational equity. In this sense, every school in the system becomes a magnet school.
- Teachers and principals must also be able to select the kind of schooling they wish to practice, again insofar as such choice promotes staff desegregation and affirmative action.
- The provision of such choice will require regular surveys of parents and teachers to determine the range of educational choices or options their system will offer.
- If this system of educational excellence through educational diversity and parent/teacher choice is to succeed, individual schools must have both the autonomy and the resources to develop their own individual educational approaches— philosophy, teaching style, curriculum, staffing pattern, governance, and so on.

- Providing the necessary autonomy to individual schools means that school system management must be based at the individual school level. Schools must be able to a large degree to determine how their allocated budgets will be spent, how their school will be staffed, how professional development will take place, what the curriculum will be and how it will be taught. Parents must play a strong and responsible role in these decisions.
- Every school system must develop a long-range (at least five-year) plan for achieving educational excellence, desegregation, and educational equity. This systemwide plan, while essentially being the sum total of the individual school plans, must be developed by all segments of the community—school board, central administration, parents, teachers, students, local government leaders, the business and cultural communities, and so on.
- This systemwide plan must set forth the system's general goals (including goals and expectations for academic achievement), define the ways in which the parent/teacher choice system (including all student assignment procedures) will work to achieve and guarantee permanent desegregation and the ways in which the individual school planning process will work.
- It is the job of the central administration, as part of the long-range plan, to develop and operate a strong, districtwide system of *evaluation and accountability* applying to all schools. This system should be based on the academic goals and expectations for all students as set forth in the long-range plan but should not impose a standardized, uniform curriculum that all schools must follow.
- This system of accountability should assess annually each school's progress toward the achievement of the goals set forth in the school's individual school plan. Schools that consistently fail to meet either their individual goals or the systemwide standards should be reorganized (including restaffing) or, if necessary, disbanded.

Have these Massachusetts school systems actually installed this new system of American public education? Not yet. But several of them are moving toward it, having instituted the crucial principles of parental choice and, to a growing degree, professional choice.

Whether this new system of public education based on choice will actually come to pass and be adopted nationally is, of course, anyone's guess. The record so far does suggest that in those cases where parents and our educational practitioners have had a taste of the power and the educational results that diversity and choice offer them, the old authoritarian system is gradually withering away.

REFERENCES

Blank, Rolf K. "Community Participation in Urban Public Schools: Analyzing Effects of Magnet School Programs." Paper presented at the Annual Meeting of the American Educational Research Association, New Orleans, 1984a. ERIC ED 247–358.

Blank, Rolf K. "Effects of Magnet Schools on the Quality of Education in Urban School Districts," *Phi Delta Kappan* 66 (December 1984b): 270–272.

Blank, Rolf K.; Dentler, Robert A.; Baltzell, D. Catherine; and Chabotar, Kent. *Survey of Magnet Schools: Analyzing a Model for Quality Integrated Education.* Report prepared for the U.S. Department of Education by James H. Lowry and Associates. Washington, D.C.: U. S. Department of Education, 1983.

Carnegie Task Force on Teaching as a Profession. *A Nation Prepared: Teachers for the 21st Century.* New York: Carnegie Forum on Education and the Economy, 1986.

Chubb, John E., and Moe, Terry M. *What Price Democracy? Politics, Markets, and American Schools.* Washington, D.C.: Brookings Institution, 1988.

Gallup, Alex M., and Clark, David L. "The Nineteenth Annual Gallup Poll of the Public's Attitudes toward Public Schools," *Phi Delta Kappan* 69 (1987): 20.

National Governors' Association. *Time for Results: The Governors' 1991 Report on Education.* Washington, D.C.: National Governors' Association, 1986.

New York State Education Department. *New York State Magnet School Research Study, Final Report.* Report prepared for the New York State Education Department by MAGI Educational Services, Larchmont, N.Y. Albany: New York State Education Department, Division of Civil Rights and Intercultural Affairs, 1985.

Worcester Conference on Equity and Choice. *The Pursuit of Excellence: Improving the Quality of Our Urban Schools through Desegregation, Equity, and Choice.* Final report from the Program Committee. Worcester, Mass.: Worcester Conference on Equity and Choice, 1984.

CHAPTER 9

Site-Based Management: Disconcerting Policy Issues, Critical Policy Choices

Betty Malen and Rodney T. Ogawa

INTRODUCTION

The term "site-based management" means different things to different people. Generally speaking, site-based management can be viewed as a form of decentralization that designates the individual school as the unit of improvement and relies on the redistribution of decision-making authority as the primary means through which improvements will be stimulated and sustained. Essentially, site-based management implies that (a) some formal authority to make decisions in the central domains of budget, personnel, and program is delegated to and frequently redistributed among site-level actors; (b) a formal structure (council, committee, team, board) often composed of principals, teachers, parents, and, at times, students and community residents is created so that these actors can be directly involved in schoolwide decision making; and (c) site participants are afforded substantial discretion. Even though their formal authority may be circumscribed by existing statutes, regulations, accountability requirements, and/or contractual agreements, site participants presumably have great discretion.

Site-based management is not a new notion. For decades, policy analysts, academics, parent associations, activist organizations, and other interested parties have argued that some formal authority to make decisions regarding budget, personnel, and program should be delegated to and distributed among various combinations of site-level actors (Bundy, 1967). For decades, individual school districts and some state legislatures have debated, enacted, rescinded, or reinstated various site-based governance arrangements (McLeese, 1991).

While site-based management is not a new notion, it has gained a prominent position on the current agenda for educational reform. At times, the idea is nested in proposals to redefine professional roles so that teachers become participants in school policy decisions. At other times, the idea is packaged with proposals to establish school improvement councils.

It seems that, once again, a host of forces such as the intense pressure to locate "solutions" to pressing problems, the ideological appeal of calls to "decentralize and democratize" decision making, and the popular presumption that "restructuring schools" will improve schools have converged to make site-based management a salient, salable slogan as well as a prevalent policy option in numerous arenas. Many commissions, task forces, organizations, and individuals are advocating this reform. Many state legislatures and school districts are encouraging or requiring schools to implement some version of site-based management. Many people are working intensively and diligently to install or reinstate some form of this approach to governance (Malen, Ogawa, and Kranz, 1990).

A number of interesting and important questions stem from the current emphasis on site-based management. One of the most fundamental questions being raised is whether site-based management is really a substantive as well as a salient approach to educational reform. Although this chapter does not provide a definitive answer to that question, it does confront disconcerting issues and critical choices that must be addressed if site-based management is to have a chance to become a potent as well as a prevalent policy option, a viable as well as a salable vehicle for educational reform.

We focus on disconcerting issues and critical choices because we are concerned about this reform. Like others, we are attracted to the idea of site-based management. We subscribe to democratic principles and participatory processes, and we believe that sensible solutions to the pressing problems confronting schools reside in the heads and hearts of the dedicated educators who work in the schools and the concerned patrons in the schools' communities. We want this reform to be implemented in ways that will make schools better places for the people who work and learn in them and rely on them. We hope site-based management will be given a full and fair chance to do so.

With that hope in mind, we identify here some of the disconcerting policy issues that repeatedly surfaced in case studies of site-based governance arrangements in Salt Lake City (McLeese, 1991; Mc-Leese and Malen, 1987; Malen and Ogawa, 1988) and in a recent review of case studies and diverse writings on site-based governance arrangements in other locations (Malen, Ogawa, and Kranz, 1990). Then we pose some of the critical policy choices that are likely to shape the fate of site-based management.

DISCONCERTING ISSUES

Recognizing that case studies and literature reviews often raise more perplexing issues than they resolve, we address three of the most troubling issues that relentlessly reappeared in studies of site-based management and reviews of diverse writings: (1) Do site-based management plans actually alter the formal decision-making arrangements in school systems? (2) Does the formal adjustment of decision-making arrangements actually alter the influence relationships typically and traditionally found in school settings? (3) As presently configured, do site-based management ventures de-bureaucratize schools and empower professionals and patrons or do they re-bureaucratize schools and overpower participants?

We focus on these three issues because they embrace the major premises, operational assumptions, and popular promises of site-based management. More precisely, they reveal the complexities embedded in efforts to design, implement, and assess site-based management plans, and they underscore the challenges inherent in attempts to make such reform ventures viable policy options.

We frame these issues as debatable questions because empirical evidence regarding how site-based management plans actually operate is severely limited, with only a few systematic investigations available. Furthermore, these investigations are based on case studies of a relatively small number of elementary and secondary schools.

The vast majority of accessible writings on the topic base appraisals of
the reform on testimonials from a single individual regarding changes
made in or inventories of activities spawned in a very small number of
select, exemplar schools.[1] A sizable portion of these sources acknowledge that comprehensive, conscientious evaluations have not been
conducted even though site-based management plans have been
underway for some time (e.g., Clune and White, 1988; Richardson,
1988). Moreover, in some settings where evaluations have been
carried out, assessments are not being released, in part because the
programs did not produce the desired results and parties responsible
for the evaluations do not believe that such disappointing information
can serve a useful purpose.[2]

---

[1] The limitations of the data base are apparent in our own work. For example, the
case studies conducted in Salt Lake City describe site-based council operations over a
fifteen-year period (1970–1985). Based on over two hundred in-depth interviews with
site council participants and district administrators, these studies offer empirical
evidence regarding the long-term effect of site-based governance councils, but they do
not support firm generalizations regarding the impact of site-based councils in other
settings.

The review of literature we conducted encompassed over two hundred documents.
Most of these documents were project descriptions, status reports, or position papers
that described current and previous attempts to institute site-based management,
sketched the general features of site-based management plans, articulated the
rationales used to advocate the plans, and offered judgments regarding the impact of
these arrangements. Unfortunately, these writings were often based on impressions
acquired from a single individual who was instrumental in initiating or held primary
responsibility for overseeing a district's site-based management experiment. They
typically focused on the activities spawned, the adjustments made, or the achievements attained in a relatively small number of exemplar schools.

In our literature review, we found only eight systematic investigations of site-
based management. While these investigations provide some empirical evidence
regarding how site-based management plans actually operate in school systems, they
are based on case studies of a relatively small number of elementary and secondary
schools (from 6 to 32) located in very different settings. They examine different
versions and focus on different aspects of site-based management. Related literature on topics closely associated with site-based management (e.g., effective schools,
participatory decision making, decentralization) augmented the information base.
However, the related literature sources consulted were confined to those most frequently cited in writings on site-based management.

[2] In order to carry out a comprehensive, even-handed review of the literature on
site-based management, we tried to acquire all available information on site-based
management programs. While many of our requests for information were honored,
some were not. Some follow-up telephone conversations indicated that documents

The reliance on testimonials, anecdotes, activities, and exemplars; the reluctance to establish formal assessment systems; the incidents of withholding disappointing results; and the dearth of large-scale systematic investigations constitute stark limitations on the existing knowledge base. Although these limitations preclude firm answers to the questions we raise, we offer provisional responses within the confines of the limitations. In developing the responses, we concentrate on the dominant patterns and discuss the reasons for and implications of those patterns.

Issue 1: Do Site-Based Management Plans Fundamentally Alter the Formal Decision-Making Arrangements in School Systems?

Dominant Pattern. If site-based management involves a redistribution of decision-making authority in school systems, then a careful analysis of documentary data should reveal what authority has been delegated, how that authority has been distributed, and the degree to which site participants have been granted discretion. However, in many instances, we found it extraordinarily difficult to determine whether site-based management provisions actually alter formal decision-making arrangements, let alone whether those plans really afford site participants any meaningful degree of discretion. The following comments illustrate the dominant pattern.

First, plans make general reference to greater latitude but often fail to articulate the degree to which site participants have been granted any greater latitude than they previously possessed. The emphasis is on vague depictions that may capture the spirit of the approach but do not delineate details. As a result, it is not at all apparent what site participants can do that they could not do before site-based management was adopted.

Second, plans tend to cast established options as new opportunities.

---

were out of print. At other times, documents were not released for the reasons we have noted in the text of this chapter.

For other indications of the reluctance to publicize disappointing results, see Diegelmueller (1990). If her account is accurate, there is concern that release of such results might jeopardize the credibility of, and undermine support for, site-based management.

Either by noting that it is cumbersome to determine, up front, which decisions are building decisions and which decisions are district decisions or by claiming that it is unwise to do so because such specificity might stifle the creativity of site participants, plans simply permit site actors to develop proposals for new ventures and submit those proposals to district offices or state agencies for approval. Since schools have had at least the intermittent option to write proposals and seek support for those proposals under the auspices of various experimental project categories lodged in district budgets, state funding formulas, federal statutes, or foundation grants, these plans simply cast established options as new opportunities.

Third, plans tend to shift task responsibility but not delegate decision-making authority. Site-based management provisions may permit or require site participants to take on certain tasks. For example, they may be assigned responsibility for developing school improvement plans, organizing in-service sessions, revising report cards, sponsoring student recognition programs, arranging tutorial programs, and the like. But designating particular tasks is not the equivalent of delegating decision-making authority. At least in some settings, site-based management provisions encourage site participants to take on additional tasks or insist that they do so, but they do not appear to grant formal authority to make decisions in the central domains of budget, personnel, or program.

Fourth, where plans do alter the formal decision-making arrangements, the adjustments are often confined to select domains of school policy. Although most site-based management plans do not delegate formal authority to make decisions in *all* matters relating to budget, personnel, and program, many do delegate formal authority to make decisions in *some* of the central domains. For example, plans may delegate to site participants the authority to make decisions regarding discretionary funds and, at times, operating budgets, but not expand their authority to make decisions in the areas of personnel and program. Or, plans may alter the formal authority relationships in the area of program but make few if any adjustments in the areas of personnel and budget. This rather segmented, compartmentalized delegation of decision-making authority limits latitude and creates a partial, piecemeal framework for decision making rather than a comprehensive, coordinated one.

Finally, even where plans expand formal decision-making authority in all the central domains, the degree of discretion afforded site participants is circumscribed by the rules and resources of the context. In all cases, the district or state retains the right to approve plans and inspect results. At times, compliance with existing statutes, policies, regulations, and contractual agreements is expected. In some instances, governmental requirements and contractual provisions are temporarily lifted; in other instances, waivers can be requested on a case-by-case basis.

Where opportunities to procure exemptions from existing rules afford site participants greater discretion, the impact of these options is certainly moderated, often muted, by the shortage of critical resources. Site participants may get to decide where to cut the budget, how to handle reductions in staff positions, and whether they are willing to increase class sizes to preserve what they deem to be essential support services. But they are hardly given the opportunity to address how existing programs might be enhanced or how school performance might be strengthened. Decades of research on policy implementation and school improvement documents that time, technical assistance, logistical support, and financial reserves are essential ingredients (e.g., McLaughlin, 1987). Unfortunately, these essential ingredients are scarce commodities in most school systems. As a result, site participants often struggle just to keep their day-to-day operations intact. While formal policy provisions may grant site participants an additional measure of discretion, the shortage of critical resources may severely limit the real range of choice, the actual degree of discretion afforded site actors.

There are, admittedly, exceptions to the above themes. The site-based management provisions in Chicago, for example, seek to specify the authority that has been delegated to site participants, the manner in which that authority is distributed among administrators, teachers and parents, and the degree to which discretion is circumscribed by the rules and resources of the context. Site-based management plans in several other locations attend to these matters in some detail as well. But such specificity is rare. Further, some states and districts do offer planning grants or permit site participants to seek external funds. But the grants tend to be meager and temporary and the responsibility for seeking supplemental resources resides with the site. Thus, the dominant features of most site-based management plans appear to be ambiguous policy provisions and modest financial allocations.

Reasons for and Implications of the Dominant Pattern. The tendency to keep these plans ambiguous is certainly understandable. It is both technically troublesome and politically risky to specify arrangements.

On the technical side, it is hard to determine who should decide what, let alone who can decide what. What criteria does one apply? What evidence is available to suggest that one set of arrangements is superior to another? How does one work through the thicket of legal and constitutional issues inherent in efforts to reconfigure intergovernmental relationships? As the case studies of site-based governance arrangements in Salt Lake City and the recent challenges of site-based management provisions in Chicago illustrate, the legal and constitutional issues embedded in attempts to redefine and redistribute decision-making authority in school systems are not easily untangled. The district board of education in Salt Lake City wrestled with conflicting legal opinions regarding what formal powers could be delegated to site councils and whether any delegation of formal powers might be an abrogation of the board's statutory responsibilities or the state's constitutional guarantees (McLeese, 1991). The legislature in Illinois faced the challenge of revising some aspects of the Chicago School Reform Act, which was declared unconstitutional by the Illinois Supreme Court because of violation of the principle of one man, one vote (Schmidt, 1991).

On the political side, it is unsettling to reopen the "who controls what" debate and rekindle the administrator-teacher and professional-patron contention that the control question frequently evokes. It is much safer to keep initiatives ambiguous. Ambiguity enables the initiatives to subsume diverse and competing interests and absorb concerns regarding a variety of pressing problems.

However understandable, the pronounced tendency to keep site-based management plans ambiguous is problematic. When these plans are little more than vague references to elusive but appealing notions of empowerment and participation, site actors have no basis for determining whether they have any greater power to affect schools than they possessed before the plan was adopted. Unless plans specify what authority is delegated to site participants, how that authority is distributed, and the manner in which the discretion of site participants is conditioned and constrained by contractual agreements or by district, state, or federal policies, procedures, and/or accountability provisions, site participants have no basis for determining whether they have a meaningful increase in discretion and authentic opportunity to make policy decisions. When site participants are not clear on the parameters of their power, or when they are not convinced that they have been given greater power, they become frustrated by the ambiguity, skeptical of the new arrangements, and disillusioned by the pretense of reform. Under these conditions, site participants are prone to adopt decision-making roles that conform to familiar practice, rather than assume decision-making roles commensurate with the concept of site-based management.

It is also both understandable but problematic to keep financial allocations modest. Many states and districts are plagued by the dilemmas that result from the intense demands for finite fiscal resources. It is often economically difficult and almost always politically difficult to expand the revenue base or redistribute the available resources. However, the pronounced tendency to keep site-based management plans modestly funded is problematic. As the following sections demonstrate, the shortage of critical resources constrains the discretion of site participants and constricts the impact of site-based management plans.

Issue 2: Does the Formal Adjustment of Decision-Making Arrangements Actually Alter the Influence Relationships Typically and Traditionally Found in School Settings?

The central premise of site-based management plans is that the formal adjustment of decision-making arrangements will alter the influence relationships typically and traditionally found in school settings. Since site-based management plans delegate formal decision-making authority to governing bodies at the school level, site participants should become principal policy actors, addressing and affecting decisions pertaining to budget, personnel, and program. Since these plans distribute decision-making authority among teachers and parents as well as to principals, site-based management should enable teachers and parents to exert significant influence on significant issues.

The related premise is that by altering influence relationships in these ways, site-based management will produce other benefits as well. For example, it will enhance morale and motivation, strengthen the quality of planning processes, stimulate instructional innovations, and foster the consonant implementation of those changes. In these and perhaps other ways, site-based management will make schools more successful with their students, more responsive to their constituencies, and more deserving of public support. Because the alteration of influence relationships is both the primary premise of site-based management proposals and the principal prerequisite for a series of additional benefits, it is important to know whether site-based management plans actually alter influence relationships.

Dominant Pattern.   As we have argued elsewhere, the case studies of site-based governance councils in Salt Lake City constitute a critical test of the ability of site-based management plans to alter fundamentally the influence relationships typically and traditionally found in school settings (Malen and Ogawa, 1988). We reasoned that if such plans are likely to work anywhere, they ought to work here. The formal arrangements were highly favorable. The district's site-based management policy had addressed the barriers to teacher and parent influence in recommended ways. The district's policy had received national recognition as a model of bold and effective building-based governance.

But the research findings did not fit the research expectations. Site councils operated more as ancillary advisors or pro-forma endorsers than as major policymakers or potent policy actors. Neither teachers nor parents exerted significant influence on significant issues in site-based decision arenas. The conventional pattern wherein principals control building policies and procedures, teachers deliver instruction, and parents provide support was not disturbed (Malen and Ogawa, 1988).

These observations are generally consistent with the findings of other studies and the findings from the review of literature on the topic. These sources also suggest that while site-based management creates opportunities for principals, teachers, and parents to be involved in schoolwide decision making, it does not fundamentally alter the policymaking influence of site actors generally, the relative influence of principals and teachers, or the relative influence of professionals and patrons. Rather, site-based management may operate to maintain rather than alter the influence relationships typically and traditionally found in schools. The following comments reveal the dominant pattern.

First, site participants rarely address central, salient policy issues in their school council or committee meetings. Teachers and parents frequently characterize the topics raised as "routine," "blasé," "trivial,""peripheral." Council members do address subjects related to the operation of the building or the implementation of district directives. For example, council members develop procedures for handling disruptive student behavior, set times for parent conferences, adjust school schedules, sponsor fundraising projects, make facility improvements, augment extracurricular activities, determine how reduction in workforce directives might be implemented or how utility costs might be reduced. But, even on these more tangible, tangential matters, council members typically characterize their involvement as "listening," "advising," "endorsing the decisions others have already made," taking "rubber stamp" or "token" action.

Second, on councils composed of teachers and principals, teachers do not exert meaningful influence primarily because principals control council meetings. By virtue of their position in the school, principals are inclined to protect their managerial prerogatives and are able to use low-cost, routine strategies to control interactions. In most instances, principals control the agenda content, meeting format, and information flow. The principals' capacity to exert control is enhanced by the tendency of teachers to defer to the principal. Even when teachers identify issues they would prefer to discuss, they permit the principal to set the agenda. During discussions, teachers tend to "accept the boss's opinion" or "take the principal's lead." When responses are selected, teachers often "approve what the principal wants." In short, the propensity of principals to protect their prerogatives and the reluctance of teachers to challenge this dynamic combine in ways that permit principals to control decision processes and thereby control decision outcomes.

Third, on councils composed of principals, teachers, and parents, professional-patron influence relationships were not substantially altered, primarily because principals and, at times, principals and teachers controlled council meetings. Since professionals can set the agenda, manage the meeting time, disperse the information and shift potentially contentious issues to more private arenas, they essentially control decision processes and ultimately control decision outcomes. Parents are, for a variety of reasons, reluctant to challenge this dynamic. As a result, the familiar pattern wherein administrators make policy, teachers deliver instruction, and parents provide support is not changed.

Fourth, site-based councils may operate to maintain rather than alter influence relationships in school systems. It appears that site councils serve a number of important maintenance functions. For example, councils create forums through which conflict can be moderated, diffused, or contained. Councils provide channels through which participants can share information, air irritations, and vent concerns. Councils become vehicles that principals and professionals can use to buffer themselves from the repercussions of potentially divisive issues.

Councils generate opportunities for participants to be involved in activities that garner support for the school, and they provide opportunities for teachers and parents to develop an appreciation for the complexity of school problems and the difficulty of the principal's position. Moreover, councils symbolize the right of teachers and parents to have a voice in school decision making. As such, councils communicate the schools' commitment to recognize if not accommodate their concerns. In these and other ways, councils operate to regulate conflict, restore confidence, and stabilize the system. They also operate to reduce the likelihood that traditional influence relationships will be challenged, and they increase the likelihood that these relationships will be maintained.

While there may be some exceptions to these dominant patterns, there is, to date, little evidence that site-based management operates to alter influence relationships. It may effectively maintain these relationships. The one systematic investigation we could locate that examines the impact of site-based governance arrangements over time indicates that the primary, long-term effect of site-based management was just that—the maintenance rather than the alteration of influence relationships, the gradual restoration of system stability rather than apparent improvement in system performance (McLeese, 1991).

However discouraging, these provisional observations are not altogether surprising. We know that previous efforts to decentralize and democratize school systems through the creation of community school boards, advisory councils, and other participatory decision-making structures often failed to alter influence relationships and, at times, functioned effectively to maintain them. We know that the link between structural arrangements and desired effects is highly tentative (e.g., Meyer and Rowan, 1983). We know that numerous forces can converge and interact to numb if not nullify the impact of structural adjustments in many settings, not just in school systems.

Reasons for and Implications of the Dominant Pattern.   The available information on site-based management indicates that several sets of factors intervene to restrict the ability of this reform to alter the influence relationships in school systems. Some of those factors relate to the composition of site councils, the predisposition of site participants, and the nature of site-based management provisions. Other factors relate to the strength of deeply ingrained norms, to well-established unwritten rules that guide and govern behavior. Many of the factors relate to capacity. While sponsoring systems do delegate formal decision-making authority, they tend not to address participant capacity. Sponsoring systems rarely infuse councils with critical resources such as technical assistance; independent sources of information; continuous, norm-based training; funds to assess current programs or to develop and implement new programs. Further, sponsoring systems rarely redistribute existing resources in ways that might balance the positional advantages of principals vis à vis teachers or the positional advantages of professionals vis à vis parents.

We need not be taken aback by the discrepancy between the appealing promises of structural changes and the actual impacts of those efforts. We need not be set back by the recognition that a variety of factors combine to restrict the ability of site-based management to alter substantially the influence relationships in school systems. Since there are a number of site-based management experiments underway, we have the opportunity to see if efforts to address the web of factors that offset the impact of structural adjustments will enable site-based management plans to alter the influence relationships in school systems. If we want to give site-based management a chance to accomplish its principal promise, we can seize the opportunity to determine what, in addition to a formal redistribution of decision-making authority, might increase the probability that this reform will alter the influence relationships typically and traditionally found in school systems.

Issue 3: As Presently Configured, Do Site-Based Management Ventures De-bureaucratize Schools and Empower Participants or Do They Re-bureaucratize Schools and Overpower Participants?

A promise of site-based management is that it will de-bureaucratize schools and empower participants. By delegating decision-making authority to the site, by easing the constraints imposed by centrally devised policies and procedures, site-based management allows schools to become more autonomous. By involving professionals and patrons in decision-making processes at the building level, site-based management empowers participants. The assumption is that site participants will be free to, inspired to, and equipped to address schoolwide problems in creative and constructive ways. They will have the incentive and the opportunity to develop school improvement plans that capitalize on the expertise of site participants and the benefits of group interaction. They will have the incentive and opportunity to develop innovative programs that meet the unique needs of students in their school. And, they will be more inclined and more prepared to implement these instructional changes in the classroom.

Dominant Pattern.   At this time, it is not at all clear that site-based management meets any, let alone all, of the above expectations. It is not at all clear that current attempts to implement site-based management frees, inspires, or equips site participants to address school problems, engage in schoolwide planning, or develop and implement major changes in the instructional component of schools.

First, site-based management plans may not free site participants to deal with school problems. As previously noted, the plans may not be delegating substantial decision-making authority to site councils, relaxing bureaucratic constraints, or expanding the decision-making discretion of site participants. Moreover, in most instances, site participants are not relieved of any of their other duties. All the responsibilities associated with site-based management tend to come in addition to, not in lieu of, regular classroom teaching assignments and related tutorial, supervisory, or extracurricular responsibilities. Given these conditions, site participants are not any more "free" to attack schoolwide problems with site-based management than they were without it.

Second, site-based management plans may not inspire significant numbers of site participants for extended periods of time. Site-based management does appear to have an initial, energizing impact on some participants, but that effect dissipates. Although many individuals are often skeptical, some principals and teachers are excited by the idea. They are eager to tackle the tough problems facing their schools and are optimistic about their capacity to do so. But this initial, energizing effect tends to get offset by the time-consuming character of the process, by the confusion, anxiety, and contention generated as people attempt to define their roles and work through complex problems, by the dissonance created as committee demands compete with teaching responsibilities, by the resentment generated if participants perceive they have only modest influence on marginal matters, and by the frustration produced by fiscal constraints. Simply put, over time participants get worn down. Exhaustion overcomes enthusiasm. Overload dilutes efficacy. The human costs tend to overshadow the ideological appeals, leaving participants feeling more drained than inspired, more overburdened than empowered (McLeese, 1991).

Third, site-based management plans tend to impose intense demands but not provide commensurate supports. In many settings, site-based management gets promoted as an all-purpose solution to a potpourri of problems. It is seen as a mechanism for handling virtually any issue that arises, from the incidence of vandalism in the neighborhood or violence in the classroom to the presence of garbage in the lunchroom or litter on the playground. It is advanced as a means for handling virtually all the ongoing responsibilities embedded in quality planning, program development, and instructional improvement. It also is promoted as a way of handling many of the seemingly endless, ever-present activities associated with the day-to-day operation of schools.

While plans impose intense demands, they rarely provide commensurate supports to help meet these demands. As previously noted, site participants are expected to attend to all these matters and more in addition to their regular assignments and ongoing obligations. They are expected to solve all kinds of problems without the benefit of additional time to think, time to bring their own expertise to bear, or time to acquire and analyze other potentially useful information. They are often expected to attend to all these matters and more, without the benefit of technical assistance, supplemental funds, or other types of support. Given these conditions, it is hard to see how site-based management equips site participants to attend to school problems.

Fourth, site-based management may direct attention to aspects of schoolwide planning in some settings, but there is little evidence it stimulates interest in or enhances the quality of that process in a significant number of settings. While site-based management can serve as a catalyst for conducting needs assessments and designing school improvement plans, that effect does not appear to be widespread. The full range of activities associated with quality planning are not often apparent. Where they are present, these activities may not be well integrated. For example, information acquired in needs assessments may not be carefully analyzed or effectively used in constructing school improvement plans, and information acquired from reviews and evaluations is not often reflected in the revised plans.

Finally, site-based management precipitates a wide range of activities (e.g., student recognition programs, discipline policies, workshops, newsletters), but there is little evidence that it stimulates the development or enhances the implementation of major changes in the instructional component of schools. Site participants rarely address subjects central to the instructional program in their school council or school committee meetings. Where instructional program issues are discussed by councils and addressed in plans, it is often difficult to see how the plans depart from or improve on existing practice. Where instructional changes are proposed in plans, they are rarely implemented in classrooms. Where teachers incorporate the recommended adjustments, they tend to drift back to conventional practice in a fairly short period of time. Moreover, in some cases, the move to site-based management impedes the development and installation of instructional improvements. It diverts attention from teaching and learning as site participants take on activities and responsibilities that are only remotely related to the instructional component of schools.

We recognize there may be some exceptions to these general patterns. Several documents we examined in the literature review alluded to exceptional cases, isolated instances where site-based management might be empowering participants and engendering improvements. Several reports have appeared since we completed the review to indicate that some sites may be making real progress.[3] But even these more optimistic accounts acknowledge that "thus far results of restructuring efforts [site-based management, shared decision making] have been more rhetorical than real. Most schools that have been involved in empowerment reforms don't look much different from schools that have not been involved" (Glickman, 1990, p. 69).

However disappointing, these findings are not particularly surprising. Hopes that the creation of more autonomous units and the involvement of stakeholder groups in decision making would unleash the creative talents of professionals and parents, strengthen planning, stimulate innovation, and engender improvements in the instructional component of schools were rarely realized in previous experiments with this approach (e.g., Stein, 1971). We know from these early

---

[3] See, for example, the illustrations offered in Glickman (1990), MacPhail-Wilcox, Forbes, and Parramore (1990), and Elmore (1990). Dr. Richard Wallace, Superintendent of the Pittsburgh schools, shared with us some encouraging assessments of ongoing projects in those schools.

experiences with district decentralization, more recent experiments with site-based management, and repeated efforts to implement change that a variety of factors shape reform effects in any complex organization, not just in school systems.

Reasons for and Implications of the Dominant Pattern. The available information indicates that several sets of factors can intervene to offset the ability of site-based management plans to de-bureaucratize schools and empower participants. Some of those factors relate to the predispositions of participants. At times, site participants are inclined to see school improvement as an individual responsibility rather than a collective pursuit. Participants may be reluctant to engage in collaborative planning activities and critical assessments of the instructional program. However, most of the factors relate to the nature of site-based management provisions and the lack of attention to capacity issues. In some cases, district and/or state requirements are viewed as so extensive or confining that site participants focus more on compliance and survival than innovation and improvement. In most instances, site participants lack the time, technical assistance, requisite skills, and supplemental funds needed to engage in comprehensive, coordinated planning processes. They also lack the time to develop innovative ideas and the funds required to procure the materials, training experiences, and professional development programs needed to install major changes in the instructional program. The shortage of resources often merges with views of regulations in ways that prompt site participants to go through the recommended or required procedural motions and develop plans that help them keep their basic, day-to-day operations intact.

Whether attention to these and other factors will bolster the ability of site-based management to achieve the broad range of heady objectives that have been assigned to it is another open, empirical question. That neglect of these factors will diminish, if not deny, the promises of this reform is, however, another fairly tentative but clearly tenable proposition.

Again, we need not be taken aback by the recognition that thus far, site-based management has yielded modest and mixed results. Change is a complex process and improvement is an elusive product. Given the complexity of change processes and the breadth of reform goals, it is unrealistic to assume that any single action, such as a move to site-based management, will accomplish ambitious aims or fulfill sweeping promises. Given the widespread interest in and numerous experiments with site-based management, we have the opportunity to determine the conditions under which this strategy might be able to achieve some, if not all, of its stated objectives.

CRITICAL POLICY CHOICES

Our discussion of these most disconcerting issues suggests that policymakers face several critical policy choices. We frame those choices as direct questions that warrant careful consideration, not as precise prescriptions that guarantee goal attainment. We recognize that even the most well-conceived, carefully crafted policies can only create conditions; they can not ensure results. We also recognize that, at best, the available knowledge on site-based management offers only general guidelines for policy, not specific remedies for particular situations. Within the confines of those limitations, we highlight three interrelated policy choices that are likely to shape the fate of this reform.

Choice 1: Retain Vague Policy Provisions or Clarify Structural Arrangements?

At the present time, the ambiguity of provisions for site-based management makes it extraordinarily difficult to tell whether this reform actually alters decision-making arrangements, actually grants site participants greater discretion, or actually enables schools to become more autonomous units. One option is to allow site-based management provisions to remain elusive notions. Another option is to clarify the formal provisions.

Our analysis suggests that the formal policy provisions must be clarified. Site-based management plans must delineate what authority is delegated to site participants, how that authority is distributed, and the manner in which the discretion of site participants is conditioned and constrained by the rules and resources of the broader context. Without this detail, site participants have no basis for determining whether site-based management is a rhetorical appeal or a real change, whether it is a hollow strategy or a genuine opportunity. Without this detail, policymakers have no basis for determining whether they are creating the conditions the concept connotes, whether they are adding more structures to the system rather than creating autonomous units in the system. If policy provisions specify the formal arrangements, at minimum all parties will be in a better position to see how site-based management modifies decision-making structures and whether it actually alters and de-bureaucratizes or essentially replicates and re-bureaucratizes the system.

Choice 2: Rely on Structural Mechanisms or Couple Structural Adjustments with Capability-Building Strategies?

At this time, the reliance on structural adjustments as the instrument of educational reform is pronounced. One option is to count on the structural strategy. Another option is to couple this strategy with other, complementary strategies.

Our analysis suggests that reliance on structural strategies as the principal if not sole instrument for educational reform is at best an incomplete game plan. The inability of site-based management plans to alter the influence relationships typically and traditionally found in schools serves as a poignant reminder that the link between the formal alteration of decision-making arrangements and actual changes in influence relationships is neither direct nor dependable. Since a variety of forces interact to shape influence relationships in school settings, it is unrealistic to assume that a structural adjustment alone will noticeably or necessarily affect them. The inability of site-based management plans to achieve the related benefits (many of which are contingent on, indeed flow from, changes in influence relationships) also serves as a reminder that the link between restructuring schools and empowering people is neither self-evident nor self-sustaining. Since a variety of factors interact to shape both the sense of empowerment and the extent of improvement, it is unrealistic to assume that a structural adjustment will in itself automatically and inevitably affect them.

Throughout our discussion of site-based management, we have noted that many of the factors that restrict the ability of this reform to achieve its objectives are related to capacity issues. Our work suggests that attention must be given to these issues. Site-based management plans must provide site participants the critical resources they need to carry out the additional responsibilities they are given. Without sizable and stable financial investments, site participants cannot purchase the time, technical assistance, instructional materials, or other forms of support they need to make major changes in schools. Site participants end up trying to transform schools on overtime, tired time, or "spare" time. They end up trying to engender improvements without the resources needed to realize improvements in schools.

With all due respect for the stories and studies of the dedicated individuals and the grassroots groups that make impressive improvements despite chronic shortage of resources, it is unrealistic to assume that these feats can be emulated or sustained in a large number of settings. Ingenuity, esprit, courage, conviction, and endurance are commendable qualities. They are important elements, but they are not the sole ingredients of broad-scale or long-term improvements in schools. The available evidence on site-based management clearly indicates that its ability to achieve its aims is constricted by the tendency to neglect capacity issues, by the propensity to depend on a stand-alone strategy—a structural adjustment only—rather than a multipronged strategy—a structural adjustment accompanied by financial investment.

Since the policy that embraces as many of the relevant factors as possible holds more promise than a policy that confines itself to a few, we urge policymakers to couple restructuring ventures with intense, capability-building strategies. At minimum, policymakers must take a more robust approach, which is essential if we want to give site-based management a chance to become an effective reform.

Choice 3: Rely on Casual Appraisal or Capitalize on Opportunities for Systematic Assessment?

Our review of literature on site-based management suggests that the tendency to rely on casual appraisal, anecdotal data, and ideological appeal is pronounced. One option is to continue to rely on this information base. Another option is to develop a stronger knowledge base.

Our analysis underscores the importance of developing a stronger knowledge base. While the existing literature on site-based management identifies factors that impede the ability of this reform to achieve its stated objectives, there are no assurances its promises will be fulfilled even if some or all of these factors are addressed. Therefore, continuous, systematic, empirical assessments of programs must be conducted to determine the conditions under which site-based management might be able to achieve its objectives and operate to improve the performance of schools.

Moreover, those assessments need to be shared. We can understand the reluctance to disseminate disappointing results (i.e., the perception that such information serves no useful purpose, the fears that this information might jeopardize the support for or shake the faith in this reform). We are, however, convinced that we can learn as much from our disappointments as we can from our successes and that confronting the disappointments may help us develop strategies that increase the probability of success.

We recognize the difficulty of the choices we present. The issues are complex. The data are thin. The stakes are high. And, in some respects, we may have set ourselves up on this reform in much the same way we may have set ourselves up in the development of community action programs in the 1960s. As Moynihan described these efforts:

> Wishing so many things so, we all too readily come to think them not only possible, which very likely they are, but also near at hand, which is seldom the case. We constantly underestimate difficulties, overpromise results, and avoid any evidence of incompatibility and conflict, thus repeatedly creating the conditions of failure out of a desperate desire for success. More than a weakness, in the conditions of the present time it has the potential of a fatal flaw. [P. xii]

While we may have set ourselves up, we need not set ourselves back. We ought not abandon our commitment to democratic principles and participatory processes. We ought to affirm it and renew it through policy choices that might help make site-based management become a viable as well as a prevalent policy option, a substantive as well as a salable approach to education reform.

REFERENCES

Bundy, McGeorge. *Reconnection for Learning: A Community School System for New York City.* New York: Praeger, 1967.

Clune, William H., and White, Paula. *School-Based Management: Institutional Variation, Implementation, and Issues for Further Research.* New Brunswick, N.J.: Center for Policy Research in Education, Eagleton Institute of Politics, 1988.

Diegelmueller, Karen. "Report Raps Shared-Decision Making Effort in Los

Angeles," *Education Week*, 21 November 1990, p. 5.

Elmore, Richard. *Community School District 4, New York City: A Case of Choice*. New Brunswick, N.J.: Center for Policy Research in Education, Eagleton Institute of Politics, 1990.

Glickman, Carl D. "Pushing School Reform to a New Edge: The Seven Ironies of School Improvement," *Phi Delta Kappan* 72, no. 1 (1990): 68–75.

Malen, Betty, and Ogawa, Rodney T. "Professional-Patron Influence on Site-Based Governance Councils: A Confounding Case Study," *Educational Evaluation and Policy Analysis* 10, no. 4 (1988): 251–270.

Malen, Betty; Ogawa, Rodney T.; Kranz, Jennifer. "What Do We Know about School-Based Management? A Case Study of the Literature." In *Choice and Control in American Education*, edited by William Clune and John Witte. New York: Falmer Press, 1990.

McLeese, Patricia. "The Decentralization of Conflict and Consensus: Salt Lake City Shared Governance Arrangements 1970–1985." Doctoral dissertation, University of Utah, 1991.

McLeese, Patricia, and Malen, Betty. "Site-Based Governance: The Salt Lake City Experience 1970–1985." Paper presented at the Annual Meeting of the American Educational Research Association, Washington, D.C., 1987.

MacPhail-Wilcox, Betty; Forbes, Roy; and Parramore, Barbara. "Project Design: Reforming Structure and Process," *Educational Leadership* 47 (April, 1990): 22–25.

McLaughlin, Milbrey W. "Learning from Experience: Lessons from Policy Implementation," *Education Evaluation and Policy Analysis* 9, no. 2 (1987): 171–178.

Meyer, John W., and Rowan, Brian. "The Structure of Educational Organizations." In *Organizational Environments*, edited by John W. Meyer and Richard Scott. Beverly Hills, Calif.: Sage, 1983. Pp. 71–98.

Moynihan, Daniel. *Maximum Feasible Misunderstanding*. New York: Free Press, 1969.

Richardson, Claiborne T. *School-Based Management: An Informal Study*. Falls Church, Va.: Fairfax County Public Schools, Office of Research and Evaluation, 1988.

Schmidt, Peter. "Short-term Fix Approved for Chicago School Reform Law," *Education Week*, 16 January 1991, p. 18.

Stein, Annie. "Strategies for Failure," *Harvard-Educational Review* 41, no. 2 (1971): 158–204.